A POLITICAL BIOGRAPHY OF DANIEL DEFOE

EIGHTEENTH-CENTURY POLITICAL BIOGRAPHIES

Series Editor: J. A. Downie

FORTHCOMING TITLES

Joseph Addison
Alexander Pettit

Henry Fielding
J. A. Downie

Eliza Haywood
Rachel Carnell

Delarivier Manley
Rachel Carnell

Alexander Pope
Pat Rogers

Jonathan Swift
David Oakleaf

John Toland
Michael Brown

A POLITICAL BIOGRAPHY OF DANIEL DEFOE

BY

P. N. Furbank & W. R. Owens

LONDON
PICKERING & CHATTO
2006

Published by Pickering & Chatto (Publishers) Limited
21 Bloomsbury Way, London, WC1A 2TH

2252 Ridge Road, Brookfield, Vermont 05036, USA

www.pickeringchatto.com

BRITISH LIBRARY CATALOGUING IN PUBLICATION DATA

Furbank, Philip Nicholas
    A political biography of Daniel Defoe
    1. Defoe, Daniel, 1661?–1731   2. Authors, English – 18th century –
    Biography   3. Journalists – Great Britain – Biography   4. Great Britain –
    Politics and government – 1660–1714   5. Great Britain – Politics and
    government 1714–1760
    I. Title II. Owens, W. R.
    823.5

ISBN-10: 1851968105

Typeset by Pickering & Chatto (Publishers) Limited
Printed in the United Kingdom at the University Press, Cambridge

CONTENTS

THE AUTHORS

P. N. FURBANK is Emeritus Professor of Literature of the Open University. He is the author of studies of Samuel Butler, Italo Svevo, E. M. Forster and Diderot, and of *Reflections on the Word 'Image'* (1970), *Unholy Pleasure: The Idea of Social Class* (1985) and *Behalf* (1999).

W. R. OWENS is Professor of English Literature at the Open University. His publications include editions of John Bunyan's *Grace Abounding* and *The Pilgrim's Progress*, and two volumes in the Clarendon *Miscellaneous Works of John Bunyan*. He is co-editor of *John Bunyan and His England 1628–88* (1990) and of *Shakespeare, Aphra Behn and the Canon* (1996).

Together, P. N. Furbank and W. R. Owens have written over twenty articles on Defoe. Their joint books include *The Canonisation of Daniel Defoe* (1988), *Defoe De-Attributions* (1991) and *A Critical Bibliography of Daniel Defoe* (1998). They have edited Defoe's *Tour Through Great Britain* (1991) and *The True-Born Englishman and Other Writings* (1997), and are General Editors of *The Works of Daniel Defoe*, 44 vols (Pickering & Chatto, 2000–8), in progress.

ACKNOWLEDGEMENTS

This book builds upon work on Defoe carried out over a number of years. Some chapters include revised or adapted versions of material previously published in journals, and we are grateful to the editors for permission to reprint. Parts of chapter 2 were published in the *Review of English Studies*; parts of chapter 7 were published in *Publishing History* and *British Journal for Eighteenth-Century Studies*; and the three letters by Defoe in Appendix A were first published in *The Scriblerian*. We have also made use of parts of Introductions written for our own volumes in the Pickering & Chatto *Works of Daniel Defoe*, 44 vols (in progress, 2000–8), and have drawn with profit upon the work of our fellow editors.

We are grateful for financial assistance from the Research Committee of the Arts Faculty at the Open University, and would also like to thank the staff of the Open University Library for their help and forbearance over many years.

Many friends and colleagues have given us advice and help of various kinds. Not all of them will agree with all our arguments here, but we have appreciated their encouragement and the interest they have taken in our work. We thank in particular Arne Bialuschewski, David Blewett, Alex Cain, Roger Day, Alan Downie, Katherine Frank, David Hayton, J. Paul Hunter, Chris Mounsey, John Mullan, Patti Owens, John Richetti, Manuel Schonhorn, Geoffrey Sill, George Starr and Ian Willison. We are especially grateful to Annick Erlos, who helped us by keying in the appendices; John McVeagh, who kindly read and commented upon the whole book in draft, and who made available to us copies of the electronic text created for his magnificent edition of *Defoe's Review*, 18 vols (Pickering & Chatto, in progress, 2003–11); and Douglas Matthews, who compiled the index.

ABBREVIATIONS

Letters *The Letters of Daniel Defoe*, ed. George Harris Healey (Oxford: Clarendon Press, 1955)

PEW *Political and Economic Writings by Daniel Defoe*, gen. eds W. R. Owens and P. N. Furbank, 8 vols (London: Pickering & Chatto, 2000)

Review *Defoe's Review Reproduced from the Original Editions*, ed. Arthur Wellesley Secord, Facsimile Text Society, 22 vols (New York: Columbia University Press, 1938)

SFS *Satire, Fantasy and Writings on the Supernatural by Daniel Defoe*, gen. eds W. R. Owens and P. N. Furbank, 8 vols (London: Pickering & Chatto, 2003–4)

TDH *Writings on Travel, Discovery and History by Daniel Defoe*, gen. eds W. R. Owens and P. N. Furbank, 8 vols (London: Pickering & Chatto, 2001–2)

INTRODUCTION

Our book is about Daniel Defoe's political career, but this phrase may be thought to call for some defining. Evidently, someone who functions mainly by means of his pen does not have a political career in the same sense as a statesman, whose daily and nightly preoccupation is power. There was indeed a brief and extraordinary moment in 1701 when Defoe might be said to have wielded power and have become a man of action: the time when he presented himself at Westminster, guarded by sixteen 'gentlemen of quality', to deliver a paper of grievances and demands (*Legion's Memorial*) on behalf of 'two hundred thousand Englishmen'. No doubt, too, by his advice to his patron Robert Harley, he exercised influence, but influence is not the same as power. By Defoe's 'political career', therefore, we are meaning his influence, or attempts at influence, as a purveyor of ideas and opinions, and also the influence, sometimes very unnerving, of political events on him. In consequence – the fact might seem like an irony but of course is not – we know a great deal more about Defoe's political ideas than we do about Harley's. Whatever ideas Harley had, and sometimes one wonders whether he actually had any, as distinct from instincts or schemes, he would have been inclined to keep to himself.

We must be clear, also, about another distinction. Defoe wrote voluminously on very many different topics, and one of them, from early on, was social reform. In 1697 he published a book-length *Essay upon Projects*, in which he made proposals for the development of banking and highroads, friendly societies and insurance; for setting up academies (and in particular an academy for women); and for improvement of the system for employing seamen and the law regarding bankruptcy.[1] He claimed to have been working on these ideas for five years, and there is no doubt that 'improvement' of this kind was a lasting interest on his part. He would pursue it, or anyway economic improvement, on a lesser scale as regards Scotland; and late in life he would produce a series of writings – under the persona of 'Andrew Moreton' or 'Squire Moreton', a crusty old bachelor living with his sister in Highgate – making proposals for a 'Protestant monastery' or old peoples' home, a secular university for London, the improvement of street-lighting, correcting the insolence of servants and shoe-cleaners, and the reforming or abolishing of select vestries. Such proposals would certainly have political implications today, but this was hardly so true in Defoe's day, and it seems best to regard them as coming from a different part of his mind, thus as not belonging in the present book.

As for Defoe's political ideas and actions, we get a very full picture of them from his pamphlets, his periodical the *Review* (launched on 19 February 1704) and his letters to Harley. But the *Review* expired on 11 June 1713, and the letters to Harley run out in September 1714; and from this point on it becomes much harder to follow his political activities. Indeed we used sometimes to be told that, after the accession of George I, they more or less came to an end – which is very far from the case.

The root of the problem, for biographers, is attribution. For there is reason to think that the Defoe 'canon' – as defined in John Robert Moore's *Checklist of the Writings of Daniel Defoe*,[2] where it ran to some 570 titles – is highly questionable, more questionable by a long way than the canon of any other major English writer. The present authors have gone as far as suggesting that nearly half of the works included by Moore may have no right to be there, in the sense that no really convincing reason has ever been offered for their being by Defoe.[3] Ours may be an extreme view, but the relevance to biography is clear. In the case of a writer, and particularly a political writer, his writings are, after all, important events in his life, possibly even the most important ones, and a biographer can hardly tell the story of his life without deciding which writings are by him.

As regards Defoe, in the years following 1714, this is not easy. Indeed the problems, at least where politics are concerned, grow really daunting – as indeed they might have done earlier had there been no *Review* or letters to Harley which often provide convincing evidence. We have here the reason why, as it strikes us, the later pages of most biographies of Defoe tend to lose direction. It is not (it hardly needs saying) that Defoe was just a political writer. He had a myriad of interests, casual or more sustained. He produced weighty historical works, religious treatises, writings on trade, finance and social reform, on travel, manners, magic and the supernatural; and for a brief period, from 1719 to 1724, he wrote novels. But it is with political matters that attribution becomes most problem-ridden. Biography and bibliography here become inextricably intertwined, and our effort throughout has been to elicit a coherent story. We have a feeling that no biographer, up to now, has quite succeeded in this, and that is why we are making a new attempt.

There are, indeed, certain major obstacles to getting this particular story right. We are thinking, for instance, of the influential theories or fantasies woven around his later years by Defoe's Victorian biographer William Lee.[4] Biographers have recently grown more cautious about Lee. We no longer hear the stirring narrative he related about Defoe's relationship with the journal-editor Nathaniel Mist: his noble generosity towards Mist, the disgraceful ingratitude displayed by Mist in return, their furious quarrels over religion and politics, and their eventual duel. We also hear less about Defoe's relationship with John Applebee the publisher, as imagined by Lee, another colourful story: how he worked for Applebee as a hired crime-reporter, as an author of criminal lives and as Applebee's 'man', and how he stood in for Applebee in conducting interviews with prisoners at Tyburn. But what we do not find is any wholesale rejection from the canon of the huge mass of articles from *Mist's Journal* and *Applebee's Original Weekly Journal* which Lee reprinted as Defoe's 'recently discovered writings'. Yet, as we pointed out some time ago, to accept these articles *en bloc* as Defoe's is to add some very peculiar features to our picture of him, not least politically.[5] Would one think it likely, judging from the rest that we know about him, that Defoe would (1 December 1722) offer a straight High Tory defence of 'passive obedience' to monarchs; or (16 December 1721) describe the execution of Charles I as 'the most unnatural Murder that ever was committed since the Crucifixion of our Blessed Saviour' (this being the same Defoe who teased Charles Leslie, champion of the 'divine right of monarchs', with a joke about 'wet' martyrdom, as suffered by Charles I, as opposed to 'dry' martyrdom, as suffered by James II[6])? Does it seem probable that Defoe would (20 May 1721) speak bitter words about 'Sectaries and Dissenters', blaming them for the spread of the infamous Arian heresy, 'as if the Schism they had already made in the Church was not sufficient'?

But an even more important obstacle to the right understanding of Defoe's later life is his famous letters to Charles Delafaye, the Whig Undersecretary of State, in which he claims to have been commissioned by Lord Townshend, Secretary of State in 1716, to insinuate himself into the management of Tory journals to restrain and 'enervate' them.[7] Most modern biographers, very understandably, construct their account of Defoe's later political career round these letters – the fact that they seem to be confessing to somewhat shady behaviour makes them, though this is illogical, seem all the more likely to be true – but we shall be arguing that they are, rather, a dazzling piece of mendacity. They are, in our view, a fiction only equalled by his claim to have known, and even been intimate with, King William.

It appears to us, then, that Defoe's political career calls for some rethinking, and we have done our best to retrace its progress step by step. As hardly needs saying, this is not the same as writing a new biography in the ordinary sense. Indeed, as we shall argue, Defoe seems to have turned his back on politics (no doubt with some relief) at the end of 1720 – ten years before his death, and before many of his most impressive writings. For this reason, that is where we end our book.

CHAPTER 1

POETRY, PAMPHLETEERING AND THE PILLORY

Daniel Defoe's upbringing was, it might be suggested, an almost sure recipe for the forming of a Whig; and as a Whig is certainly how, throughout his tangled political career, he would always regard himself, though it was not invariably the picture his enemies would form of him. He was born into a Dissenting family, of strict religious principles, living in the London parish of St Stephen Coleman Street. The Defoe family worshipped in the congregation of a distinguished Presbyterian preacher, the Rev. Samuel Annesley, whom Defoe would later regard as a personal friend and whose death in 1697 he commemorated in a poem. Initially the idea was that he should become a Dissenting minister, and at the age of sixteen or thereabouts he entered a Dissenting academy at Newington Green, run by the Rev. Charles Morton. It was an untraditional establishment in which the teaching was done in English and students were given grounding in physical science and political theory.

Precisely why, or when, he gave up the idea of the ministry is not known. At all events, in 1684 he married Mary Tuffley, daughter of a well-to-do citizen and cooper of London, and with the aid of her very substantial dowry (£3,700) he set up as a wholesale merchant, with a house and warehouse in Freeman's Yard, Cornhill.

Defoe's father James Foe, a successful butcher and tallow-chandler, was a freeman and liveryman of the City of London, as in due course Daniel himself would be, and it was in the political struggle between King Charles II and the City that Defoe had his first experience of tyranny, the theme that would dominate his political philosophy. The City was a stronghold of militant Protestantism, with many rights and privileges. It enjoyed the right (until King Charles succeeded in suspending it[1]) to elect its own sheriffs and justices of the peace, and it controlled appointments to the lieutenancy of the militia. It had also been a strong supporter of the Exclusion Bill, designed to exclude the King's brother, the Roman Catholic Duke of York, from the succession. Defoe would recall, years later, the terrors he and his fellow Dissenters felt at the threat of 'Popery, and its Introduction into this Kingdom, Hand in Hand with Slavery', and how they set to work to copy out the Bible in shorthand, in case they were not allowed the use of it under the new regime.[2] The City was in the habit of plaguing King Charles with petitions, for instance calling on him to summon a new Parliament; and it was partly for this reason that he convened his fourth and last Parliament in Oxford rather than London. Charles, in his designs for absolute monarchy and attempts to impose his own candidates in shrieval or mayoral elections, found the City a troublesome and formidable antagonist.

From the opening years of Charles II's reign Dissenters had been subjected to various severe religious and civic disabilities. The Conventicle Act of 1664 prohibited more than five persons meeting together for any form of worship not recognised in the Prayer Book; the Five Mile Act of 1665 forbade any Dissenting minister from coming within five miles of any place where he had preached or taught since 1660; and the Test Act of 1673 precluded all but members of the Church of England from accepting any civil or military office. In practice these laws had – to use Defoe's own words – 'not been much insisted on till about the Year 82 and 83'.[3] But in the last few years of Charles's reign they were applied in full force, and it became altogether a time of persecution for Dissenters. Government spies and informers were busy everywhere; many Dissenters perished in prison; and Charles Morton felt compelled to emigrate to America.[4]

With the accession of the King's Roman Catholic brother James to the throne in February 1685, and the threat that he posed, not so much to the Dissenters as to Protestantism in general, matters quickly rose to a climax. It had been rumoured for some time that the Duke of Monmouth, an illegitimate son of Charles II, at present in exile in Holland, was contemplating invading England, with a view to dethroning his uncle James II. Monmouth was a Protestant, and for this reason, as well as for his winning looks and personality, he was a hero for many ordinary English citizens. Thus when he put his plan into action, landing at Lyme Regis on 11 June 1685 with a small party of armed companions, he was joined within days by several thousand supporters from the country round about. They described themselves as 'in arms for the defence and vindication of the Protestant religion', and their cry was 'Fear Nothing but God'.[5]

Reactions in the City of London seem to have been somewhat less whole-hearted. So at least Defoe suggested years later in the *Review*:

> I remember, how boldly abundance of Men talk'd for the Duke of *Monmouth* when he first Landed; but, if half of them had as boldly joyn'd him Sword in Hand, he had never been routed at *Kings-sedgmoor*, and as they kept their Hands off from acting, so when he was defeated, we heard but little of their Tongues neither afterwards.[6]

Whatever the truth of this, several of Defoe's classmates from Morton's academy joined Monmouth's army and were executed as rebels, and Defoe himself took up arms on Monmouth's behalf. The fact is well attested, for not only do we have his word for it, he is named in a royal pardon dated May 1687.[7] Beyond that, however, nothing whatever is known about his part in the rising, and – perhaps because of Monmouth's ignominious behaviour after his defeat and capture – he does not seem to have made a cult of him. What has a certain interest, however, is that, much later, he claimed Monmouth to be the popularizer of the term 'Whig'. Monmouth had in 1681 been sent to subdue a Scottish rising at Bothwell Bridge, but instead of thanks for his success he was abused for treating the rebels too mercifully.

> D[uke] Lauderdale told King *Charles*, with an *Oath*, That the Duke had been so Civil to the *Whigs*, because he was a Whig himself in his Heart. – This made it a Court Word, and in a little while all the Friends and Followers of the Duke, began to be called *Whigs*.[8]

The reign of James II, even more than that of his brother Charles, would be the dominant influence on Defoe's political thinking, and it would, over the ensuing years, be his text for innumerable analyses and homilies. It was here he acquired his contempt for the High Tory doctrines of the 'divine right' of monarchs and the sin of 'resistance' and that he explored the evils of oath-imposing and oath-taking. His claim, made many years later, was a true one.

> For my part, I thank God, that when he [James II] was King I never own'd him, never swore to him, never pray'd for him (as King),

never paid any Act of Homage to him, never so much as Drank his Health, but look'd upon him as a Person who being Popish, had no Right to Rule.[9]

Much can be learned about a person from a study of his heroes, and this is certainly true of Defoe. Highest among his idols would be King William, but there were also one or two from the past: the great Gustavus Adolphus, champion of Protestantism in the Thirty Years' War,[10] and a certain Alderman William Love, of the reign of Charles II. What he will write about Love in the *Review* for 12 June 1705 tells us much about Defoe himself. He relates a speech, made in Parliament in 1673, by 'that truly *English Roman*, Mr. Alderman *Love*', which, he says, ought to be 'wrote in Letters of Gold, and remember'd, to the Honour of his Family, as long as Citizens and Parliaments remain'. The King had issued a proclamation granting liberty of conscience to the Dissenters, who 'Greedily and Unwarily Embrac'd their Liberty, Rejoyc'd, Built Meeting-Houses, and Throng'd to them in Publick', but when this dispensing of the law by Charles came up for debate in the House of Commons, Love vigorously opposed it and wanted it declared arbitrary and illegal. This provoked a testy rebuke from a member of the Court party: '*Why, Mr. Love, you are a Dissenter your self, it's very Ungrateful, that you that received the Benefit, should object against the Manner*'. To this Love replied:

> I am a Dissenter, *and thereby Unhappily Obnoxious to the Law; and* if you catch me in the Corn, you may put me into the Pound; *the Law against the* Dissenters, *I should be glad to see repeal'd by the same Authority that made it; but while it is a Law, the King cannot Repeal it by Proclamation; and I had much rather see the* Dissenters *suffer by the Rigour of the Law, tho' I suffer with them, than see all the Laws in* England *Trampled under the Foot of the Prerogative in this Example; and, I hope, the* Dissenters *understand their Liberty as* English Men, *better than to accept of it in an Illegal manner.*[11]

Love's reasoning here, taking the high ground and rejecting an easy advantage in the cause of a wider good, would become a favourite with Defoe. It is at work in much of his writing about the Dissenters – frequently to their resentment – though he would employ it in many other contexts too.

*   *   *   *   *   *

This leads us neatly to the beginnings of Defoe's career as a writer. His first known pamphlet, published with a fictitious imprint in 1688, was *A Letter to a Dissenter from his Friend at the Hague, Concerning the Penal Laws and the Test*.[12] It was an appeal to his fellow Dissenters not to swallow the bait of James II's offer to repeal the Test Act; and, in its contrariness, it was a characteristic début. He would always love to show his independence of those who, conventionally, would have been considered to be his friends. Very probably this is the pamphlet he refers to in the *Review* for 24 November 1711, where he describes the offence he caused to his Dissenting brethren 'when, in print, I oppos'd at the utmost hazard, the taking off the Penal Laws and Test'.[13] It was not the last time he would fall out with his fellow Dissenters.

Three years later, following the 'Glorious Revolution', when James had fled to France and been replaced by William and Mary, Defoe was to make a larger-scale venture into politics with a lengthy satirical poem, *A New Discovery of an Old Intreague* (1691).[14] It is a strange affair, oddly discontinuous in its style (its phrasing in places seems grammatically only half-formed), and stiff with ephemeral and, at least for the modern reader, almost impenetrable allusions.[15] Yet on the other hand it contains a number of memorable lines and passages, some of which he would re-use in later poems.[16] Its subject is City politics, in particular the nefarious handling of City elections and appointments to the lieutenancy of the militia, during and after the Restoration. More immediately, it is a response to a petition presented to Parliament on 2 December 1690 by 117 Common Councillors, complaining that the present Lord Mayor, Sir Thomas Pilkington, and several aldermen were holding offices they were not entitled to. The petitioners, so Defoe is at pains to imply, are all Tories and Jacobites (covert or otherwise), and include a number of the jurymen who sentenced to death the Whig martyrs Lord William Russell and Henry Cornish.

The poem gives a burlesque depiction of England's defenders, the City militia, with their weighty baggage-train of provender to sustain them on their long day's march, being reviewed by Queen Mary in Hyde Park on 21 July 1690, a day of great peril for England, the English and Dutch fleets having just been defeated by the French at Beachy Head; and it goes on to present a series of savage lampoons of certain of the petitioners. Or rather, it would appear, that was the form the poem took, when on 1 January 1691 there came the sensational news of the discovery of a Jacobite plot and the arrest of its leader, Lord Preston – caught, with his companions, carrying treasonable letters to King James at St Germain. Defoe evidently saw the relevance to his poem and added a few lines about the event, and more particularly featured it – though in somewhat riddling fashion – on his title-page, which would now bear the sub-title '*A Satyr Level'd at Treachery and Ambition: Calculated to the Nativity of the Rapparee Plott, and the Modesty of the Jacobite Clergy. Designed by Way of Conviction to the CXVII Petitioners, and for the Benefit of those that Study the Mathematicks*'.[17]

The poem is Defoe's first statement of several themes of permanent importance to him. For example, the absurdity and falsity of the doctrines of 'divine right' and 'passive resistance',[18] as invoked at the time of the deposing of James II. With what remarkable alacrity, he notes, those who had taken the oath of loyalty to the King (and most of all the clergy) forgot these doctrines when they saw danger to their own interests.

Further, it is plain from the poem that one of his great standbys as a satirical poet will be lampoon. In a passage in his poem *The Pacificator*, assigning English writers to their appropriate genre, he was to write:

> Let P[rio]r Flatter Kings in Panegyrick,
> R[atcli]ff Burlesque, and W[icherl]y be Lyrick:
> Let C[ongrev]e write the Comick, F[o]e Lampoon …[19]

A New Discovery is, appropriately, full of most merciless lampoons of Jacobite petitioners, for instance Sir William Dodson, on whom

> 'Twas thought the King bestow'd his Spurs in spight,
> And spoild a Captain to compose a Knight;
> … Nature has wisely blazon'd on his Face,
> The Escutcheon of his Family, an Ass:
> From ear to ear the Mantling does extend,
> *Crested* to show the Goat's the Asses Friend;[20]

or Sir Ralph Box,

> With Ruby Face, and old abhorring Nose,
> So Copper mix'd with Stone, does Brass compose.[21]

Defoe, a reckless man, began here a practice that would bring much trouble on him. When in 1703 he was put on trial for seditious libel, one of his judges was to be Sir Salathiel Lovell, of whom he had written in *Reformation of Manners* (1702)

> L[ove]l, the *Pandor* of thy Judgment-Seat,
> Has neither Manners, Honesty, nor Wit;
> Instead of which, he's plenteously supply'd
> With Nonsense, Noise, Impertinence and Pride.[22]

In the same poem he had been equally rude about the man who was to be his prosecutor, Sir Simon Harcourt.[23] He was convicted, and as one of the penalties of his conviction he was banned from polemical writing for seven years – no doubt precisely with his lampooning bent in mind – and at first he looked upon this as the end of his poetic career. But the habit was too engrained, and his lampooning satire on Parliament, *The Dyet of Poland* (1705) would be, if anything, more ferocious than anything of his before.[24]

The presiding genius in *A New Discovery*, antithesis to the traitorous miscreants in the lieutenancy, is King William ('great Nassau'). Defoe, who prays to Jupiter to inspire his satire, evokes William as another Jupiter, armed with thunder and able to hurl conspirators down to hell as Jupiter did the Titans.

> Great *Nassau* from his envied Throne look't down,
> And view'd their busie Malice with a Frown.
> Their Impotent Fury view'd with just disdain,
> *And ask'd if he had Sav'd them all in vain?*[25]

We have here the first taste of another major theme in Defoe's political life: that William represented the true gospel of statesmanship. He was a model of vision, personal nobility and self-abnegation, whose judgements, bitterly contested as they often were during his lifetime, almost always turned out to have been right. Olympian though he is depicted as in *A New Discovery*, he is also a paragon of gentleness; and there are moments when Defoe hints at his being another Messiah, his saving of England resembling Christ's salvation of mankind.

*   *   *   *   *   *

During the early part of his reign, King William had been engaged in the Nine Years' War with France. In December 1697, a month or two after the Peace of Ryswick and his triumphant return from the continent, the House of Commons debated the size of his army and, to the King's chagrin, proposed a very drastic reduction, Robert Harley suggesting that all land forces raised since 29 September 1680 should be disbanded. The rights and wrongs of a standing army became the issue of the day, and Defoe vigorously entered the controversy, publishing three pamphlets designed to give support to the King.[26] They argued, in sober fashion, a middle or 'moderate' way. Kings, they said, could tyrannize whether or not they had a standing army, and the idea that England could be sufficiently defended by a militia was ludicrous. The proper solution was a balance, the monarch having responsibility for making war and the People holding the purse-strings. (In writing these pamphlets it is always possible that Defoe received some encouragement from the Court, but we know of no actual evidence for this.)

He then turned his attention to what was to become a burning political issue and a preoccupation of his throughout much of his career, the 'Occasional Conformity' of Dissenters. Under the Corporation Act of 1661 and the Test Act of 1673 no-one might hold a municipal or national office without first qualifying by taking the sacrament according to the rites of the Church of England. These civil disabilities had remained in force even though, under the Toleration Act of 1689, Protestant Dissenters had been granted statutory freedom to worship outside the Church of England. There had thus grown up a practice among Dissenters, when appointed to municipal office, to take communion in an Anglican church on a single occasion, while continuing their membership of a Dissenting congregation. It had not attracted much notice until, upon becoming Lord Mayor in 1697, the Presbyterian Sir Humphrey Edwin took communion in St Paul's and on the same Sunday attended a Dissenting communion service at Pinners' Hall, in full mayoral regalia, compelling his indignant sword-bearer to do likewise. His action provoked an outcry from the High Church party, who regarded toleration as the cause of a serious decline in attendance and financial contributions to the Church of England, and from Tories, who saw Occasional Conformity as a means by which Dissenters and their Whig allies could exercise political power. It fell to Defoe, however, to attack Sir Humphrey's action on serious religious grounds.

In a subtle and sardonic pamphlet, *An Enquiry into the Occasional Conformity of Dissenters*, published in January 1698, he told Sir Humphrey that if the rights of his sword-bearer were infringed by Sir Humphrey's making him attend a Dissenting meeting house, his own liberty of conscience was equally violated, by his being forced to take communion at St Paul's. Why did Sir Humphrey put up with it? When we saw him at St Paul's, Defoe writes ironically, we were in hopes that he had seen the error of his Dissenting ways. (To suspect he was doing it to curry favour with both political parties was too base.) But to see him immediately afterwards worshipping in a meeting house left one simply bewildered. What was this '*new sort of a religion that looks two ways at once*'?[27]

The Dissenters, wrote Defoe, were the heirs of the Puritans, but in some respects unworthy heirs. To be a Protestant under Mary Tudor was a genuine test of conscience, and the debates between the Reformers in the age of Elizabeth were singularly earnest and devout. Their tone was very different from that of later debates. Indeed, the present day offered a unique spectacle.

> There is a sort of Truth which all men owe to the Principles they profess; and generally speaking, all men pay it; a *Turk* is a *Turk* zealously and entirely; an Idolater is an Idolater, and *will serve the Devil to a tittle*: None but Protestants halt between *God* and *Baal*.

It was, he wrote, such a 'Bantering with Religion', such a '*playing Bo-peep* with God Almighty', as could not but fill any modest Christian with horror.[28]

*   *   *   *   *   *

In November 1700 Defoe ventured, for the first time, into foreign policy. In the previous month King Charles II of Spain had died and in his will he was found to have bequeathed his entire empire to Louis XIV's grandson, Philip of Anjou. It thus became an urgent question, whether Louis would support Philip's claim to the Spanish throne; and Defoe published an anonymous pamphlet, *The Two Great Questions Considered*, asking 'What the French King will do, with Respect to the Spanish Monarchy?' and 'What Measures the English ought to Take'.[29] His answer was that, if Louis were to support the Spanish

King's will, King William would inevitably have to form a continental alliance to preserve the balance of power. All the same, this might not be easy, since England, in its present army-less state, was cutting a very 'mean' figure abroad, and if it were not for King William no nation would want her as an ally. An anonymous rejoinder, *Remarks upon a Late Pamphlet*, admitted that the author 'has gotten abundance of reputation by writing his book' and speculated, perhaps perceptively: 'If ever man petitioned in print for a Place, surely our Author does in this book'.[30]

In September 1701 the exiled James II died, and Louis XIV of France declared James's thirteen-year-old son to be his lawful successor and the rightful King of England. Defoe, in *The Present State of Jacobitism Considered* (1701), seized the occasion to address a persuasive and diplomatic argument to Protestant Jacobites: that the death of James had released them from their vows of loyalty, and they could now honourably *'come into the Bosome and protection of the Government'*.[31] Their previous commitments, even if foolish, were worthy of respect, and their fellow citizens would welcome them back. He added (a characteristic touch) that the behaviour of Louis XIV, that wise king, towards the Stuarts, father and son, was a perfectly rational piece of statecraft, and the Jacobites would be fools to take it for more than it was worth. Defoe would be notably flexible in his approach towards the Jacobites, shifting, as circumstances required, between friendly persuasion, menace and ridicule; though in the end ridicule would predominate.

The King's troubles with Parliament steadily worsened. In April 1700 it was voted that the grants of Irish land he had made to friends and supporters after his victory at the battle of the Boyne should be revoked; also Parliament voted that an address be made to the King requesting him to appoint no foreigners, apart from Prince George, to his Privy Council. These insults prompted him to contemplate abdication. Then in the following year an attempt was made to impeach his leading ministers, Portland, Orford and Somers, for their part in drawing up the second of two Partition treaties, concerted by William without Parliamentary warrant, for a prospective division of Spain and its dominions.

Meanwhile Defoe's preoccupation with King William steadily grew, and it spurred him to write the poem *The True-Born Englishman*, which rocketed him to fame. The poem was a very personal and heart-felt tribute to the King, though it expanded beyond this into a joyous wholesale denunciation of English chauvinism and ingratitude. He was to describe its origin later in his autobiographical *An Appeal to Honour and Justice*. In August 1700, he explains,

> there came out a vile abhor'd Pamphlet, in very ill Verse, written by one Mr. *Tutchin*, and call'd THE FOREIGNERS: In which the Author, *who he was I then knew not*, fell personally upon the King himself, and then upon the *Dutch* Nation; and after having reproach'd his Majesty with Crimes, that his worst Enemy could not think of without Horror, he sums all in the odious Name of FOREIGNER.
>
> This fill'd me with a kind of Rage against the Book, and gave birth to a Trifle which I never could hope should have met with so general an Acceptation as it did, I mean, *The True-Born-Englishman*.[32]

The poem is the supreme example of a favourite manouevre of Defoe's, a joyous savaging of the follies of his own side or party – no less, in this case, than the English people. Why are the English so factious, it asks, and more restless in peace than in war? Why are they so scornful of foreigners? Why do they never recognise their own good fortune, '*And always have been sav'd against their Will*?[33] These are questions which 'Satire' is best fitted to answer, and it entails going back to ancient times – when it would have been a puzzle what the words a 'True-Born-Englishman' could possibly mean.

The truth, so Satire explains, is that the Devil was always a most successful monarch, providing his subjects with an easy reign. Unlike mortal rulers, he suffers no annoyance from nonconforming sects, nor is he in need of a standing army. For he has discovered a secret: the art of ruling each nation by their favourite sin. With the Spaniards it is Pride, for the Italians Lust, the Germans chose Drunkenness and the French ('A *Dancing Nation*, Fickle and Untrue') opted for Passion. He binds the Irish, the Danes, the Swedes and Muscovites, the Portuguese, the Dutch and the Scotch, the Persians, Tartars, Turks, Moors and Chinese by chains suited to their genius and inclinations.[34]

And the English? No question about their darling sin, it is Ingratitude: 'An Ugly, Surly, Sullen, Selfish Spirit, / *Who* Satan*'s worst Perfections does inherit*'. England's open harbours and fertile meadows, and her too-hospitable women, invited in marauders from all quarters – Romans and their slaves, Saxons, Scots, Picts and Irish, and

William's Normans – each introducing their own language and manners and leaving behind their barbarous offspring. It is from this 'Amphibious Ill-born Mob' that sprang '*That vain ill-natur'd thing, an Englishman*'.[35]

William the Conqueror, indeed, made his obscure troopers into lords and freeholders, so blessing England with a nobility. It was, nevertheless, a paradoxical one. 'A *Turkish* Horse can show more History, / To prove his Well-descended Family', than True-Born Englishmen boasting of their Norman ancestry, yet it is these who despise 'newcome Foreigners' and look down upon their rescuers, the Dutch! For it is not as if the invasions ceased with the Normans. England continued to be '*Europe*'s Sink, *the Jakes* where she / Voids all her Offal Outcast Progeny'. Religion (God be thanked) sent droves of 'Priests, Protestants, *the Devil and all* together' to England to find refuge; and soon, in turn, they would complain loudly of the Scots, who crowded hither in the wake of King James I.[36]

Here Defoe's poem – spun along by the continual return, swelling in irony at each repetition, of the refrain 'True-Born Englishman' – reaches a magnificent crescendo of comic insult.

> *Scots* from the *Northern* Frozen Banks of *Tay*,
> With Packs and Plods came *Whigging* all away:
> Thick as the Locusts which in *Egypt* swarm'd,
> With Pride and hungry Hopes compleatly arm'd:
> With Native *Truth*, *Diseases*, and *no Money*,
> Plunder'd our *Canaan* of the Milk and Honey.
> Here they grew quickly Lords and Gentlemen,
> And all their Race are *True-Born Englishmen*.[37]

As we wrote some years ago, the verb 'Whigging' here is, hedgehoglike, designed to sting whoever takes hold of it.[38]

Having told us of the origins of the 'True-Born English', Satire next describes them and their foibles in the present day: their drunkenness, their refractoriness, their fine words in favour of friendship ('None talk on't more, or understand it less') and their detestation of whoever does them a good turn.[39] What more typical than their rapturous welcome of King William and the way that, safely restored to their rights and possessions, they turned to harassing and traducing him and began to find excuses for the exiled King James?

It was in vain that they did so, for King James had un-kinged himself. The poem passes from satire for a moment to a memorable statement of Whig political principle: that the source of power resides in the People (the 'Original').

> If to a King they do the Reins commit,
> All men are bound in Conscience to submit:
> But then that King must by his Oath assent
> To *Postulata*'s of the Government;
> Which if he breaks, he cuts off the Entail,
> And Power retreats to its Original.[40]

There follows a hymn, sung by Britannia, in praise of King William:

> *Princes for Pride and Lust of Rule make War,*
> And struggle for the name of Conqueror.
> *Some fight for Fame, and some for Victory.*
> He fights to Save, and Conquers to set Free.[41]

After this, Satire resumes its work, giving us a matchless modern example of the True-Born Englishman's sin. Sir Charles Duncombe, a ploughboy turned millionaire who rose by cheating his own patron, explains with pride how in one year he was expelled from Parliament for forgery and in the next awarded a knighthood, how as a sheriff he hired gaol-birds to proclaim his glory, and as a public benefactor he 'gives to God what he has stole from Kings'.[42]

The moral of this reckless and liberating poem is a simple one:

> Then let us boast of Ancestors no more,
> Or Deeds of Heroes done in days of Yore …
> For Fame of Families is all a Cheat,
> *'Tis Personal Virtue only makes us great.*[43]

The poem provoked a whole string of rejoinders. The larger part of these were condemnations of the author for anti-patriotism and for 'fouling his own nest',[44] and some, like the anonymous *A Satyr upon Thirty Seven Articles*, supposed, or pretended to suppose, that the author had sold himself to the Dutch.

> What makes an *English Sat'rist* losely [*sic*] write
> Against his *Country-men* with so much spite;
> Revile their *Honour* and their *Blood* debase,
> To please the Quagmire of a *croaking Race?*[45]

From William Pittis, a somewhat drunken High Church pamphleteer, it provoked a long poem of some 720 lines entitled *The True-Born
Hugonot*, in which he represented Defoe as an example of the locust-
like proclivities of the Huguenot refugees in England.

> Out of this *Rebel Herd* our *Rebel* sprung
> And brought the Virtues of the Soil along,
> A mild Behaviour and a fluent Tongue.
> With up-lift Eyes, and with ambitious Heart,
> On *England*'s Theatre to act his Part.
> How well he acted, witness ye that saw,
> How wresting *Gospel*, and provoking Law!
> A true Malignant, Arrogant and Sour,
> And ever Snarling at establish'd Pow'r;
> More famous for *Ill-Nature* than for *Wit*,
> And like a *Bull-Dog* lik'd, because he Bit,
> As he got in with the *Dissenting Tribe*,
> And from a Broken *Hosier*, turn'd a *Scribe*.[46]

Pittis was to devote much of his later career to writing answers to
Defoe.

* * * * * *

'I believe no Man in the World was ever *the Peoples King* more than his
present Majesty', writes Defoe in one of his standing-army tracts.[47]
The remark has a bearing on the brief period in which he himself took
on the role of intrepid demagogue or 'tribune of the people'. On 29
April 1701, at the Kent Quarter-Sessions at Maidstone, the Grand
Jury and justices and freeholders signed a petition to the Commons
about 'the dangerous estate of this kingdom', humbly imploring the
House to 'have regard to the voice of the people' and to turn their
loyal addresses into votes of supply, so that the King might be 'enabled powerfully to assist his allies before it is too late'. Five Kentish
gentlemen were deputed to deliver the petition, which they did on 7
May, and the House, highly incensed, voted it 'Scandalous, Insolent,
and Seditious' and threw the petitioners into prison.[48]

This was the cue for Defoe to emerge in a new role. A week after
the arrest of the 'Kentish Gentlemen' he made an appearance at Westminster, accompanied by a guard of sixteen 'gentlemen of quality', and

– 18 –

delivered to the Speaker (Robert Harley) a paper known as *Legion's Memorial*. It presented, as from 'The People of England' and in the most threatening terms, an 'abridgement' of the nation's grievances against the Commons. Among its demands were that all just national debts should be discharged, all persons illegally imprisoned be released or bailed, vigorous resistance be given to the growing power of France, and the thanks of the House be offered to the gallant Kentish petitioners. The Speaker was commanded '*by Two Hundred Thousand English-men*' to put the *Memorial* before the Commons and told that if he refused, he would '*find cause in a short time to Repent it*'. '*Our Name is Legion*', the Memorial ended threateningly, '*and we are Many*'.[49]

This astonishing ultimatum appears to have terrified the House; at all events it seems that no steps were taken to punish the authors. The impeachment of William's ministers was dropped; the King eventually got his 'supplies'; and on the prorogation of Parliament the Kentish gentlemen were released from prison, and immediately afterwards they were entertained at a lavish dinner in Mercers' Hall. Defoe sat next to the guests of honour, and – as a Tory journalist remarked – 'one might have read the downfall of parliaments in his very countenance'.[50] The philanthropic projector[51] and amused satirist had become a formidable radical activist and self-appointed spokesman for 'the People'.

What exactly he meant by 'the People', however, needs to be spelled out, and this is very clearly done for us in a tract which Defoe published at the end of same year, 1701, entitled *The Original Power of the Collective Body of the People of England*. It is one of his most important writings, an idiosyncratic statement of an extreme Whig theory of sovereignty.[52] Framed as a sequence of brief maxims, it is not only an attack on 'divine right' theory but more particularly on a recent pamphlet by the Tory financier and MP Sir Humphrey Mackworth, entitled *A Vindication of the Rights of the Commons of England* (1701). Mackworth had asserted that all political authority in England lay with the King, Lords and Commons. Their respective powers served as checks and balances to one another, but they were 'not to be limited by any authority besides their own' and the ordinary citizen had no right to criticize them.[53] Defoe, by contrast, asserts the 'original right' of the 'People' of England to govern themselves. They may depute this right to a monarch, a nobility, or a house of representatives, but if those governors betray the 'public good' their authority ends, and (as he had phrased it in *The True-Born Englishman*) 'Power retreats to its Original'. For there is, and must be, 'some Power *Prior* to the power of King, Lords and Commons, from which, as the Streams from the Fountain, the Power of King, Lords and Commons is derived'; and if the People cannot retrieve this power from bad governments by peaceful means, they may reasonably resort to force or ask for help from a neighbouring nation.[54]

There is, nevertheless, an important qualification to be made. The power or 'original right' that Defoe speaks of belongs essentially to freeholders. They are the proper owners of the country, the other inhabitants being merely 'Sojourners' or lodgers, who must either accept the laws that the freeholders impose or leave the country. ('If any single Man in *England* should at any time come to be Landlord of the whole Freehold of *England*', Defoe adds with a touch of fantasy, 'he would immediately be the full Representative of all the Counties in *England*, and might Elect himself Knight of the Shire for every County, and the Sheriff of every County must Return him accordingly'.)[55]

In March 1702 King William died, and it became clear that, with the accession of Queen Anne, the country had taken a swerve towards Tory and High Church views. The Church of England had by this time become bitterly divided into 'High Church' and 'Low Church' parties, the High Church being aligned with the Tories, and the Low Church with the Whigs and their Dissenting supporters. Thus the Dissenters could expect trouble. Anathemas against them, and hints that it was time to reconsider William's Act of Toleration, were to be heard from Anglican pulpits, and, in a sulphurous sermon, Henry Sacheverell, a fellow of Magdalen College in Oxford, called upon all good sons of the Church to 'Hang out the *Bloody Flag*, and *Banner* of Defiance' against Dissenters amd members of the Low Church.[56] By November a legal blow had been aimed at the Dissenters, in the shape of a Parliamentary bill to outlaw the practice of Occasional Conformity.

Defoe's first reaction to this was characteristic and significant. In an anonymous pamphlet published in November 1702, *An Enquiry into Occasional Conformity, Shewing that the Dissenters are no Way Concern'd in it*, he argued that everybody, in either camp, was strangely mistaken about the bill – everybody but himself, which was an awkward thing to say, but happened to be true.[57] The fact was, the bill was thoroughly unjust and malicious but it could do no possible harm to conscientious Dissenters, who would not dream of practicing Occasional Conformity anyway. It might even strengthen them in their faith; and, if it prompted weaker brethren to desert the Dissenting fold, the Church was welcome to them. The Queen had promised to maintain the Act of Toleration, wrote Defoe. The Dissenters deserved more, but this was their essential and precious protection, and they must content themselves with it.

His tract was aimed at his fellow Dissenters whom, characteristically, he was very happy to enrage (he was never a 'joiner'). For High Church readers he was constructing a different engine of war. On 1 December 1702, three days after the bill passed the Commons, he published an anonymous tract entitled *The Shortest Way with the Dissenters*, in which the imaginary author, in the very accents of Sacheverell and his like, outlined what would really be the simplest solution as regards the Dissenters. For fourteen years (that is to say, since the Revolution) had the Dissenters not bullied the Church of England with their Act of Toleration and set up their 'Canting-Synagogues' at the very church-door? Now, with a new 'Royal, *English*, True' friend of the Church (i.e. Queen Anne) on the throne, it was time, the writer said, for retribution. The Dissenters realized it themselves, crying out self-pityingly about '*Peace, Union, Forbearance*, and *Charity*, as if the Church had not too long harbour'd her Enemies under her Wing, and nourish'd the viperous Brood, till they hiss and fly in the face of the Mother that cherish'd them'. The simple answer was that they must be rooted out. The King of France had managed it with his Protestants, and they had been more numerous. Moreover, it would be the Dissenters' own fault; for in the days of their ascendancy during the Commonwealth what charity had they ever showed to their enemies? '*Alas! the Church of England!* What with Popery on one Hand, and Schismatics on the other; how has she been Crucify'd between two Thieves. Now *let us Crucifie the Thieves*.'[58]

Defoe's plan was for some at least of his High Church readers to be taken in and believe these very welcome views to come from one of their own number. In this he succeeded magnificently. According to Defoe, one country clergyman wrote that he prized *The Shortest Way* above any book he owned except '*the Holy Bible, and Sacred Comments*' and prayed to God to put it into the heart of Queen Anne to carry out its recommendations.[59] Indeed Defoe had succeeded too well for his own comfort. When it dawned on High-flying readers, who had praised the tract, that they had been gulled, their fury was intense. Moreover Defoe's Dissenting brethren were almost equally resentful. They smarted at having been fooled (as many of them were) and told themselves that such terrible things ought not to be said, even in jest or irony. Even the Whig John Tutchin, who wrote with relish in the *Observator* (23–6 December 1702) that the tract must be by one of the 'Inferior Clergy', was enraged when he discovered that he had been fooled. 'Perhaps there was never a greater piece of Villany impos'd upon Mankind', he said (30 December–2 January). 'This is a Cheat that even a Heathen would have blush'd to expose to the World.' The Government, for its part, took the matter very seriously, and on 3 January 1703 a warrant was issued for Defoe's arrest. He fled from justice, and a week later a proclamation was issued in the Queen's name offering a reward for his capture. In this emergency Defoe wrote an eloquent appeal to the High Church Secretary of State, the Earl of Nottingham, saying that to flee from the Queen's justice seemed to him to be 'a kind of Raiseing Warr Against her' and begging Nottingham to help him in 'Laying Down These Arms' or in making a truce, also offering, in exchange for a pardon, to raise and lead a troop of horse for the Queen at his own expense.[60] It was to no avail.

Eventually, in May, he was tracked down and arrested in Spitalfields, at the house of a friend of his, a silk weaver named Sammen. He was lengthily interrogated by the haughty and gloomy Nottingham, who appeared to be fishing for secrets about Dissenting conspiracies. A large quantity of his papers was seized for examination; and he was appointed to be tried at the Old Bailey, bail being granted, but in the very large sum of £1,500.

As defending counsel he engaged his friend William Colepeper, a rash choice seeing that he had been one of the Kentish petitioners, and on Colepeper's persuasion he agreed to plead guilty. In his own words, he 'agreed to give the Court No Trouble but to plead Guilty to the Indictment, Even to all the Adverbs, the Seditiously's, The Malitiously's, and a long Rapsody of the Lawyers et Ceteras; and all this upon promises of being us'd Tenderly'.[61] Colepeper's turned out to have been bad advice; and as a result of his trial (a dramatic and highly-publicized affair) he was fined and sentenced to stand three times in the pillory, and to remain in Newgate until he could 'find good sureties to be of good behaviour for the space of seven years'.[62]

The trial had impressed the eminent Quaker William Penn. He was not personally known to Defoe, but he had been a fellow-sufferer on behalf of Dissent, and through his influence in high places he managed to have Defoe's punishment delayed. Writing to Penn from Newgate (12 July), to thank him for his 'Extraordinary Kindness', Defoe gave an account of the position he had maintained under official questioning, which was that, not only was he unwilling to betray innocent men, he really had nothing of significance – no conspiracy – to reveal. 'I Sollemnly Affirm that Other than what passes in Conversation, and Perhaps There is ill blood among people of my Opinion More than Enough, but other Than that I have no Accomplices'.[63] He had reason to brood over 'ill blood' and disunity among his fellow Dissenters, for he had invited three eminent Dissenting divines (John Howe, John Spademan and Robert Fleming, all favourers of Occasional Conformity) to join him in prayer in his prison cell in Newgate, but they had refused.[64]

Five days later, however, Godolphin informed Nottingham that Penn had come to see him and told him a very different story: that 'De Foe was ready to make oath to y[r.] L[p] of all that he knew, & to give an Account of all his Accomplices in whatsoever he has been Concerned, for the information of the Queen, & the Lords of the Councill, provided that by so doing, he may bee excused from the punishment of the pillory, & not produced as Evidence against any person whatsoever'.[65]

What, in the end, Defoe did, or did not, 'confess' must remain an unsolved problem. Even after the interrogation at Windsor, the indefatigable Nottingham, together with the Lord Privy Seal, visited him in his cell in Newgate; but they could extract no more information. Defoe, however, would bear a long-lasting resentment against Nottingham and what he regarded as his harsh and deceitful treatment, and would pursue him over the years in a long sequence of savage gibes and blackenings of his reputation.[66] Defoe's appearances in the pillory turned out, in fact, to be a personal triumph. According to contemporary accounts, the crowd pelted him, not with rotten eggs, but with flowers; and copies of a poem, *A Hymn to the Pillory*, which he had composed for the occasion, were handed round and recited by ballad-singers. The theme of this poem, which is in the form of an irregular Pindaric ode, is the rights and grandeur of authorship and its power to turn even the pillory to advantage. By a brilliant succession of conceits the pillory is made to stand for all the institutions of society: the pulpit, the stage, the bar, the pageants and the '*opening Vacancys*' (in other words, jobs) of a corrupt state system. The poem even dares to insult the 'Mob', whom the powers-that-be intended to shower the victim with filth, and challenges the crowd to act, not as a 'Mob', but as the 'People'.[67] This was, nevertheless, the end of Defoe's career as a public agitator.

It was evidently the moment for a new start; and providentially one was offered. The ambitious Robert Harley, leader of the so-called 'Country' party and, since 1700, Speaker of the House of Commons, had realized the potential usefulness of such a skilled writer and, with the assistance of the Lord High Treasurer, the Earl of Godolphin, he secured his release from Newgate and engaged him as an unofficial agent and adviser.

Harley was a dominating political figure, said to have an unrivalled knowledge of Parliamentary procedure. His father Sir Edward Harley, a country squire in Herefordshire, had been prominent on the Parliamentary side during the Civil War, and Robert had been brought up (in the words of David Hayton) in a 'heavy atmosphere of Puritan religiosity'.[68] The marks of this persisted throughout his life, though to what extent, in his later years, he was at heart a religious man is not clear. For he was also notably secretive. Some time after the Hanoverian succession Richard Steele, very much Harley's enemy, wrote of him harshly: 'It is an hard thing to unlearn gestures of the body, and though [Harley] has quite got over all the prejudices of his education, not only as to superstition, but as to religion also, he makes a very queer figure, and the persecuted sneak is still in his face, though he now sets up for a persecutor'.[69]

Harley already employed several other journalistic agents (among them John Toland and Charles Davenant), and he was a pioneer in the control of Parliament through the press.[70] There was a piquancy, however, in his making this approach to Defoe, in that he had been the architect of the anti-Williamite measures – the drastic reduction of the armed forces and the resumption of the King's Irish grants – against which Defoe had been writing so industriously. But he was a man of graceful and affable manners, and Defoe evidently felt he was being offered not only financial salvation but friendship.

Part of the bargain or understanding they entered into was that Defoe should launch a political journal, the one we know as the *Review*

CHAPTER 2

DEFOE AND THE DEAD KING

Defoe emerged from Newgate ruined and humiliated but, so he liked to let it be known, with one impressive claim to respect: that he had known, and even been intimate with, King William. Writing much later in *An Appeal to Honour and Justice* (1715) he asserted that their relationship dated from the publishing of *The True-Born Englishman*.

> How this Poem was the Occasion of my being known to his Majesty; how I was afterwards receiv'd by him; how Employ'd; and how, above my Capacity of deserving, Rewarded, is no Part of the present Case, and is only mention'd here as I take all Occasions to do for the expressing the Honour I ever preserv'd for the Immortal and Glorious Memory of that Greatest and Best of Princes, and who it was my Honour and Advantage to call Master as well as Sovereign, whose Goodness to me I never forgot, neither can forget; and whose Memory I never patiently heard abused, nor ever can do so, and who had he liv'd, would never have suffered me to be treated as I have been in the World.[1]

From the time of his release from Newgate onwards, Defoe's relations with King William became one of his most cherished themes. He evidently spoke about it to Harley, for in a letter of May or June 1704 he writes to him, 'All my prospects were built on a Manufacture I had Erected in Essex; all The late kings Bounty to me was Expended. There I Employ'd a hundred Poor Familys at work, and it began to Pay me very well.' On 2 November 1704 he tells Harley of the timely advice he gave the King at a fraught political moment ('Your Majtie Must Face About, Oblige your Friends to be Content to be Laid by, and Put In your Enemyes ...'), advice which 'his Majtie had the Goodness to Accept, and Over Vallue by Far'.[2] He does not so far allude to his friendship with the King in print. This has to wait for quite a few more years; but at last, in a dozen *Reviews* from 1707 onwards, the year in which he began regularly to celebrate William's birthday, he expatiated on it, as also in pamphlets. He writes, for example, of his privilege in being 'heard and valued by the best King that ever reign'd over you', of his being 'BELOV'D by that Glorious Prince', of 'the Bounty of his late Majesty' and how, in the space of half a year he had 'tasted the difference between the Closet of a King, and the Dungeon of *Newgate*'.[3] In his *History of the Union* (1709) we are told how, in the course of a discussion with the Monarch on 'a Scheme of General Peace among the Protestant Interests in Europe', he 'had the Honour' to mention the advantages of Union between England and Scotland, and how the King replied sadly '*I have done all I can in that Affair, but I do not see a Temper in either Nation that looks like it*', adding '*It may be done, but not yet*'. Also in the *History of the Union*, we are told that Defoe heard something of the inner story of the Glencoe massacre 'from Persons very near the King, and perhaps from His Majesties own Mouth'.[4] In his poem 'The Storm' he recalls how

> I've heard the sighing Monarch say,
> The Publick Peace so near him lay,
> It took the Pleasure of his Crown away.[5]

By the year 1705 he was claiming that, in his troubles over *The Shortest Way*, he was suffering for his loyalty to King William. He was, so he wrote to Lord Halifax, one 'who scorn'd to Come out of Newgate at the Price of betraying a Dead Master'.[6]

Allusions to this friendship served him as an effective rhetorical put-down. 'If I should say I had the Honour to know some things from his Majesty, and to transact some things for his Majesty, that he would not have trusted his Lordship with', he tells his adversary Lord Haversham, 'perhaps there may be more Truth than Modesty in it'.[7] 'I am not at all vain in saying', he remarks on another occasion, 'I had the Honour to know more of His Majesty, than some of these that have thus insulted His Character, knew of *His Horse*'.[8]

Some have felt that he goes on rather too much about all this, and also that perhaps he embroiders the truth.[9] Certainly there are some problems about the story, and especially the fact that every bit of it comes from Defoe himself. It seems strange that (with one possible exception) no-one at the time made the slightest reference to this remarkable association. We do not even know where their meetings are supposed to have taken place.

But indeed there must undoubtedly have been some embroidering. Although in *An Appeal to Honour and Justice* Defoe says that he got to know King William through *The True-Born Englishman*, he claims in *The Succession of Spain Consider'd* (1701) to have witnessed the drafting of William's Second Partition Treaty and speaks of having some of the original drafts in his possession.[10] He goes even further in the *Review* for 28 April 1711, where he seems to claim to have taken part in the drafting process: 'I remember in that Famous Treaty, *which I had the Honour to see, and something more in its Embrio* [our italics] – This Fundamental Maxim is laid down ...'. Now, *The True-Born Englishman* came out in January 1701 or thereabouts, and the Second Partition Treaty was being drafted in the autumn of 1699.

Plainly, all is not well with Defoe's story, and it looks as if he must have made some of it up. Which leads to the question, did he perhaps make it all up? We have reason to ask, since in 1708, when the author of the *Observator* challenged 'Mr. *Review*' over his alleged services to King William, he was quick to back down. The *Review* for 3 January 1708 had complained of a passage in the *Observator* for 17–20 December 1707, criticizing William for being bad at taking advice, and in turn the *Observator* replied (3–7 January 1708): 'his [Defoe's] Charge of my reflecting upon K. William, 'tis all of a Piece with the rest of his Ignorance and Malice. I had better opportunities of knowing that Great Prince than ever the Slanderer could pretend to; and did him more Service than ever he was capable of, tho' the Scribler has boasted of large rewards from him, for libelling our native Country, in his *True-born* English-man'.

Defoe's response to this in the *Review* for 13 January is decidedly meek.

> As to his [the *Observator*'s] comparing himself to the *Review*, the *Review* does not say he was ever so honour'd as Mr. *Observator*, in the Favour or Service of the late King; but this he says, he knows that His Majesty was a good Master, and if the *Observator* has had the Honour to be one of his Servants, it is so much the more Barbarous for him to fall upon his Masters Memory, with such a Scurrilous and Scandalous Reproach.

This, allowing for a certain vagueness in the phrasing, seems to be granting the *Observator* its point; and so, by default at least, does what he goes on to say in the next issue of the *Review*, for 15 January, which is merely a denial that he ever boasted of receiving bounty from the King.

> His plain Forgeries on me are too mean Things to name here, only still as they reflect on the King, such as that I have boasted of Rewards from the King, for libelling our Native Country in the *True-Born-Englishman* … That the King should reward any Man for libelling his Native Country, there's another Piece of Dirt thrown at his Majesty, which at the same time I challenge him to prove; or secondly to prove, that ever I boasted of any Rewards from His Majesty on that Poem, or for any thing else.[11]

If his account of his friendship with the King had been true, Defoe would have surely made some defence against this challenge – would have claimed to have evidence in the form of documents in the King's handwriting, or the like.

One strong reason for doubting Defoe's stories about himself and King William is that, as we have said, they contain flagrant contradictions. But of course another is that some of them, and especially the business of the King discussing the Partition Treaty – that most momentous, most top secret of documents – with Defoe, and of his actually helping in the drafting, are almost impossibly hard to swallow. It does seem proper, then, in regard to this particular story, to let scepticism do its worst. Surely, for one thing, the drafting took place not in England but in Holland? Then, in *The Succession of Spain Consider'd*, Defoe puts forward two possible schemes of partition of the Spanish monarchy, of which one would assign the throne of Spain to the son of the Duke of Savoy and both would give the kingdom of Lombardy to the Duke of Savoy himself. He asks the reader not to think his suggestions too arrogant, as coming from a private citizen, for 'these Schemes are drawn from, and with very little difference, are a faithful Abstract of those Original Drafts, from which the late *Treaty of Partition*, which he had the Honour to see form'd, was after many Consultations and Alterations Concluded; and which he has still by him to produce'.[12] However, in the Treaties as they were finally drawn up, we look in vain for mention of any such donations to the House of Savoy; and anyway the reason given for rewarding the Duke in this way (his 'Faithful Services to the House of *Austria*[13]) plainly relates to the Duke's conduct in the present war (i.e. an event much later in date than the Treaty).

What also makes for difficulty is the timetable. *The True-Born Englishman* came out in January 1701, or conceivably the previous month,[14] and by June 1701 the King had sailed for Holland, not returning till November and dying the following March. This does not leave much time for Defoe to have become 'beloved' by the King, or, as he claims, to have travelled about England on the King's affairs.[15]

One would, in fact, hardly be tempted to believe Defoe at all were it not for one striking piece of evidence – first published by Paula R. Backscheider – which might possibly support his story. This is a note from the Earl of Nottingham to Godolphin of 22 July 1703, referring to his interrogations of Defoe at the time of *The Shortest Way with the Dissenters*. He writes: 'I askt him when his advice about dissolving the Parliament was given, and he cd not at first recollect but concluded that he verily believed 'twas before the King went into Holland'.[16] The most natural interpretation of this would be that the advice was given to someone close to the King, or to the King himself. However, against this is the fact that when, over four months later (on 11 November), William did dissolve Parliament, it was a quite unforeseen decision, prompted by the news that James II had died and Louis XIV had recognized the Pretender as King of England, events which entirely transformed the political situation.

As we saw, the main object of Defoe's interrogation at the time of his arrest and trial was to discover whether he had any accomplices in the *Shortest Way* affair, and if so who they were. It may be, as Backscheider assumes, that Nottingham also tried to fish out other secrets about the previous reign. However, an alternative explanation seems also feasible: i.e. that Defoe himself had hinted, during an earlier interrogation, that – in addition to writing pamphlets on King William's behalf[17] – he had known and advised the King personally. To claim a personal relationship with the King would have been an ingenious, though extremely audacious, ploy on Defoe's part, bestowing lustre on himself if it were believed; and Nottingham was now trying to test the truth of this. The story, according to our hypothesis, would have been a fiction invented to save himself from the pillory – a fiction that, once it had proved its value, he grew extremely fond of and would embellish lovingly over the years to come.

His boldness in this affair (if we are right about it) is certainly staggering. We suggest that it may be connected with another trait of his, which we discuss later: his fascination with the possibilities of public credulity.[18] It would certainly be no disgrace for his biographers to have been hoodwinked by him. But further, it would suggest an explanation for an all-important fact about Defoe, experienced by all who write about him: that it is impossible to reach any close intimacy with him or to read his heart. A man capable of a deception of the scale of Defoe's over King William would be perpetually on his guard against intimacy and on the defensive against the world.

In 1955 the executors of Mrs E. Defoe Latham deposited with the Bodleian Library, on permanent loan, some letters from Daniel Defoe, hitherto in the possession of the Defoe family, and with them a thin manuscript book containing two remarkable letters of political advice addressed to King William, dated (from 'Hampton Court') 24 November and 12 December 1701.[19] They had been brought to light by George Healey, in the course of his work as editor of Defoe's letters, and at first he had naturally assumed that the letters to King William were by Defoe. Then, in a flash of inspiration, he realized that they must be by Defoe's friend William Paterson – the Scottish financier and projector of the ill-fated Darien scheme.[20] The envelope containing the volume was inscribed, in an unknown hand, 'This is the Identical M.S. Presented to King Wm in 1701', but there seems no way of telling whether this was true, or of establishing how the manuscript came into Defoe's possession. However there is good evidence that the King invited Paterson to meet and advise him in 1701, and that Paterson made proposals much like those put forward in the two letters, recommending the seizing of the isthmus of Darien or Panama, with Cartagena and the Havannahs of Cuba.[21]

Now, a broadly similar scheme was what Defoe would repeatedly (and eloquently) advocate in the *Review*, and he claimed to have laid such a plan before King William. He refers to this in the *Review* for 18 January 1711 ('I have the Schemes still by me'); and in the issue for 28 June 1711 he writes, apropos of the launching of the South Sea Company:

> I have told the World in a late *Review, long before this Project was on Foot,*
> how I had the Honour to lay a Proposal before his late Majesty *King*
> *William,* in the beginning of this War, for the carrying the War not
> into *Old Spain,* but into *New Spain;* not into *Catalognia,* but into *Amer-*
> *ica;* which Proposal his Majesty approv'd of, and fully purpos'd to
> put in Execution, had not Death, to our unspeakable Grief, pre-
> vented him.

Defoe evidently came to know of the privileged role Paterson had
been invited to play, as unofficial adviser to the King, and, as we have
shown, he had some 'schemes' by Paterson in his possession. One
wonders whether this might not have encouraged him, or helped to
encourage him, to invent a similar role for himself. If so, it would con-
stitute one of the more amazing facts about this extraordinary man
and prove, once again, the soundness of William Minto's admiring
remark: 'He was a great, a truly great liar, perhaps the greatest liar that
ever lived'.[22]

CHAPTER 3

THE AUTHOR OF THE *REVIEW*

Defoe's journal the *Review* was launched at an auspicious time. In 1695 the Licensing Act of 1662, by which books and pamphlets had to receive official approval before they could be published, had been allowed to lapse, and the result had been a great upsurge of pamphleteering and journalism. Newspapers (to use the words of Laurence Hanson) began to 'encroach on the whole field of politics'.[1]

Attempts, now and later, were made to revive the licensing system, but without success. The High Church party brought a bill to 'restrain the licentiousness of the press' before the Commons in January 1704, only a week or two before the launching of the *Review*; and a few days before the bill's first reading Defoe published an *Essay on the Regulation of the Press*.[2] In this he took what would always remain his stance over the matter. He granted there must be some restriction on the press, and that authors who broke the laws of libel or blasphemy ought to be punished; but pre-publication licensing, he contended, was to make the press 'a slave to a Party', and to put 'an absolute Negative on the Press' into the hands of a licenser would be 'the first step to restore Arbitrary Power in this Nation'. The right method was, rather, to spell out what matters of Church and State were not to be criticized and to punish offending authors after publication. As a help to this, it should be enacted that the name of author, printer or bookseller must be placed on the title-page, and anyone selling an anonymous work should be deemed the author and held responsible for it.

His *Essay* was a well-argued but sober piece of writing, aiming at an appearance of strict impartiality. But what is pleasant is that we also have his uncensored thoughts on the question. An anonymous spy reported to Robert Harley, as Speaker of the House – evidently not suspecting any personal link between him and Defoe – that he had been present by accident at a secret meeting of avowed Dissenters and heard Defoe read out an ironical *Petition* to the Commons (later printed for private circulation) begging the Commons, in the legislation now pending, to restore the licensing system and place it firmly in Church of England's hands. There were, the petitioners said, so many good reasons for their request. For one thing, the Whigs and moderate churchmen were always 'Bullying the CHURCH of *England* in their Pamphlets and Writings about Law, Liberty, Property and Conscience, things we find it absolutely necessary, our present Circumstances Considered, not to be so much concern'd about as much as we use to be'. For another, given a Church of England licenser, the petitioners and their friends would be able to publish what they liked without the danger of a reply, a useful privilege 'Because we do find that these Damn'd Whigs are a little too hard for us, when we come to Down Right Arguments, Demonstration, *&c*'. Truly, the petitioners averred, 'Freedom of Speech ought not to be allow'd to any body except the Members of your honourable House and *us of the Pulpit*. And since the just Law of speaking Treason was Unhappily Expir'd, 'tis absolutely necessary to lock up the Pen of the Party since we cannot otherwise stop their Mouths'. The spy evidently hoped this new *Shortest Way* could land Defoe in Newgate and the pillory again – as indeed it might have, had it not been for Harley's protection.[3]

Defoe's *Review* was to be not a newspaper but a journal of opinion, like its rivals Tutchin's *Observator* and Ridpath's *Flying Post*, and this was not an undertaking for the timid. Governments resented the very existence of such productions, and there were stern penalties, targeting all concerned with them – editors, authors, booksellers and printers – for misdemeanours. In strict theory, criticism of the Government was the prerogative of Parliament and was not permitted to the common citizen; and for several more decades it would remain the rule (though a rule often evaded or broken) that Parliamentary speeches could not be published. But in practice many politicians were just as eager to exploit the new freedom of the press as journalists were; and seasoned journal-editors, such as Defoe would become, played a subtle game or duel with the libel laws. Much could be done by naming the famous only by their initials; and Defoe would always piously deny 'directing' Parliament.

The first number of his *Review* came out on 19 February 1704, under the title *A Weekly Review of the Affairs of France: Purg'd from the Errors and Partiality of News-Writers and Petty-Statesmen, of all Sides.*[4] This original title – it went through a number of changes, ending up as *A Review of the State of the British Nation* – was intentionally provocative, given that England was at war with France. It was meant to assert the need to face facts and to learn from one's enemies. (Julius Caesar's injunction never to despise one's enemy had been a watchword for Defoe from the time of his juvenile 'Historical Collections' and, as may be seen, was the complement of his rule to eschew all flank-rubbing as regards his own side.) Nevertheless it was an accurate title, for Defoe began with a grandiose historical scheme, that of tracing the rise of France to its present formidable greatness. How absurd, its drift was, for the English not to recognize the superior efficiency, civility and prudence of present-day France, not to mention the greater patriotism of her nobility, or to be unwilling to learn from them. They might do this notwithstanding the fact that the sagacious and large-minded French King, Louis XIV, was also a ruthless despot who aimed at hegemony over Europe and was the unceasing and dangerous enemy of Protestantism.[5]

Before long, being obliged to keep up with current events, 'Mr. *Review*' had to break off from his history of French greatness. By a logical transition, nevertheless, his main theme, through much of the later part of 1704, became the all-importance of the Protestant cause, a matter always central to his thinking. It was the failure of the Protestant nations to defend the cause of their religion, he maintained, that was the source of French greatness, and none were more guilty in this than the English. James I's failure to support the Protestant Frederick of Bohemia at the start of the Thirty Years' War and Charles I's betrayal of the Huguenots at the time of the siege of La Rochelle, in 1628, had had long-term and tragic consequences. How little, Defoe argued, does religion seem to count for the combatants on the European scene. The Hungarians, who recently had risen against the Austrian Empire, claimed to be fighting for the Protestant cause, but this was a mere pretence. Theirs was a war simply for liberty and aggrandizement; and those who wished them victorious were forgetting the importance of the Imperial armies to a quite different war, the one against France and against Catholic encroachment and tyranny.

Likewise Charles XII of Sweden, though a descendant of Gustavus Adolphus, the great champion of Protestantism, was ready to invade Poland and meddle with the Polish crown, leaving his own Protestant subjects in Livonia to be destroyed by the Russians. From now on the character of the young 'Gothick Hero' Charles XII, whose dazzling military escapades so riveted his contemporaries, became a sort of malign portent to Defoe. 'If this is to be a Hero —, if this be to make a King Great and Terrible in the World', he would write later, 'God Almighty grant, England may never be Govern'd by Heroes'.[6]

Such theories could hardly be directed at action, nevertheless Defoe was fascinated by the life of political action – for instance as it might be lived by his new employer, Robert Harley. Our evidence for this is the remarkable paper of advice he submitted to Harley in July or August 1704, when Harley had just been appointed Secretary of State.[7] (He would not often write to Harley with such boldness.) He had been reading the *Life* of Richelieu by Le Clerc,[8] and not only did he draw conclusions from Richelieu's example, he may also, one feels, have dreamed of playing a Richelieu-like role towards Harley. He begins by saying that the reason that England has no great and 'capital' men in her civil administration, no Richelieus, Mazarins and Colberts, is that the English have a rooted prejudice against favourites. But this difficulty, he says, could be overcome. Richelieu did not seek people's favour and got his way, defeating his adversaries, by 'mere force'; and whereas that would be impossible here, something equivalent was needed. It was essential for Harley to pursue popularity, and in this, after all, there was much to learn from Cardinal Richelieu. Richelieu took care never to appear involved in matters of punishment, but if a pardon were to be granted, he would manage to get the credit for it. 'A popular statesman', said Defoe, 'should have the obtaining all the favours and let others have the management of offences, and the distribution of justice'. He should be ready to disappoint his friends, if it was safe to do so, but to surprise his enemies with 'voluntary kindness'. Popularity must be based on genuine merit, but it would be no crime to try to persuade every Party that he was on their side – to 'obtain from them all a general esteem'. People might call this dissimulation, but that was a misconception; 'a lie does not consist in the indirect position of words but in the design by false speaking to deceive and injure my neighbour'.

The drift of all this is that Harley should make himself a 'Prime Minister', channelling most Government business through his own office. It was 'a method to make the office of Secretary of State an inner cabinet, and execute necessary parts of private affairs without the intervention of the Privy Council, and yet have their concurrence as far as the law requires'. In 'doubtful' affairs, the Privy Council would be a protection and screen. 'But in matters of war, treaties, embassies, private instructions, expeditions, how many such has the delay, the hesitations, the ignorance, or something worse, of Privy Councillors overthrown!' If Harley objected that he did not want to be a prime minister, then, said Defoe, he could not be a Secretary of State. 'The Secretary's office well discharged makes a man Prime Minister of course; and you must be Prime Minister with applause, or you will be Secretary with disgrace.' What Defoe was recommending here was, as we know, to become the modern system.

What, further, Defoe insists upon is the need for a really well-organized intelligence system, something that Richelieu considered of the first importance and upon which, so Defoe hears, Louis XIV spends eleven millions a year. A Secretary of State, says Defoe, ought to have

> 1st, a perfect list of all the gentry and families of rank in England, their residences, characters, and interest in the respective counties; 2nd, of all the clergy of England, their benefices, their character and morals, and the like of the Dissenters; 3rd, of all the leading men in the cities and boroughs, with the parties they espouse ... [He] should have a table of all the ministers of state, lists of the households, the privy councils, and favourites of every court in Europe, and their characters, with exact lists of their forces, names of the officers, state of their revenue, methods of government, etc. ... A hundred thousand pounds *per annum* spent now for 3 year in foreign intelligences might be the best money ever this nation laid out; and I am persuaded ... if some money had been well applied, neither the insurrection in Hungary nor the war in Poland should have been so fatal to the confederacy as now they are ... [The lack of a] settled intelligence in Scotland, a thing strangely neglected there, is without doubt the principal occasion of the present misunderstandings between the two kingdoms ...[9]

In this picture of an intelligence system Defoe was describing
something he felt that, given suitable funds, he might himself create
for Harley and would be his great contribution as Harley's servant.
Indeed, over the next year or two, he proceeded to set up a network of
correspondents all over England and Scotland, with fitful encouragement from his employer.

*   *   *   *   *   *

Defoe's pamphleteering during 1704 was much concerned with the
Dissenters and their wrongs. Charles Leslie, a non-juror and High
Church champion, had recently, in *The Wolf Stript of his Shepherd's
Cloathing* (1704), accused the Dissenters of leaguing together against
Church and State in a conspiratorial 'Society of Writers'; he
reproached them, moreover, for showing no desire for reunion with
the Church. Defoe answered him in *The Dissenters Answer to the High-
Church Challenge* (January 1704), lamenting that, on the contrary, the
Dissenters were all too disunited, and claiming that, anyway, they had
twice made proposals for reunion and been brutally rebuffed.[10] In *A
New Test of the Church of England's Honesty* (July 1704) he also pointed
out, with stinging irony, the dishonesty of the Church in ignoring the
large part played by the Dissenters in inviting King William to England.[11] At the same moment, however, Defoe, who felt he had been
badly let down by his fellow Dissenters at the time of the *Shortest
Way*,[12] was giving Harley Machiavellian advice on how to 'manage'
them and their Whig supporters. 'Sir', he wrote to Harley (2 November 1704) 'the Whigs are weak'.

> They may be Mannag'd, and Allways have been So. What Ever you
> do, if Possible Divide Them, and they are easy To be Divided.
> Caress The Fools of Them Most, There are enough Among Them.
> Buy them with here and there a Place; it may be well bestow'd.[13]

Or again,

> I allow ... That 'Tis Not Necessary in the present Conjuncture to
> Restore the Dissenters to Offices and Preferments.
>   This would Make the Govornmt Seem Byast in Their Favour.
> The high Church Men would reflect on her Majtie as Not True to
> her Own Principles or her Promise ...

> I Premise Also by the Way That I am Perswaded Freedom and
> favour to the Dissenters is the Directest Method to Lessen Their
> Numbers and bring Them at last into the Church. I Verily Believ the
> 18 yeares Liberty They have Enjoy'd has weaken'd Their Interest. A
> Tenderness and Moderation to Them will Still Lessen Them and I
> Could Say Much on This head.[14]

In August, on Harley's orders, Defoe set off on a fact-finding and
propaganda-making tour through the Eastern counties. He was feeling much gratitude towards his employer, who had recently secured
him a 'bounty' from the Queen – though, not for the last time, he was
wondering what exactly they expected of him. 'I Confess it Afflicts
me', he wrote, 'to See the Day Appear and My Self Unfurnisht with
The Main Thing, the Very Substance of all the Rest, *your Instructions*'.[15]
However, so he told Harley, he hoped his journey would be the foundation of such an intelligence service as England had never known.
The tour would also be a welcome escape from his creditors who, as
usual, were harrying him.

From Hertfordshire he reported on the state of the parties in the
county and on the activities of a Tory drinking club in Royston, the
members of which 'Settle all the affaires of the Country and carry all
before them'.[16] Proceeding from there to Norwich, he 'Perfectly Dis-
sected' the city for Harley's benefit.[17] But at this point he received a
shock. He came across a report in a newsletter saying that he had been
taken into custody for libelling the High Admiral Sir George Rooke.

We need to digress here, to explain the circumstances. Rooke was a
very influential High Tory, nevertheless he was considered by some to
be a timid and incompetent admiral; and when, just before Defoe's
trial in 1703, Defoe's friend and lawyer William Colepeper went to the
royal palace at Windsor, in connection with a petition on Defoe's
behalf, he became involved in an affray with a friend of Rooke's, Sir
Jacob Banks. Colepeper inquired of Banks, with what the latter took
to be a sneer, where Rooke was just at present, and Banks took his
cane to him; and not long after this, at the instigation of Rooke or his
cronies, Colepeper was set upon in the street by ruffians and nearly
murdered.[18]

Defoe had already satirized Rooke in *The Spanish Descent* (1702), a
poem concerning Rooke's bungled expedition to Cadiz;[19] but now,
with this added personal reason for hostility, it became for him a

positive vendetta. Before he left for his tour of the Eastern counties, he presented Harley with a lengthy diatribe, 'Of the Fleet and Sir Geo: Rook', cataloguing Rooke's failures, which, he wrote, were seriously endangering the nation's war-effort, and urging Harley to press the Queen to dismiss him.[20] In fact, though Harley would not have known this, he had even gone further: he had launched an anonymous periodical, *The Master Mercury*, largely for the purpose of lampooning Rooke. It was this journal of which he was now suspected of being the author.

On reading the report, according to his own account,[21] he instantly made his way to London, confronted the 'Messenger of the Press' Robert Stephens, whose duty it was to arrest misbehaving authors, and forced Stephens to admit he had no warrant. Nevertheless, it had put him in an awkward situation, and he begged Harley to take him into his protection, declaring himself ready to make such acknowledgement to Rooke as Harley thought reasonable.[22]

As it happened, Defoe had already been in bad odour with the Government earlier in the year. He had then come under suspicion (rightly) of being the author of, or a collaborator in, an inflammatory petition, *Legion's Humble Address to the Lords* (1704) and of an equally subversive poem, *The Address* (1704).[23] Both the petition and the poem were philippics against the Tory-dominated House of Commons for its Occasional Conformity bills, its interference with national voting rights and the invidious resumption of King William's Irish grants. Their titles were an allusion to the address of the Commons to the Queen (21 December 1703) urging her to extend her prerogative at the expense of the House of Lords. There was an unsuccessful attempt to find and arrest Defoe, but at the time, perhaps reminding himself of his powerful protector, he had been breezily scornful about the matter. In the *Review* he denounced a 'very Scandalous Letter' which accused him of writing *Legion's Humble Address*, and proposed, so as to scotch rumours that he had fled from justice, to exhibit himself to view at stated hours 'for Two Pence a time'.[24]

However, with this new piece of trouble, he felt things were getting rather hot for him. If he received no message from Harley, he wrote from Bury St Edmund's, he would hardly know how to behave, for he still risked being arrested and having his papers seized, or at least seen, 'which would be as bad'.[25] Thus he decided to lie low for a while, hid-

ing away in seaside towns. In the *Review* for 21 September he had
made cruel fun of Rooke's part in the recent sea-battle off Malaga, but
in his present mood of caution, or perhaps under pressure from Harley, he backed down and declared in the *Review* for 7 October that it
had been a victory for England.

*   *   *   *   *   *

In November, returned to London, Defoe published *Giving Alms no
Charity*, one of his most closely argued pamphlets, a counterblast to
the Tory Sir Humphrey Mackworth's bill (subsequently published as a
pamphlet) authorizing the overseers of the poor in every town or
group of towns to provide means of employment to the destitute, setting up 'parish stocks' and workhouses for the purpose. Claiming the
right of an English freeholder to address Parliament about a bill in
progress, Defoe declared that the scheme was calculated to ruin the
English wool-trade without benefiting the poor. There was, he argued,
no shortage of work in England, so the proper solution was not to try
to create work for the workless but to compel them to look for it
themselves, by enforcing the laws against beggars. To set up the same
trades everywhere would not merely wreck the delicate mechanism of
English trade but ruin innkeepers and carters and others dependent
on the circulation of trade.[26] Defoe's arguments effectively demolished Mackworth's bill, and it was killed in the House of Lords.

The end of this year saw a serious crisis for the Dissenters, when
for the third time the Tory majority in the House of Commons
brought in a bill against Occasional Conformity. Defoe responded
with several pamphlets. In one of them, *Queries upon the Bill against
Occasional Conformity* (1704), he adopted the persona of a Churchman
confessing shame at his own Church for bringing in such a bill. Did it
not reveal a quite irrational fear of the Dissenters, when the real danger to the Church came from within? He followed this with a punchy
tract, *The Dissenter Misrepresented and Represented*,[27] attacking the hypoc-
risy of High Church calumnies of the Dissenters. After all, it argued,
the most flagrant Dissenters on the scene were not the nonconform-
ists but the non-jurors (those who had refused to take the oath to
William and Mary and the Revolution settlement). Also, unlike the

Huguenots, the Dissenters had never been a united body; thus it was unfair to charge them, as a body, with crimes.

It then became clear that the managers of the Occasional Conformity Bill intended to 'tack' the bill to the one for the Land Tax. (In Parliamentary language, a 'consolidated' bill is one in which two or more bills are 'tacked' together, and to tack another bill to a finance one – a scheme already mooted, though abandoned, at the time of the first Occasional Conformity Bill – was generally held to be unparliamentary.) The outcry against this move was loud and furious, and the bill was soundly defeated, by 251 votes to 134. From now on, in the *Review* and elsewhere, Defoe's recriminations against the High Church Tories would take the form of savage satire of the 'Tackers'.

In particular this debacle gave him the idea for an extravagant satirical fantasy entitled *The Consolidator: or, Memoirs of Sundry Transactions from the World in the Moon.*[28] This supposes that the great discoveries in science and technology made in China several millennia before they reached Europe were in fact introduced from the moon – otherwise the Chinese would be no further advanced than Europeans. The author of the *Consolidator* has been to China and has read there some remarkable treatises or encylopaedias donated by lunar authors, and from these it would appear (as indeed our traveller finds when he gets there) that the atmosphere on the Moon is so clear, and their telescopes are so powerful, that all is seen there; and appropriately they conceive of the Deity as the Great Eye. The lunar beings attach great importance to memory and have a wonderful engine which enables a merchant to write his letters with one hand and copy them with the other and allows a shorthand writer to put down everything a preacher says, even before he has said it. In some parts of China, through lunar influence, people can even read one another's thoughts, which proves a marvellous preservative against those European inventions (in which England takes the lead) of fraud, cheating and sharping. In a word, the men in the moon have made extraordinary advances in mental science. They even have an engine, the Cogitator, in the form of a chair, which will '*screw a man into himself*',[29] allowing him to think with perfect concentration. 'I cannot but tell my Reader,' writes the author, 'That our Sublunar World suffers Millions of Inconveniencies, for want of this thinking Engine: I have had a great many Projects in my Head, how to bring our People to regular thinking, but 'tis in vain without this Engin; and how to get the Model of it I know not'.[30]

It became the hobby of the lunar scholar from whom the Chinese learned all their science to devise different forms of transport between China and the moon, and among them his favourite was a vehicle called 'The Consolidator'. It was formed in the shape of a chariot, held on the backs of 'two vast Bodies with extended Wings, which spread about 50 yards in Breadth, composed of Feathers so nicely put together, that no Air could pass', and the flapping of their wings was fuelled by a burning spirit. The number of the feathers (like that of the English House of Commons) was 'just 513', all of a length except for one much larger feather in the middle, and it was essential that the two bodies should be evenly balanced.[31]

The Consolidator was an admirable invention, but various things might go wrong with it. A certain kind of 'fluttering hot-headed Feathers', which struggled hard to raise the engine to 'extravagant heights', were a danger to it.[32] Another problem was that some of the feathers (though never, to the author's knowledge, more than 134 of them: the number of the 'Tackers'), might prove to be rotten, and in the past a certain King, 'being deceiv'd, by the unhappy Miscarriage of the deficient Feathers ... fell down from so great a height, that he struck himself against his own Palace, and beat his Head off'.[33] His elder son, equally, found the feathers of his Consolidator too stiff to manage; and the latter's brother, who succeeded him, unwisely tried to reach the moon without a Consolidator at all.[34]

It is discovered by our traveller that they have divisions on the moon somewhat similar to ours at home. The main ones are between the Solunarians (resembling the inhabitants of southern Britain), the Nolunarians (who correspond to the Scots) and the Crolians (corresponding to the Dissenters in England and the Kirk in Scotland). A few years ago a '*very mean, obscure and despicable Fellow*, of no great share of Wit, but that had a very *unlucky way of telling his Story*', wrote an ironic tract, '*The shortest way with the Crolians*', which brought infinite trouble upon his head; but on this occasion, sadly, the people of the moon behaved no better or more clearheadedly than their counterparts on Earth.[35]

Nevertheless, says the author, the present state of affairs on Earth, where the brave but impoverished nation of the Scots has brought in an Act of Security, by which they reserve the right not automatically to follow England's choice of a monarch upon the death of Queen Anne, shows just how badly the Cogitator is needed. Some that have been very forward to have us proceed the shortest way with the Scots, that is to say to threaten the Scots with war, 'may be said to stand in great need of this Chair of Reflection, to find out a just Cause for such a War, and to make a Neighbour-Nation making themselves secure, a sufficient Reason for another Neighbour-Nation to fall upon them. Our Engine would presently show it them in a clear sight, by way of Paralel, that 'tis just with the same Right as a Man may break open a House, because the People bar and bolt the Windows.'[36]

*   *   *   *   *   *

Relations between Scotland and England had, as this suggests, recently become exceedingly fraught, indeed they were teetering on the verge of war. In March 1705 the English Parliament, in retaliation against the Scottish Security Act, passed an Alien Act, which offered the Scots a choice, giving them till Christmas to decide either to enter into negotiations for a Treaty of Union, or, alternatively, commit themselves unreservedly to the Hanoverian succession. Failing their agreement to one or the other they would be treated as aliens, their staple imports to England would be banned and any attempts on their part to trade with France would be blocked by English men-of-war. Defoe, who blamed the Alien Act entirely on the High Tories (in fact it also received some support from the Whig Junto), was unrelentingly hostile to it, writing later that it was 'an Act in my Opinion the most Impolitick, I had almost said unjust, that ever past that great Assembly'.[37]

Through all the earlier part of the year there had also been another source of friction between the two kingdoms. The Edinburgh authorities had impounded an English ship, the *Worcester*, in Leith harbour and arrested and brought proceedings against its captain and some of his crew, convicting them (on thin evidence) of being pirates and of seizing and destroying a Scottish ship in East Indian waters. English opinion over the affair was, for the most part, violent against the Scots; and in and around Edinburgh, in return, it aroused such intense mob fury against England that, though the Queen sent orders for a reprieve, the Scottish Privy Council was too scared to obey. Thus on 11 April 1705 Captain Green and two companions were hanged on Leith Sands. Reactions in England were in general bellicose, but Defoe, in the *Review* (26 April), took a notably statesmanlike and irenic attitude, urging that there should not be a rush to judgment against the Scottish authorities.

> Nothing can be more horrid, than that the Scots should Execute these Men on a meer Pique at the English Nation.
>
> Nothing can be more like it, than to conclude rashly, that it is so, and improve it on purpose to Exasperate our People against the Scots.

*   *   *   *   *   *

Defoe was, in all this, making his mark as a political writer. He was also acquiring many enemies. It was rumoured that he was contributing to other journals as well as the *Review* and had taken over the *Observator* during November while its editor Tutchin was in trouble. The *Review* was inclined to praise a column in the *London Post* entitled 'Truth and Honesty', and on 9 April 1705 'Truth and Honesty' himself wrote plaintively that he was 'a little distasted' at friends' saying his column was merely 'a detachment of his [Defoe's] Scandalous Club'. However there may well have been something in this rumour, since, in a letter of about 1 May 1705 to his Norwich friend John Fransham, Defoe offered to place a story of Fransham's about a Tory Mayor in the 'Truth and Honesty' column.[38] It is a sign of Defoe's increasing prominence on the journalistic scene that entire serials would be launched with the sole purpose of making a running report on him. There was the anonymous *The Reviewer Review'd* in 1705, though it expired after three issues, and in the following year Joseph Browne published, anonymously, *A Dialogue between Church and No Church: or a Rehearsal of the Review,* which declared open war on the author of the *Review* and ran to seven issues.

His best-known rival among Whig journalists was John Tutchin (*c.* 1661–1707), whose xenophobic poem *The Foreigners* had spurred Defoe on to write *The True-Born Englishman.* Tutchin came from a long line of Dissenters, his grandfather, his father and his father's two brothers all having been Dissenting ministers.[39] He himself, after some years under a private tutor, had attended a Dissenting academy in Stepney. He took arms for the Duke of Monmouth in 1685, and in the aftermath of Sedgemoor – it is a celebrated episode – he came before the infamous Judge Jeffreys. Jeffreys sentenced him to prison and to be flogged through every market town in Dorset each year for seven years, and in his anguish Tutchin asked if, instead, he might be hanged. The monstrous sentence drew tears from the spectators; but then, a few days later, Tutchin developed smallpox, and eventually Jeffreys was bribed to recommend a pardon. According to Macaulay, 'the temper of Tutchin, not originally very mild, was exasperated to madness by what he had undergone'.[40]

During the reign of King William Tutchin published patriotic odes and an account of the 'Bloody Assizes', and he obtained a post in the navy victualling office, which however he lost when he laid a complaint against his superiors. Then in April 1702 he launched the periodical entitled *The Observator*. It took the form of a dialogue between the learned 'Observator' and a sturdy 'Countryman' named Roger, both of them violent Whigs. 'Countryman' is a hearty, downright xenophobe, apt to vociferate against High Churchmen and the 'Tacking clergy' and growl abuse of the French: he held that all Frenchmen were asses and so lean and half-starved they would eat anything. He loves his master Observator and listens with reverence to his opinions, though is not averse to teasing him, and on occasion even subsidises him when he is hard up. Observator spends many of his waking hours studying ancient charters and rolls and is an authority on the English Constitution. The two fight shoulder-to-shoulder against their remorseless foe Charles Leslie.

When Defoe attacked Tutchin as 'Shamwhig' in *The True-Born Englishman* (saying that Tutchin's poem on the subject of honesty could have been very good if he had understood the subject better[41]) he did not know much about him, and his grudge against him was not a lasting one. He found they had causes in common, and the two would have acquired an extra motive for friendship as fellow victims of Charles Leslie. Thus, though he would complain of Tutchin's scurrilous remarks about himself, he persistently aimed for a truce with him. When Joseph Browne and Tutchin accused him of being an ignoramus who knew no Latin, and of having been a hosier's apprentice, his response was the good-tempered one of challenging Tutchin to a translation competition. They should take passages from any Latin, French and Italian author that Tutchin would like to name, translate them into English and then re-translate them 'crosswise' (i.e. the English into French and so on), he who did it soonest and best standing to win £20 from the other.[42] Tutchin declined the challenge; and it seems as if, in fact, he was made to feel a little inferior by Defoe. He writes with defensive sarcasm that Mr. *Review* may think he [Tutchin] ought to leave off writing, 'when so Great a Man has undertaken the Office of an Observator' and wise men will not expect that someone who spends his days 'tumbling over the Musty Rolls of Antiquity' will have such 'Quaint Expressions and Beau Language' as Defoe.[43]

The two had a substantial dispute at the same period over the rioting and tumult in Coventry during the 1705 election. (Defoe had a group of Whig friends in the city, among them the ex-mayor Edward Owen, and they kept him well informed about political in-fighting there.[44]) In the *Review* for 10 May 1705 he reported that, at the height of the election, the parties had deployed little armies, five hundred or a thousand to a side, which fought 'with all the Fury and Animosity imaginable', breaking heads and limbs and trampling the magistrates underfoot. How was this permitted, he asked? But all he could get out of Coventry folk when he exclaimed against it was the 'weak and most ridiculous' reply, 'HOW CAN WE HELP IT?'. Yet (surely?) it was the supreme function of sheriffs and officers to keep order, and if this proved beyond their power it was their duty to alert the Queen, who might feel forced to send in a troop of horse.

Tutchin replied by asking 'our Great *Statesman*' by what laws her Majesty had the right to bully electors. 'Our Ancestors us'd to remove the Red-Coats from *Towns Corporate* and *Burroughs* sending Members of Parliament, at the time of the election.' Does Mr. *Review* pretend to show himself wiser than them by bringing them in? Since he had written so much against 'Tackers', was it not a strange plan to bring in a pack of men likely to terrorize anyone who would not vote for them?[45] To this Defoe retorted (22 May 1705) that, since the election had taken place at least two months ago, there was not 'the least Shadow, or Circumstance' to justify Tutchin in thinking he was urging any such thing. He reproached Tutchin, as much in sadness as in anger, for his rudeness and slanders. It was most unjust, he wrote, seeing that whenever letters complaining of Tutchin reached his office he always either passed them on to him or answered for him 'with Decency and Respect, and to his Advantage'.

The leaders of the Coventry election were, almost a year later, at last brought to trial – that is to say to two mutually contradictory trials. First (to Defoe's feigned incredulity) the rioters indicted the Mayor and the magistrates for provoking tumult; and then the rioters themselves were brought to court. Tutchin took Defoe's report on this, in the *Review* for 17 August 1706, as a renewed attack on himself, but Defoe answered in the *Review* for 31 August that he was very sorry for this, for he neither intended it as such nor would pursue it as such, 'resolving if possible, not to differ with him, at least not so as to contend'; and on 7 September he wrote again in the *Review*, begging the 'Countryman' Roger – a nice touch – to intercede on his behalf with his irritable master. ('He is so woundy touchy and so willing to quarrel with a body', Defoe wrote in 'Countryman' language, 'that let one give him the best Words in the World, there's no keeping the Peace with'n'.)

Tutchin died in the following year, as the result of a ferocious assault by ruffians, set on by his political enemies, and Defoe gave him a generous obituary in the *Review* (20 November 1707). Tutchin, he wrote, was a 'Man of Misfortunes', but he was an honest man, was no fool, and was a most zealous enemy of tyranny and friend to the Revolution establishment. His chief fault was 'want of temper' – 'And where is the Man, that under his Pressures may not be embittered, and lose himself sometimes among the Croud of his own provoking Misfortunes?'. As for Tutchin's ill-treatment of himself, he forgave it heartily and supposed it might have been the result of misinformation. For all his irascibility Tutchin, he said, was 'really a very valuable Person'. There were those who said that their later hostilities had been a pretence, and this could conceivably be true.

*   *   *   *   *   *

In early April 1705 Lord Halifax, who had been William III's great Chancellor of the Exchequer, wrote to Defoe, saying he had been praising Defoe to Godolphin, the Lord High Treasurer, and would be glad of his support (presumably meaning writing something in the *Review*) for a forthcoming Parliamentary bill, about promissory notes.[46] Halifax was now out of office, as he would remain throughout Queen Anne's reign, and, not long before, he had been threatened with impeachment for neglect of duty as Auditor of the Exchequer. He was still, nevertheless, influential in the Whig Junto, the tightly-knit group of Whig grandees, formed during the reign of William and Mary, which was to dominate the Whig party during the latter years of Queen Anne's reign.[47] Defoe was effusively grateful at this approach and, with much rigmarole of humility, for he knew Halifax was a vain man, he offered him his services (if necessary in secret) should his Lordship ever 'Think this Despicable Thing, who scorn'd to Come Out of Newgate at the Price of betraying a Dead Master, or Discovring those Things which No body wou'd ha' been the worse For, fitt to be Trusted in your Presence, Tho' Never so Much Incognito'.[48] But, flatteringly, he told his prospective patron that he would willingly wait till such time that the nation, in its wisdom, had reappointed Halifax to public office. He asked his new benefactor for details of the bill and for the titles of relevant books and promised to discuss it in the *Review*. He also sent him a copy of the *Consolidator*. It was a gift which bore fruit, for Halifax passed the copy on to the Duchess of Marlborough, who was impressed and sent Defoe, by Halifax's hand, a gift of £100 as from an unknown admirer. Defoe, in his grateful reply, reaffirmed his desire to help Halifax in opposing the High Tories, 'a Stupid, Distracted Party that are for Ruining themselves Rather than not Destroy Their Neighbours'.[49]

Defoe still felt uncertain how he could really be most 'serviceable' to Harley – so at least he told him. 'Make me Merit Sir all you Do for me', he writes in a letter 9 July 1705, 'If I Can do Nothing, why assist me at all?'.[50] It was agreed that he should go on another fact-finding and propagandizing tour, this time in the West Country. It would be a chance to improve his intelligence network, and also to make practical use of it, by lodging with his correspondents, the majority of whom were Dissenting ministers. He got Harley to provide him with an official 'pass', in case of emergency, and asked Harley to feed him scraps of inside information, with which to impress his hearers. By 14 August he could proudly announce: 'I Think I may say I have a perfect skeleton [political map] of this part of England and a Settled Correspondence in Every Town and Corner of it'.[51]

The political message he was bringing was 'Peace and Union', a doctrine which the Queen had urged from the throne and which he himself had already propounded in many *Reviews* and in *A Challenge of Peace Address'd to the Whole Nation* (1703). Might not peace and union, he asked there, be achieved without involving religion at all? 'Men would be Gentlemen as well as Christians, and the Union of Conversation and Interest would make a little Heaven in the Nation'.[52] Some people, he wrote in the *Review* for 7 July 1705, grew quite angry at his incessant harping on Peace, his continual urgings of voters in the coming election to choose men 'Bless'd with Healing Principles'. They even threatened him with violence; but it was not worth their while, he told them, 'to kill a poor Mortify'd Author, one that the Government had Kill'd before'.

> I move about the World Unguarded and Unarm'd, a little Stick not strong enough to Correct a Dog, supplies the Place of Mr. O[*bservato*]*r*'s Great Oaken-Towel, a Sword sometimes perhaps for Decency, but it is all harmless to a meer Nothing; can do no hurt any where but just at the Tip of it, call'd the Point – And what's that in the Hand of a Feeble Author?

But these enemies, he said, had also found another way to bully him, and for Party reasons, and that was through his creditors – by 'a more Scandalous Assassination, Studying to Ruine and Embroil him, Crowds of Sham-Actions, Arrests, Sleeping Debates in Trade of 17 Years standing Reviv'd', and so on. The tour, as he frankly told Harley, would be an escape from these persecutions.

The greatest obstacles to moderation and union, next to the clergy, he reported, were the Justices of the Peace. 'Wherever There happens to be Moderate Justices The People live Easy and The Parsons have the less Influence, but the Conduct of the Justices in Most parts in Intollerably scandalous.'[53] In Lutterworth he heard how Mr Justice Bradgate had ridden on horseback into a Dissenting meeting house and 'told the parson as he was preaching he Lyed';[54] and in Chippenham all the high-flyers, 'who here act like Devills more than Men', were intriguing to get 'that scandall of the County' Colonel Chivers into Parliament – not so much for the good of Parliament as to shelter him from the Bishop of Salisbury, who was threatening to prosecute him for impudent language. Defoe urged Harley to have Chivers, who 'Influences the Town, Sitts Dilligently at Every petty sessions, and Aws the people', removed from the Commission of Peace, which could be managed 'Obliquely' and without publicity, for in that case he would certainly lose the election.[55]

Defoe suffered a mishap during his tour. He had given instructions for his letters to be sent to him care of a friend of his, Captain Turner, in Weymouth, but they were delivered into the hands of a different Captain Turner, the commander of a Guernsey privateer. This 'Ignorant Tar', as Defoe labelled him, was puzzled by the mysterious allusions in the letters and talked to half the town about them. As a result, the affair came to the ears of the Mayor, who remanded several of Defoe's local hosts to the Dorchester Assizes for questioning; and subsequently a Justice of the Peace at Crediton, named Hugh Stafford, issued a warrant for Defoe's arrest as 'a Person of ill Fame and Behaviour', lurking about and suspected of distributing seditious libels.[56] Defoe seized the occasion to use his pass and, confident in its protection, wrote Stafford a swingeing letter, castigating his 'unjustice-like as well as ungentleman-like warrant'. He did not 'lurk' about, he told Stafford, but dared to show his face to him or to any man.[57] One gets the impression that Defoe distinctly enjoyed the affray.

Having failed to catch Defoe or to get sight of the letters, Stafford wrote to Charles Hedges, the Secretary of State for the South. He told him that, according to his informers, Defoe

> deals very freely in his common conversation with the young parliament men, in basely reflecting on them lately in my neighbourhood, by Saying, as for them, they generally lay drinking at Some Tavern or other near the house, and leave the concerns of the Nation to half a Score Old Stagers to mannage; till any business of moment, and then they are Sent for, who as soon as they come into the house imeadiatly whisper to one, and soe to another, to know how Sir Edward, Sir Humphry, or Sir John, how they voted, and haveing learnt that, without ever hearing the merits of the cause, or indeed any thing of the matter Says he, imeadiatly cry out they give their vote the same way. [58]

One overhears Defoe's contumacious accents in this; but he can be believed, too, when he says that, though people tend to expect him to have a cloven foot and horns, he has 'Had the honour, with small Difficulty, of Convincing some Gentlemen over a Bottle of Wine, That the Author of the *Review* was really no Monster, but a Conversible Sociable Creature'.[59]

In October he stayed in Coventry for a day or two with his friend and agent Edward Owen, whom we mentioned earlier, and despite the furious party-politics of the city they spent an evening with some local High Tories. Defoe found them, politically speaking, remarkably reasonable, though, not realizing who he was (he was travelling incognito), they discussed a rumour that he was £3,000 in debt and was playing false with his creditors. (But if he owed £3,000 and could not pay, he wrote to Owen, was that a crime?[60]) He was writing in exultation that, as he had prophesied, the Whig John Smith had beaten the Tory candidate William Bromley for the post of Speaker of ther Commons, and his letter catches for us his joshing tone of voice among his cronies.

> What Cowards are these Coventry Whigs that now Barcelona is taken,[61] Mr Smith chosen, and all the Torys Dead hearted, yet they Dare not so Much as make a bonefire – or ring the Bells.
>
> Nay there's that Ned Owen is such a Cowardly R— that he Dares not go to Greens Coffee house and read a balad there.
>
> Fye Ned, Coventry Men Cowards! Fye! Fye!
>
> If you are So Dastardly now, what wou'd ha' become of you if B B B Bromley had been Chosen.
>
> Courage! men of blew,[62] the job is Done. Rouze up Jere Withers,[63] the Gold is all your Own.
>
> What a Toad is this de foe. He is old Dog at a guess. He Said we should have a majority of 60 - and behold 52, which put against 63, which they had of us last parliamt, makes near the 120 I Computed.
>
> And about 25 more Recovred by Controverted Elections secures the Nation, bewildres the Jacks,[64] Disheartens the high Church, and I hope makes an End of all these brangles.
>
> Amen[65]

*   *   *   *   *   *

During Defoe's spell in Newgate in 1703 he had begun a long poem (in twelve books, like the *Aeneid* and *Paradise Lost*, though he called it a 'satyr'), attacking the 'divine right' theory of monarchy. It was to be published by subscription and when, as frequently happened over the next few years, it was confidently asserted to be 'in the press' but failed to materialize, Defoe's enemies put it about that it did not exist and Defoe had simply pocketed the subscriptions. Exist it did, however, and copies at last reached the subscribers in the July of 1706. The work was a response to the High Church and High Tory policies of Queen Anne's first administration and the revival of the 'divine right' and 'passive obedience' doctrines at that time. 'This *Satyr* had never been Publish'd, tho' some of it has been a long time in being', Defoe wrote in his Preface, 'had not the World seem'd going mad a second Time with the error of Passive Obedience and Non-Resistance'.[66]

According to the 'divine right' theory, hereditary monarchy was the form of government prescribed by God himself. Thus all monarchs derived their authority from that bestowed on Adam, and a monarch was above the law. The doctrine was a fairly recent invention, first coming into prominence in the reign of James I and receiving its classic statement in the treatise *Patriarcha* by Sir Robert Filmer, a work written some time around 1642 though not published until 1680. The Filmerian theory, however, though itself new, was linked to the older and hallowed doctrine of the Anglican church which inculcated the duty of Passive (as opposed to Active) obedience to a monarch, even were he to be the most depraved and merciless of tyrants.

Jure Divino, with its copious footnotes, is the most complete statement of Defoe's political and ethical philosophy, its central subject being tyranny. The Introduction begins with the lines

> Nature has left *this Tincture in the Blood*,
> That all Men *would be Tyrants* if they cou'd:
> If they forbear their Neighbours to devour,
> 'Tis not for want of *Will*, but want of *Power* …[67]

This is not mere Hobbesian or Augustinian pessimism about the human condition, for, as the poem argues, the very fact that the instinct to tyrannize is universal makes it self-regulating and a basis for civil society.

> The only Safety of Society,
> Is, that my Neighbour's *just as proud as I*;
> Has the same Will and Wish, the same Design,
> And his *Abortive Envy* ruines mine.[68]

All the same, human beings pay a heavy price for their tyrannizing bent. For a tyrant is also by propensity a slave – a slave to vice. Vice is, precisely, a form of tyranny; and a human tyrant, however supreme his power, is a 'drudge' to his vices. Aspiring tyrants, such as we all are, are prone to an incapacitating *folie de grandeur*. *'Because they can't be Gods, they won't be Men'.*[69] The relationship of a tyrant, or potential tyrant, to vice and crime is best described as a kind of idolatry. In his Introduction Defoe has, in a word, explained all moral evil – the pride, avarice, envy, lust and rage of which we all have a share – in terms of tyranny. It is, as one might say, a quintessentially Whiggish world-view.

In rebuttal of Filmer, Defoe argues in his poem that God did not lay down any specific form of government: it was enough that he bestowed on Man the inestimable gift of reason, which equipped him to solve such problems for himself. The earliest system of government was patriarchy, but as vice and crime increased, mankind found it necessary to resort to monarchy (for laws require an executive), and the choice of a king, he writes, naturally lay with property-owners. This right is so clear that, if any man owned the fee-simple of England, the rest of the inhabitants would have to receive laws from him; and if there were any prince alive today who could show an unbroken line of succession to the throne, one might need to submit entirely to him. However, no such royal freeholder exists, and accordingly kingship cannot be based on hereditary succession. It is based, rather, on power and possession, and to legitimize it requires the people's consent. Thus the claim of tyrants to be above the law, so the poem asserts, is a kind of popery or image-worship, a superstition like transubstantiation. As for 'passive obedience', since nature has provided even the meanest creature with some power to defend itself, it is a grave sin, akin to suicide.

Defoe's poem ends with a bloodstained pageant of historic tyrants, including most of the Anglo-Saxon kings, and, in happy contrast, a eulogy of Queen Anne and her present set of wise Whiggish courtiers and counsellors. It includes a long and lavish encomium of Defoe's patron Lord Halifax, acclaiming his steadfast behaviour during his recent troubles.

* * * * * *

In his Preface to *Jure Divino* Defoe asserted that church tyranny in England, whether of the Laudian or the Puritan kind, is now a bygone evil and (short of a French invasion) would never be resurrected. The

Church had declared its new attitude in the preamble to the first Occasional Conformity Bill, of 1702, which stated that persecution for conscience's sake was 'contrary to the Principles of the Christian Religion, and to the Doctrine of the Church of England'.[70]

This leads Defoe on to the subject of Toleration. By 'Toleration', it is to be remembered, he means merely freedom of worship, a different matter from civic equality. This freedom, he says, the Dissenters enjoy as a legal right, in virtue of the Toleration Act of 1689; the pretence of High Churchmen that it is no more than a 'grace' or 'bounty' being altogether false. Their enjoyment of this precious possession, however, their critics would sometimes ask them to remember, brought with it a corresponding duty. They ought to wish to see the right extended to others, and indeed they ought to declare for a toleration for all shades of religious opinion. But in this, Defoe argues, those critics are quite wrong.

This was an issue which had arisen memorably in 1705, when the Deist John Toland (1670–1722) sent a circular letter to leaders of the three main Dissenting sects urging them to declare for a universal toleration. It would, Toland said, be an answer to the accusation sometimes made that the Dissenters did not deserve the Toleration, being so factious that they could neither tolerate anyone else, or even one another. Defoe possessed a copy of Toland's letter and, according to his reading of it, it recommended a toleration even for heathens and non-Christians.[71] But why, he asks in the Preface to *Jure Divino*, should the Dissenters want this? Surely toleration was only appropriate to those who subscribed to the fundamental Christian beliefs? Indeed, why should the Dissenters make any declaration on the subject at all? It might be unwise and suggest that they were plotting some subversive political scheme. Of course – he wrote with deft irony – he would not doubt Toland's 'sincere Regard to the Interest and Reputation of Religion in General, and of the Dissenters in particular'; but silence might be altogether a better answer.[72]

It was not the first time that Defoe and Toland had differed. Their relationship was a long-lasting and acrimonious one, reaching a bizarre climax in 1717, and we need to fill in a few details about Toland. He was born in Londonderry in 1670 and was brought up as a Catholic, but converted to Protestantism sometime before the age of sixteen. He was sent to Glasgow University by some 'eminent

Dissenters', and proceeded from there to Leyden and to Oxford, where he gained a reputation for wildness. (He was a great holder-forth in taverns and would talk against the scriptures, justify the killing of Charles I, defend commonwealths and, it was said, he burned a copy of the Book of Common Prayer on a tavern fire.) Expelled from Oxford, he was helped by the City father Sir Robert Clayton to write the lives and edit the works of Harrington and Milton, and in 1696, emboldened by the ending of the Licensing Act, he published a pro-vocative treatise, *Christianity not Mysterious*, which denied that God demanded humans to assent to what they did not understand and pointed out close parallels between Christian observances – such as fasting, initiation ceremonies and sacraments – and paganism. The book was declared heretical by the Irish House of Commons and Toland, who had returned to Ireland in early 1697, was forced to take refuge in England.

There, for a time, he was (like Defoe) employed by Robert Harley as a secret agent, becoming in the course of this *persona grata* at the court of Hanover, where he would hold philosophical conversations with the Electress Sophia. His arrangement with Harley eventually broke down, however, whereupon he turned into a virulent critic of all Harley's policies.

From the time of *Christianity not Mysterious* onwards Defoe, a stickler for religious orthodoxy, regarded Toland as a dangerous heretic and Socinian. In his satire *Reformation of Manners* (1702) he wrote about him in sulphurous terms:

> To[*l*]and, if such a Wretch is worth our Scorn,
> Shall Vice's blackest Catalogue adorn;
> His hated Character, let this supply,
> Too vile even for our University.[73]

The affair of Toland's circular letter[74] stayed in his mind, and he referred to the letter again, disparagingly, in *A Short View of The Present State of the Protestant Religion in Britain*.[75] Toland later complained that what Defoe wrote there, i.e. that Toland 'prest the Dissenters to declare for the Universal Liberty of all Christians', was a gross cal-umny, for, he says, 'the Papists and some other are excepted in the *Letter* by name'.[76] But in fact the wording of the circular was some-what ambiguous. It is true that it poured scorn on the Catholic doctrine of transubstantiation as 'the greatest Idolatry and most extravagant Absurdity', but it did not say in so many words that Catholics should be excluded from any toleration, a penalty Toland seemingly reserved for atheists and disbelievers in an afterlife. Some years later, moreover, in the Second Part of his *State Anatomy* (1717; see below, pp. 152–6), where he is speaking of the American colonies, he would suggest that, just as we tolerate '*Heathens* that are our Subjects' there, so, 'if we had *Mahometan* Subjects there, pray where wou'd be the harm to the State of tolerating them?'.[77] Thus Defoe had perhaps been not so far off the mark.

Toland's generous scheme, unrealistic in his time and presented in the persona of 'a settled member of the Church of *England* as by law establisht',[78] which he certainly was not, gives off a faint whiff of inauthenticity. The scheme was well received by the Baptists and Independents, though they did not act on it, but not by the Presbyterian Edmund Calamy, who refused to respond to Toland because of the 'obnoxiousness' of his character.[79] It is significant that, in sharpest contrast to Defoe, Toland praised Occasional Conformity as 'the noblest practice in the world'.[80] Defoe, as we know, had his own intricate but logical theory about Occasional Conformity and about the civil disabilities which led to it. He held that the disabilities were themselves profoundly unjust, considering what the Dissenters had done and were doing for the nation, yet that it would be unwise for them to demand their removal. As for bills forbidding Occasional Conformity, they were even more unjust, but with the paradox that, by putting a stop to a shameful practice, they might in the end be for the Dissenters' good. Defoe and Edmund Calamy, it is evident, were afraid that Toland's scheme might be a danger to the Dissenters – and they could have been right.

*   *   *   *   *   *

In writing *Jure Divino* Defoe had been helped, rather than hindered, by his long-running controversy with Charles Leslie. Leslie's political stance was somewhat paradoxical. He was a staunch Anglican, with an intense and mystical attachment to episcopacy, his dearest wish being to secure a union between the Anglican and Gallican churches. On the other hand he was a convinced Filmerian or 'divine right' man, upholding wholeheartedly the duty of non-resistance to princes. He had come to London, according to his biographer, with a plan to 'provide a complete armoury of defence for the Church of England against her various antagonists, within and without', beginning with Deism, Quakerism, Judaism and Socinianism, and then concentrating on the Dissenters.[81]

Defoe by now recognized Leslie as an important adversary, and particularly so because in August 1704 Leslie had launched a new journal, *The Rehearsal*, with the direct purpose of skirmishing with John Tutchin, author of the Whiggish *Observator*, and Defoe, the author of the *Review*. (Parodying the *Observator* formula, the *Rehearsal* took the form of a dialogue between 'Countryman' and 'Observator'.) As a non-juror who had sacrificed his career in the Church by refusing the oaths, Leslie was in a strong moral position as compared with his more time-serving brethren. But equally in Defoe he was faced with an untypical Dissenter, one quite as vehement against Occasional Conformity as himself. Thus their quarrel, in the pages of their journals, developed in a not altogether predictable way.

It certainly got very abusive at times. Defoe loved to enrage Leslie with anti-High Church rumours, and Leslie would go to most painstaking lengths to discredit them. Defoe, for instance, reported that a certain Oxford College had erected the Queen's royal arms (the motto of which was 'Semper eadem', or 'always the same') under a weathercock![82] Leslie instantly set up inquiries in Oxford and managed, after much effort, to obtain written denials from the college workmen that anything of the kind had occurred.[83] From now on he made a habit of raking this incident up, as a glaring example of Defoe's mendacity, and Defoe, for his part, would never frankly admit it had been a joke anyway.

More importantly, in the *Review* for 18 December 1705, Defoe drew a comparison between the 'dry martyrdom' of King James, at the hands of supposed exponents of 'passive obedience', and the 'wet martyrdom' of King Charles I, at the hands of the Puritans. The difference, he said, appeared to him remarkably small. Leslie responded to this ruthless witticism with the greatest indignation, and from then on it became another pretext for exchange of insults.

At a certain point, however, it occurred to both writers that there might be some profit in politer behaviour. For Defoe, being at work on his verse attack on 'divine right' doctrines, it was in a way an advantage to have, in Leslie, such an articulate spokesman for these doctrines. It helped to clear his own mind regarding Sir Robert Filmer's theory, as presented in his *Patriarcha* (1680), that all kingship derived its authority from Adam, and again over the thorny issue of the Israelites' choosing of Saul as king. It enabled him moreover to press the question, to which Leslie could not really find a convincing answer, whether basing the Queen's right to the throne purely on inheritance, as Leslie and his followers did, was not actually treasonable, considering how much stronger, hereditarily, were the claims of her brother the Pretender. Moreover, Leslie sometimes made intelligent criticisms. He had quite cogent things to say against Defoe's idiosyncratic theories about property and the political rights of freeholders. Defoe, he announced with triumph, had deserted the people in favour of the freeholders, a comment not altogether off the mark.[84] He came round, on the other hand, to doing a little more justice to Defoe's argument that Queen Anne had a 'divine right' to the throne, in the sense that 'Government is Divine, and Her Majesty's Title to Execute it, is Divine', but that this right was not 'personal and inherent in … Her, by Succession, Inheritance, Line or Devolution'.[85]

The two had, in short, begun to listen to each other. Leslie promised to read Defoe's poem when it came out, though in the end he did no more than mock its Dedication 'To Reason' in a heavy-handed fashion.[86] Defoe, however, chose this moment to repeat his views about monarchy at length, in the *Review*, and this sparked off an intelligent debate. Defoe had argued that an English monarch's right to the throne is not consecrated till the moment in the coronation ceremony when the People are asked if they will have him or her as ruler. To this Leslie replied, not unreasonably, that if anyone were actually to answer 'No' at this stage, they would simply be hurled into jail: the ritual was not meant to be taken literally.[87]

Leslie was also struck, as one is oneself, by a curious ambiguity in what Defoe says about Locke and Algernon Sidney. Defoe is explaining that his own theories about the origin of government are, perhaps, somewhat novel, and he continues 'I know, what Mr. *Lock, Sidney* and others have said on this Head, and I must confess, I never thought their Systems fully answer'd'.[88] As Leslie points out, it is not clear from this whether Defoe is saying that no-one had ever succeeded in answering Locke and Sidney, or on the other hand that their systems had not 'answered', i.e. had not proved convincing. He assumed, for polemical purposes, that Defoe must have meant the latter: for in their recent debates Defoe had allowed that the first monarchies were 'patriarchal', not elective. Defoe's point had actually been that, if this was so, it was not because God had issued any directive in the matter: Reason had arrived at this solution unaided. Leslie, however, seized on it as a major concession and declared, triumphantly, that he had '*Converted* the Now *Celebrated DE FOE* himself, who has, under his Hand, fairly given up to me *Lock, Sidney,* Milton &c. and all their *Schemes*'.[89] This, one may suppose, was not how Defoe saw matters. But by this time he had been despatched to Scotland, and for the moment their debate ends.

CHAPTER 4

PROPAGANDIST FOR THE UNION

To hear our People speak of *Scotland*, or of the *Scots* Affairs or People, it would make a Stranger think that this same Place call'd *Scotland* was some remote Country in the *East-Indies*, or about *Madagascar*, or some Island in the *Fretum Magellanicum*, the *North-West* Passages, the *South* Seas, or somewhere very unfrequented, where very few People ever came, and from whence, *like our News from* Muscovy, Things were very uncertainly related, and our Accounts from thence very little to be depended upon.

The learned Gentlemen of this Party, tho' skill'd in History, Masters of Geography, and have seen great Part of the World in their Travels, they'll tell you that *Scotland* is a barren, uncultivated, desolate Country; that the Land is all barren and will hardly maintain the People that live there – Nay, they will very learnedly ask sometimes, if there is any Mutton, or any Beef, or any Butter, or any such thing as Milk in *Scotland* – The *Highlanders* they take to be a Sort of Monsters, and ask, if they live upon Roots and the Bark of the Trees.[1]

This evocation of England's benighted ignorance regarding Scotland, in which Defoe anticipates Macaulay, was to be one element in his approach to the country. Another – though till 1706 he most probably had never crossed the Border – was a pretension to speak about Scotland as an authority.

The draconian English Alien Act of 1705 (see above p. 44) had had its effect. War between England and Scotland had, narrowly, been averted, and negotiations for an incorporating union between the two nations, as an alternative to total severance, had begun in earnest in the early months of 1706. The Queen had appointed a Commission of 62 members, 31 for each nation, and by 22 July they had agreed on a draft Treaty, which would then have to be ratified article by article in the two parliaments. Meanwhile in May, evidently at Harley's desire, Defoe applied himself to propaganda for the Union, and it was planned that at some stage he might continue this work in Scotland. On 4 May he published the first of six projected *Essays at Removing National Prejudices against a Union with Scotland*, this first essay offering reasons why a Union would be to England's advantage. The Church of England, it argued, far from being weakened as an established church, would actually be strengthened by a settlement which recognized 'National Establishment and Legal Toleration' in both countries; and together, England and Scotland would be safe from any foreign enemy.[2] He followed this with an essay upon taxation, urging the need for sensitive treatment of the Scots, who should not be expected to pay English debts and might need to be allowed different levels of tax, notably on malt and salt. Scotland, it argued would in return provide what was needed most of all, i.e. more people to help exploit the American colonies.[3]

Defoe was acquainted with several Scottish merchants in London, and in early May one of them, George Scott, an admirer of his writings, gave him a very valuable introduction, bringing him together with the three Dalrymple brothers, John, Hew and David, of whom Hew and David were Treaty Commissioners.[4]

The Dalrymples were a distinguished family: John, Earl of Stair, had been Scotland's Lord Advocate and was a member of Queen Anne's Privy Council; Hew was Lord President of the Court of Session; and David was Solicitor-General to Queen Anne. 'I did bring them acquainted with one Mr Deffoe', wrote Scott to his brother in Edinburgh on 14 May, 'who seeing [*sic*] to understand trade & the interest of nations very well, he was the person that wrote the pamphlett cal'd the shortest way with the dissenters & for which he was pilloryed'. According to Scott, it was in fact he and his friends who had prompted Defoe to write the first of his *Essays at Removing National Prejudices*. 'It is very well done', wrote Scott, '& is only the introduction to 2 more books he designs upon the union before the Commissioners have done'.[5]

Defoe also, at this time, perhaps through Scott or the Dalrymples, got to know John Clerk, another member of the Scottish Commission. Clerk was an aspiring young littérateur, son of a well-to-do and staunchly Presbyterian laird and son-in-law to the Duke of Queens-

berry, the Queen's High Commissioner for Scotland. He too admired
Defoe's writing and wrote to his father on 13 July urging him to come
to London to meet him. Later, Sir John Clerk the elder would show
considerable interest in Defoe's work, asking his son to send him copies of various items, including *Jure Divino*, the second volume of the
Review and the first volume of *A True Collection*.[6]

Defoe had told the younger Clerk that he would soon be coming to
Scotland, and he promised to visit their family mansion, Newbiging,
in Midlothian, 'to teach us some improvements, in which he is very
knowing'. Defoe, so Clerk told his father, was planning to write about
the improvement of Scotland. He did not think that the eastern parts
of the country could be much improved, but 'he makes himself
believe he cou'd improve moorland grounds to double their rent'.[7]

All went relatively smoothly with the Treaty negotiations until, in
July 1706, its terms were published in the press, whereupon there was
a hostile outcry in various quarters – not only among the Jacobites,
but also the more intransigent of the Presbyterian clergy, who held
prayer-meetings and fasts against it. It confirmed Harley in his idea of
sending Defoe on a mission to Scotland, to act as a spy on his and
Godolphin's behalf and to do what he could to influence opinion
there; and Defoe seems to have leapt at the chance. His situation *vis-à-
vis* his creditors had grown steadily worse, till he was more or less a
prisoner in his own house, unable to visit Harley or undertake any
work for him. (He asked if he could be given a private lodging in
Whitehall, but nothing came of this.[8]) At last he had declared himself
bankrupt once again, and in late August he had managed to come to a
composition with his creditors.[9] He was thus free to set off, and he
hurriedly made preparations – though, having for bankruptcy purposes had to surrender all his possessions, including his horse and
saddle, bridle and pistols, he had to buy them afresh. But he wrote
exuberantly to Harley: 'Refurnisht Sir with Two horses and all Neces-
sarys, I Assure you I have no fear of highway men. Cantabit Vacuus[10]
– is my Motto'. All that was lacking was any actual instructions from
Harley – not but that, he wrote to him wryly, 'Abraham went Chearfully Out Not knowing whither he went'.[11] However Harley had told
the Queen and Godolphin of his commission, so it was a frightening
prospect that, for lack of directions, he might prove useless. As the

next best thing, therefore, he drew up a list of instructions as he imagined them, asking Harley to tell him if it was correct.

> 1 To Inform My Self of the Measures Takeing Or Partys forming
> Against the Union and Applye my Self to prevent them.
>
> 2 In Conversation and by all Reasonable Methods to Dispose
> peoples minds to the Union.
>
> 3 By writeing or Discourse, to Answer any Objections, Libells or
> Reflections on the Union, the English or the Court, Relateing to the
> Union.
>
> 4 To Remove the Jealousies and Uneasyness of people about
> Secret Designs here against the Kirk &c.[12]

On reaching Newcastle he stayed with John Bell the postmaster,
Harley's chief agent in the north, who wrote to Harley that he thought
Defoe was 'a Very Engenious Man & fit for that business I guess he is
goeing about'.[13] But still no letter of instructions, and Defoe wrote
dolefully: 'Methinks I look Very Simply when to my Self I Reflect
How I am your Messengr without an Errand, your Ambasador without Instructions, your Servant without Orders'.[14]

Some instructions from Harley did eventually arrive later in October, but decidedly meagre ones. They did little more than urge Defoe
to write constantly and warn him to use 'the utmost caution that it
may not be supposed you are employed by any person in England: but
that you came there upon your own business, & out of love to the
Country'.[15] Defoe's enemies loved to depict him, as indeed modern
scholars sometimes do, as writing under Harley's instructions, but – as
painful experience would teach him in Scotland – to extract any
instructions at all out of Harley proved an almost insuperable task.

Defoe arrived in Edinburgh somewhere about 6 October and
found the city falling into tumult. Anti-Union mobs would follow the
Jacobite Duke of Hamilton's coach with huzzas and would pelt the
Duke of Queensberry's with filth and missiles. On 23 October Hamilton drove up the High Street to the house of Sir Patrick Johnston, one
of the Union Commissioners, and a great mob followed and tried to
break down Johnston's door. The Guard was summoned, making a
few arrests, but the rioters retreated only a little way and continued
'Hallowing and Throwing stones and sticks at the souldiers', badly
hurting some of them. When Defoe ventured out from a friend's

house, to return to his lodgings in the High Street, he 'heard a Great
Noise and looking Out Saw a Terrible Multitude Come up the High
street with a Drum at the head of Them shouting and swearing and
Cryeing Out, all scotland would stand together, No Union, No Union,
English Dogs, and the like'. The rioters besieged his windows and, as
he looked out, hurled a large rock at his head.[16]

In Parliament the reading-out and discussion of the Treaty had
already begun and, obtaining access to the House through the influence of his Scottish friends, Defoe attended daily. He was there for
the debate of 2 November on the first article of the Treaty, that 'the
two Kingdoms of *Scotland* and *England*, shall ... for ever after, be
united into one Kingdom, by the Name of *GREAT-BRITAIN*'.[17] It
was a great day for speechmaking. The choice, said William Seton of
Pitmedden (one of the Treaty Commissioners), was simple. History
told the grim fate of federal unions, thus the solution must either be a
full incorporating union or a continuance of the present unsatisfac-
tory system. If things remain as they are

> Our Sovereignty and Independency will be eclipsed, the number of
> our Nobility will Encrease, Our Commons will be Oppressed, Our
> Parliaments will be influenced by *England*, the Execution of our
> Laws will be neglected; Our Peace will be interrupted by Faction for
> Places and Pensions; Luxury together with Poverty (tho' strange)
> will invade us; Numbers of *Scots* will withdraw themselves to For-
> eign Countries; and all the other Effects of Bad Government must
> necessarily attend us.[18]

He was followed by Lord Belhaven who, with melancholy elo-
quence, drew an apocalyptic vision of the threatened Union.

> I think, I see *a Free and Independent Kingdom* delivering up That, which
> all the World hath been fighting for, since the days of *Nimrod*; yea,
> that for which most of all the Empires, Kingdoms, States, Principal-
> ities and Dukedoms of *Europe*, are at this very time engaged in the
> most Bloody and Cruel Wars that ever were, *to wit*, A Power to Man-
> age their own Affairs by themselves, without the Assistance and
> Counsel of any other.
>
> I think, I see *a National Church*, founded upon a Rock, secured by
> a *Claim of Right*, hedged and fenced about by the strictest and point-
> edest Legal Sanction that Sovereignty could contrive, voluntarily

descending into a Plain, upon an equal level with *Jews, Papists, Socinians, Arminians, Anabaptists,* and other Sectaries, *&c.*

I think I see *the Noble and honourable Peerage of Scotland* ... put upon such an Equal Foot with their Vassals, that I think I see a petty *English* Excise-man receive more Homage and Respect, than what was paid formerly to their *quondam Maccallanmores.*

... I think I see *the Honest Industrious Tradesman* loaded with new Taxes, and Impositions, disappointed of the Equivalents, drinking Water in place of Ale, eating his salt-less Pottage, Petitioning for Encouragement to his Manufactures, and answered by counter Petitions.

In short, I think I see *the Laborious Plow-man,* with his Corns spoiling upon his Hands, for want of Sale, Cursing the day of his Birth, dreading the Expense of his Burial, and uncertain whether to Marry or do worse.

... But above all, *My Lord,* I think I see *our Ancient Mother* CALE-DONIA, like *Caesar* sitting in the midst of our Senate, Rufully looking round about her, Covering her self with her Royal Garment, attending the Fatal Blow, and breathing out her last with *Et tu quoque mi filii.*[19]

Defoe sent Harley a printed copy of Belhaven's speech and also a verse skit on it by himself entitled *The Vision* – which, he told Harley, 'has made Some sport here and perhaps Done More Service than a More Solid Discourse'.[20] It began:

> Come hither ye Dreamers of Dreams,
> Ye South-Sayers, Wizards and Witches,
> That puzzle the World with hard Names,
> And without any meaning make Speeches:
> > Here's a Lord in the North,
> > Near *Edinburgh* Forth,
> Tho' little has been said of his Name or his Worth,
> Has seen such a Vision, no Mortal can reach it,
> I challenge the Clan of *Egyptians* to match it.

A flyting ensued, Belhaven retorting in a rumbustious ballad, *A Scots Answer to a British Vision,* and Defoe in turn offering *A Reply to the Scot's Answer to the British Vision.*[21] Later, however, when Belhaven was in trouble,[22] the two would become friends, and on Belhaven's death in July 1708 Defoe would pay handsome tribute to him in the *Review.*[23]

Belhaven was followed by the Duke of Hamilton, who challenged the supporters of the Treaty over their interpretation of an 'incorporating union'.

> I take an Incorporating Union to be, where there is a change both in the material and formal Points of Government, as, if two Pieces of Mettal were melted down into one Mass, it can neither be said to retain its former Form or Substance, as it did before the mixture. But now when I consider this Treaty, as it hath been Explained and Spoke to before us these three Weeks by past, I see the *English* Constitution remaining firm, the same two Houses of Parliament, the same Taxes, the same Customs, the same Excises, the same Trade in Companies, the same Municipal Laws and Courts of Judicature, and all ours either subject to Regulations, or Annihilations: only we have the Honour to pay their old Debts, and to have some few Persons present for Witnesses to the Validity of the Deed, when they are pleased to contract more.
>
> Good GOD! What is this an intire Surrender?

Not to be outshone by Belhaven, the Duke ended with a well-rehearsed stroke of theatre. Addressing the Lord Chancellor Seafield, he said he found his heart so full of grief and indignation that he must beg pardon for not finishing his speech – feeling as he did the need to 'drop a Tear as the Prelude to so sad a Story'.[24] With much pathos, he sat down.

*   *   *   *   *   *

It seems that Defoe's identity was known to some in Edinburgh,[25] as well as his reputation as an expert on trade and finance; and, to his gratification, he was invited to give advice to the Parliamentary committee on the 'Equivalent',[26] and also to a committee dealing with rates of taxation and excise. His opinion was asked as to an export 'drawback' (a reimbursement of duty paid upon importation) on peas and oats. It was a subject that the people were very 'clamarous' about, but he persuaded the committee that there was no need of it, seeing that England would always take all Scotland could produce. On the other hand, he argued, it would be appropriate in the case of oat meal, which the Scots exchanged for Norwegian timber (as England also might do after the Union).[27] More significantly, he managed to settle the vexed problem, made much of by the enemies of the Union, of the excise on Scottish ale. Under English excise regulations there were two rates of tax on beer or ale, a low one levied on 'small beer' and a higher one on 'strong' beer or ale. In Scotland, on the other hand, there was a single standard rate, and it was made a great argument against the Union that it might mean the Scottish so-called 'Two-penny' or 'Tippony' ale, the standard drink of the nation, being taxed at a vastly higher rate, namely that imposed on English 'strong' ale. Defoe was able to show that the value of Scottish 'Tippony' ale worked out, with fair neatness, at two-thirds the value of English strong ale, and he proposed a new middle rate of excise to reflect this. The Committee was impressed and ordered him to lay the proposal before them in writing, and at a meeting of the Scottish Parliament on 28 November 1706 an 'explanation and addition' to article VII of the Treaty was approved, framed in Defoe's own words.[28]

Defoe also gained access to meetings of the Commission of the General Assembly of the Kirk. Parliament was preparing a Bill for the Security of the Church, but the Commission, suspecting that this might not prove adequate, was preparing a 'representation' containing further demands. What especially rankled with the clergy was the Abjuration Oath, which, as it stood, entailed that the ruler of Great Britain must be a member of the Church of England – thus compelling Scots Presbyterian ministers and office holders to abjure, as their monarch, not only the Pretender but even a member of their own established Church. They also demanded exemption from the English Test Act; and the more extreme held that for Scots to adopt a consti-tution which gave seats in Parliament to bishops would be a violation of the National Covenant.

Defoe created his own informal circle among the ministers, a 'Revrend Committee with me to Answer their Cases of Conscience',[29] and they found him a sympathetic listener. He indeed thought they had a genuine grievance in the Abjuration Oath and wrote about it more than once to Harley; and Godolphin, when shown a letter of Defoe's on the subject, was convinced, saying 'it ought to guide us very much in what we are doing here'.[30] Defoe told Harley that he passed for an 'Oracle' among these fathers of the Kirk, and that they would have been surprised had they known his private thoughts. In fact, he thought them an irrationally obstinate crew. 'I work Incessantly with them', he wrote on 24 October. 'They go from me seemingly Satisfyed and pretend to be Informd but are the Same Men [i.e. their old selves] when they Come Among Their parties – I hope what I say to you Sir shall Not prejudice them; in Generall They are the Wisest weak men, The Falsest honest men, and the steadyest Unsettled people Ever I met with.' 'They are a hardened, refractory and Terrible people', he confided again to Harley on 2 November. 'They have now kept a Fast, Thursday was the Day in this City, and tho' the Ministers spoke with more Modesty than I expected, yet in the Country they Enflame the people strangely'.[31]

At the end of October he brought out in quick succession a third and fourth *Essay at Removing National Prejudices*. He explained that the previous two *Essays* had been designed to open English readers' eyes to their advantage of a Union, its advantage to the Scots being so obvious – so he had thought – as to call for no mention. But what did he find, on arriving in Scotland? His *Essays* had been reprinted there for use as an argument *against* a Union. Readers, evidently, had suffered from a deep-rooted delusion that the advantage to one partner in a Union must, of necessity, be a disadvantage to the other. There was, however, a cure for this error. It lay in a full realization of the meaning of the word 'Union'. It meant nothing less than (as Defoe eloquently puts it) 'A Sameness of Circumstances and of Sympathies; becoming one and the same Body, with one and the same Head, Life, Soul, Nutriment, Point and Period'.[32]

For the Scots, so Defoe argued, the advantages of a Union would be enormous. England's ports and customs houses would become theirs; English capital would help the Scots exploit the 'Indies' lying at their door (i.e. their incomparable wealth of fish); their linen industry would enjoy (what even Ireland was denied) a free trade to all the colonies; and the English navy would convoy their ships. It was, moreover, false to speak of Scotland as a 'barren' land. What it needed was 'Trade to whet Industry, Profit to whet Trade, Vent of Goods and Stock to produce Profit'.[33] Its lands, when enclosed, manured and cultivated, would be as rich, its cattle as large, its sheep as fat and its wool as fine as those in England.

As regards religion, could the Scots, as things were at present, feel their established church to be secure? History should warn them otherwise. True security for the Kirk lay in a Union, in which the Church and the Constitution had the same sanction and were 'Twisted and Connected together', unable to fall but by the same disaster, or to stand, but by each other's support. There seemed at present a good chance of a Union, but this has not been easy to bring about, and the High Church party was still hopeful of wrecking it, pleading 'those very things for arguments, which they own their aversion to'.

> Those very Men who wish your Church and perhaps Nation too, at the D——l, are turn'd about, and talk of the Security of the Church; the very *Jure Divino* Men talk of Liberty, the very Instruments of former Tyrannys in *England* talk of Preserving your Laws, Parliaments and Judicatorys.[34]

Scottish readers might wonder, wrote Defoe, why he wanted to involve himself in their affairs. To this his answer was that, not only had he always had a particular regard for the Scots, he even contemplated settling amongst them. If he did so – he would say unblushingly – it would be as a private gentleman, and he hoped no-one would think he came there on behalf of a party. 'I Contemn the Suggestion, as I Scorn the Employment of an Emissary, a Spy, or a Mercenary; my Bussiness is known here: Which tending to Trade, Settlement and general Improvement, I never purposed to Meddle in this Affair, and I hope I have done it so as can give no offence to any.'[35]

There were numerous tracts by Scottish authors against the Union, and especially a full incorporating union. Among the most influential were two by James Hodges, a writer thought to have been in the employment of the Duke of Hamilton. He argued, much as the Duke had done in the great debate, that the proposed Treaty left the English governmental system intact, not so much as a stone in the whole building being shaken, whereas the Scottish Government was to be totally overturned and dissolved: it would have no more power to direct its partner than toes have to manage the head.[36] He also maintained that, whatever agreements might be made now between the two nations, after the Union they would be at the mercy of the new British Parliament – which might, for instance, try to impose episcopacy on Scotland. To this Defoe replied that it was to miss the point that the Treaty would *be* the Constitution: the two things were one and the same.

They cannot put that Question [about episcopacy] in the House. –
If any Man should move it, they can not enter on the Debate; they
shake their own Foundation in the very Thought; every Motion is an
Earthquake under the Pillars of the House, and the moment they
should do it, they like *Samson* pull the House down upon their own
Heads.[37]

Hodges further argued that England was a nation simply too
wicked for a God-fearing Scotland to unite with – or as Defoe para-
phrased him, 'You must not Unite with us, for we are a Wicked
Notorious People, *Sodom* was a Fool to us, and GOD will plague you
for our National Sins'. Defoe rejects this as a 'horrid Blasphemous
Suggestion upon the Divine and Immutable Justice', as well as an
uncalled-for reflection on England.[38] Perhaps indeed she was a sinful
nation, perhaps even a more sinful one than Scotland; but it befitted
neither nation to say 'holier-than-thou'. They would do much better,
both of them, to apply themselves to reformation.

Defoe concludes with an allegory. In the reign of James IV of Scotland a woman gave birth to a strange monster.[39] It was an ordinary
male child from the navel downwards,

> But from the Belly upwards it was two distinct Creatures, divided in
> Parts, had two Heads, two perfect and separated Bodies, and
> receiv'd its Nourishment two ways, tho' it voided but by the same;
> and which was yet more wonderful, it had a Division of Souls, two
> Hearts, separate and sometimes opposite Wills, Passions and Affec-
> tions; and this so apparent, that sometimes one side would quarrel
> with its Neighbour and almost fight.

Now, says Defoe, imagine that the monster 'was pleased to be
angry with itself'. Suppose, as Hodges had pictured, a man should
whisper to one of the heads how it could subdue and destroy the
other. What would be the consequence? Would it not be that 'the
Mortality of the other would descend to the Parts that were essential
to both' and the whole creature would die – 'the Wretch become *Felo
de se*?'.[40]

*   *   *   *   *   *

Throughout October 1706 Defoe was writing to Harley every few
days, but Harley gave him no more specific orders and ignored his

hints and pinpricks. 'Want of Instructions, is a Mellancholy Reflection', wrote Defoe (22 November), 'and makes me Frequently think my self an Unworthy Instrument'.[41]

When at last he received a proper letter from Harley, Defoe was proportionately grateful. He assured Harley that he was carrying out his 'Directions' with the 'Uttmost Caution', and was entirely unsuspected of corresponding with anybody in England. 'I Converse with Presbyterian, Episcopall-Dissenter, papist and non-juror, and I hope with Equall Circumspection', he told him, with relish.

> I have faithful Emissaries in Every Company And I Talk to Everybody in Their Own way. To the Merchants I am about to Settle here in Trade, Building ships &c. With the Lawyers I Want to purchase a House and Land to bring my family & live Upon it (God knows where the Money is to pay for it). To day I am Goeing into Partnership with a Membr of parliamt in a Glass house, to morrow with Another in a Salt work. With the Glasgow Mutineers I am to be a fish Merchant, with the Aberdeen Men a woollen and with the Perth and western men a Linen Manufacturer, and still at the End of all Discourse the Union is the Essentiall and I am all to Every one that I may Gain some.[42]

Evidently, despite his disclaimers,[43] the role of spy appealed to his imagination. A little later he would tell Harley he had managed to infiltrate a circle of Jacobites round the Duke of Gordon. 'In This Little scheme of their Affaires I have acted a *True spy* to you.'[44]

He also had a spy in his own employ at this time: his friend John Pierce, with whom he had been involved at the time of the *Legion's Humble Address to the Lords* affair (see above, p. 40). Pierce was now in Edinburgh, under the assumed name of Allen, and Defoe dispatched him to the West Lowlands, to report on the anti-Union agitations there – a service that, Defoe told Harley (26 December 1706), 'No Man in Scotland by himself Could have done'.[45] He had spent three days with the fiery John Hepburn, the 'Bishop' of the Cameronians (extreme Presbyterians), and had heard him preach for nearly seven hours to a vast field meeting, nevertheless had managed, so he claimed, to have planted some new ideas in Hepburn's mind. Defoe pressed Harley to overlook the intrepid Pierce/Allen's peccadilloes and enable him to send him on further missions; but then he discovered that Pierce had been suborned by another paymaster.[46]

Harley, meanwhile, had resumed his silence, and Defoe's reproaches grew sharper. 'Nothing afflicts me so much as not to hear from you or have the least hint what Measures to take' (27 December). 'I wrott you at large about the Kirk. I hope, tho' you do not think Fitt to Replye to me, you will take that Case in thought' (2 January 1707).[47] The atmosphere in Edinburgh was, moreover, very uneasy. There had been an anti-Union rising in Glasgow at the end of November, and an attempted protest march on Edinburgh, though it was suppressed before it got near the city. Then, in another uprising soon afterwards, the rioters took the Glasgow magistrates prisoner. Meanwhile, in Edinburgh, there was a mysterious influx of armed men, and rumour had it they were considering some kind of *coup*.

However, the air suddenly cleared, and on 16 January 1707 Defoe reported to Harley in triumph that the final articles of Union had been agreed and the Treaty had been touched with the sceptre.[48] It was assumed that it would now pass easily through the Westminster Parliament, as indeed it did.

CHAPTER 5

'MAINTAINING A COUNTER CORRESPONDENCE'

The achieving of the Union was, as might have been expected, cele-brated with exultation in the pages of the *Review*. When, later, the cannons were proclaiming the great event from Edinburgh Castle, Mr. *Review* begged pardon for fancying, though he knew it was childish, that they were roaring 'UNION, UNION'.[1]

'Nothing but Union! Union! ... I am quite tired of it, and we hope, 'tis as good as over now; prithee, good Mr. *Review*, let's have now and then a Touch of something else to make us merry.' So the *Review* for 28 January imagines one of its readers complaining, but in reply Mr. *Review* offers a weighty and sarcastic rebuke.

> Pray, Gentlemen, what can you expect out of *Scotland*? Poor, barren *Scotland*! where you fancy there is nothing to be had, but wild Men, and ragged Mountains, Storms, Snows, Poverty and Barrenness. Very well, Gentlemen, and what if you should be mistaken now, and I should tell you, that *Scotland* is quite another Country than you imagine ... That the Poverty of *Scotland*, and the Fruitfulness of *Eng-land*, or rather the Difference between them, is owing not to meer Difference of the Clime, Heat of the Sun or Nature of the Soil, but to the Errors of Time and the Misery of their Constitution.[2]

The mighty Union transaction was, he said, 'a Sea of universal Improvement', and he thanked his good fortune he was among the first to reveal the blessings in store for the Scots.

> I have told them of the Improvement of their Coal Trade, and 'tis their own Fault if they do not particularly engage 20 or 25 Sail of Ships immediately from *England* on that Work.
>
> I have told them of the Improvement of their Salt, and I am now contracting for *English* Merchants, for *Scots* Salt, to the Value of above 10,000 *l. per Annum*.

> I have told them of Linen Manufactures, and I have now above
> 100 poor Families at Work, by my Procuring and Direction, for the
> making such Sorts of Linen, and in such Manner as never was made
> here before, and as no Person in the Trade will believe could be
> made here, till they see it.[3]

It was not exactly the truth, and no doubt those 100 families of linen-
workers were phantoms. Yet it was not pure fantasy either, for within
three years from this time Defoe would in fact contract with a partner
to manufacture embroidered linen tablecloths.[4]

He kept, from this time on, a much stricter incognito in Scotland,
and to casual enquirers he would explain his continuing presence in
their country in several different ways. He had fled there because of
debt and dared not return (a reason the more likely to be believed, he
calculated, in that it was humiliating); he was going to write a history
of the Union and had been given warrants to search the registers and
Parliament books; he was working on a new version of the Psalms,
secluding himself in Edinburgh University for the purpose; he was
going into business to manufacture linen. If his plans for setting up
linen manufactures succeeded, he would say, he would bring his family
to Scotland and settle there. By these 'Triffles', he told Harley, he was
serving the 'Great End, Viz. a Concealmt'; his real reason for being in
Scotland was quite unsuspected.[5]

But what above all he needed to know from Harley was whether he
was to stay on in Scotland. 'If nothing better Can be found out for
me', he wrote to him on 2 January, 'I Could Wish you will please to
Settle me here after the Union. Perhaps I might do her Majtie a Service of One Sort while I was in an office of Different Face.'[6] Judging
from his employer's silence, he might well have supposed he had been
forgotten or was to be abandoned. However, his work in Edinburgh
was in fact interesting other potential patrons. Early in November
1706 he had received an invitation from his erstwhile benefactor, Lord
Halifax, to send him reports on Scottish affairs – no doubt in return
for handsome payment, for Halifax was a munificent patron. He had
accepted with enthusiasm, though he felt in duty bound to let Harley
know. 'As I am yours Sir in Duty Abstracted from and Exclusive of all
the World,' he wrote to him, 'I Thought my Self Oblig'd to Acquaint
you of it and on your Orders shall at any Time Desist'.[7]

Then on 13 February 1707 he reported to Harley, in somewhat cryptic terms, that he had been receiving approaches from 'the Other Newly alter'd part of an office Near you Sir'.[8] By this he presumably meant the Earl of Sunderland, who, two months previously, had replaced Sir Charles Hedges as Harley's fellow Secretary of State. Sunderland's appointment was the first, and a momentous, step in an attempted take-over of Godolphin's administration by the Junto Whigs. It had been ruthlessly forced on the Queen, who detested the overbearing Sunderland and had fought the proposal tooth-and-nail.

Defoe evidently saw dangers, but also enticing possibilities, in this approach from Sunderland, and he told Harley he longed to tell him the details of it and get his advice. 'I am Not to be pumpt or Sounded', he wrote, 'and yet would be Glad to have a hint from you Where I should be wary and where not'. He assumed that Harley would not let it be to his (Defoe's) prejudice and, as a point of honour, would not reveal it to anyone else. Perhaps there was no need for caution, for he was sure that Harley and his colleagues were 'all in the True Intrest', but he would like a hint as regards his own conduct. Were he to be asked about his own prospects – for instance if people should say 'We hope he [i.e. Defoe] is Not Dropt' or 'Tis hard if the persons who *say they Employ him* do not stand by him' – might he take advantage of it? He had, he said, no right to accept favours without Harley's approval.[9]

In fact, it was far from the case that Harley and his colleagues were 'all in the True Intrest', if that means the same interest. Indeed Defoe probably hardly believed so himself, though it is hard to guess just what he did know. As early as October 1706, prompted by the Duchess of Marlborough, Godolphin had begun to suspect Harley of disloyalty and, with his friend St John and others, of planning to make trouble for him in the forthcoming session.[10] Harley, for his part, was attempting to detach Godolphin and Marlborough from the Junto and to persuade the Queen to set up a non-party administration, which could include some moderate Tories. It was about this time that Harley acquired special favour with the Queen and gained backdoor access to her through her waiting-woman Abigail Hill (later Masham). He had encouraged her in her losing struggle against Sunderland, and this would certainly have been known to Sunderland himself, who was violently against Harley and his devious ways. By the middle of 1707

Godolphin was complaining that 'Mr. Harley does so hate and fear Lord Somers, Lord Sunderland, and Lord Wharton, that he omits no occasion of filling the Queen's head with their projects and designs'.[11] Sunderland, meanwhile, together with other Junto leaders, complained bitterly of Godolphin's vacillation and feeble support for their plans.

Nothing could have been more probable than that Sunderland should try to 'pump' and 'sound' Defoe about Harley; and no doubt the idea of Defoe's corresponding with this enemy throws light on Harley's subsequent treatment of him. To have forbidden the correspondence would have been awkward and likely to arouse, or confirm, Defoe's suspicions, so he opted for silence, a silence more profound than his previous one. After a letter of 21 January 1707 he did not write again for nearly six months.[12]

Defoe was bewildered, and in almost every letter (for he dutifully continued sending reports) he begged for instructions, his tone growing more desperate as the months went by. 'I humbly Entreat your hints for my Conduct'; 'I am Impatient for your Ordrs which way to steer my Course'; 'I … Am forced to take your Long Silence for a Tacit professing your Satisfaction'; 'without your Directions I am a Meer Image without life, soul or Action'.[13] It was not that, at this period, he was without funds, for he was able to draw on Bell the postmaster. But he had what he called his 'spyes' and 'pensioners' to reward. 'I am spending your Money a Little Freer than Ordinary On the Occasion of the Assembly', he writes on 3 April.[14] Indeed it was part of his quandary that he did not know how much money Harley would approve of his spending in this fashion. However by May 1707 the supply, not only of instructions but of money, had quite dried up.

In asking for his contact with Sunderland to remain a secret Defoe no doubt meant, above all, kept from the knowledge of the Lord Treasurer Godolphin, who was his official channel to the Queen's bounty and had reason to dislike and fear Sunderland. He wished for Godolphin's good opinion above all others, and when a rumour reached him that Harley was ill, he seized the occasion to make direct contact with Godolphin, to warn him about a trade fraud connected with the Union. Since duties on imports from France were much lower in Scotland than in England, and after 1 May, when the Union became effective, there would be free trade across the Border, some merchants, both English and Scottish, had arranged large imports of

French wines and brandies to Scotland, planning to send them on to England customs-free after 1 May, thus undercutting honest traders. Likewise, some merchants were exporting goods to Scotland, for re-importation back to England after 1 May, so as to be able to claim the 'drawback' on exports to what, until 1 May, had been a foreign country. 'Your Ldship Will Find the Inconvenience Very Great and the Quantity before the first of May Incredible', he told Godolphin. 'Here Was Three Ships Entred last week and all the Wines are bought up, and I am Informed There are Eight More at the *Orcades* Waiting to Come in.' He did not presume to suggest what Godolphin should do about this dishonest business, but he offered to discover the quantity of wines brought in, and where they were stored. The matter, he warned him, was going to inflame feeling against the Union.[15]

It could well have been Defoe who first alerted the Government to this quite serious matter. At all events by April it had become a burning issue: the injured English traders were petitioning for redress and the Scottish merchants fulminated against any interference from England, as a violation of the Union. The affair also vividly reveals the rifts within Godolphin's ministry. The Tory-dominated House of Commons brought in a bill to prevent the fraud, and on the third reading Harley introduced a clause making the penalties retrospective. The 'Drawback Bill' precipitated a furious clash with the Whig lords in the Upper House, who for their own reasons were desperate not to alienate the Scots, and they threw it out. Whereupon Harley, in a curious manoeuvre, persuaded the Queen to prorogue Parliament for a few days, so enabling the measure to be passed a second time – though soon afterwards it was quietly laid to rest. The Earl of Sunderland, in a letter to Marlborough, was vitriolic about Harley. 'I believe you will be surprised at this short prorogation. It is entirely occasioned by him who is the author of all the tricks played here ... I will only say, no man in the service of a government ever did act such a part.'[16]

As for Defoe, on reflection he changed his attitude towards the fraud. 'If the Parliamt had not Dropt the Drawback bill I must ha' fled this Country', he wrote to Harley from Glasgow (15 May). 'It is scarce possible to Describe to you the Disgust that affair gave here and what Use was made of it.' The best he could do, in talking to the magistrates and clergy in Glasgow, was to stress the thoughtfulness of England in letting the Drawback Bill lapse, a reason for them to show moderation in return. He begged Harley to ensure that the Customs and Excise officers sent to Scotland were courteous and understanding men, ready to 'wink, Abate, and bear with Circumstances'.[17] The grievance over the wine and brandy, he had come to think, was a meer trifle beside the brouhaha and clamour against the Union that had been raised about it.

Hearing nothing from Harley, Defoe asked himself what his reward was going to be for his faithful service in Scotland, or whether indeed there would be any. 'My Friends write me word I shall stay here till I am Forgott', he writes to Harley on 25 April 1707. 'I Am Inform'd Sir the Custome house is Settled for this Country', he writes on 21 May. 'Is there No Room for an Absent Servant to be admitted?' On 10 June he complains that others are being appointed as Commissioners in the Customs, yet nothing seems to come his way. 'I kno' absent and Forgotten are frequently synonimous', but he would be glad to be appointed Surveyor of the 'Out ports' or perhaps the accountant or Comptroller of the Accounts, 'things I pretend to be Master of'.[18]

Then at long last, on 12 June 1707, he received a letter from Harley. It is a curious and significant document. Harley reassured Defoe that Defoe's letters were reaching him safely and that he (Harley) was giving thought to his career. 'I am sure I have taken care to represent your services in the best light from time to time where it may do you service.' It was, he tells him, a good idea to put the Duke of Queensberry in mind of him,[19] and he advises him to do it again. 'It will Serve to cover your friends in doing You justice: I need give You only a hint.' Meanwhile he advises Defoe to write a letter to Godolphin, for Harley to pass on to him, suggesting how he might be most usefully employed. '*He* thinks surveyor of one of the Ports.' Harley would also like Defoe (it would be to his own advantage as well as the public's) to draw up a paper about ways to prevent future frauds in the Customs. He asks him, nonetheless, to send him an account of the money he has drawn from postmaster Bell, with the dates; for Lord Treasurer Godolphin says that 'it is not fit you should be longer at my Charge, which I hope is for Your Good'.[20]

This last, about the handing Defoe on to a new paymaster, is plainly a reflection of Harley's growing rift with Godolphin, and the rest of his letter is self-righteous railing against the 'impotent malice', the 'inveterate' spleen and the 'notorious forgeries' of his enemies – though, if God spares his life, he is confident he will be able to 'pull off the Mask from the reall Atheists & pretended Patriots'.[21]

Harley was evidently feeling beleaguered. We have already mentioned the ferocity with which Sunderland, the Junto leader, greeted his conduct over the Drawbacks Act (see p. 78), and the truth is, this was the attitude among the Junto in general about the 'trickster' Robert Harley, and the 'Court' Whigs with their leader Godolphin were at bottom almost as hostile. Godolphin, once a warm friend, had been relatively slow to doubt his loyalty, but by October 1706, prompted by the Duchess of Marlborough, he became sure that Harley was working against him. By July 1707 matters had reached a crisis. Marlborough wrote to Godolphin on 11 July: 'You must find some way of speaking plainly to him [i.e. Harley]: for if he continues in doing ill offices upon all occasions to Lord Somers, Lord Sunderland and Lord Wharton, it will at last have so much effect upon the Queen, whose inclinations are already that way, it must occasion that no measures will be followed'.[22]

In view of all this, one can hardly doubt the meaning of Godolphin's saying that it was 'not fit' that Defoe should continue on Harley's payroll. How soon Defoe realized the full extent of the rift between Godolphin and his own employer is not clear; but from now on it is plain that his reports from Scotland, though he continued to address them to Harley, were really intended for Godolphin's eye.

It will be remembered that Harley had encouraged Defoe to write to Godolphin about his own future, and sometime in July Godolphin seems to have made him a definite offer of employment in Scotland,[23] which – for whatever reason – he had refused. His words in a letter to Harley written some years later suggest an explanation: that faced with a choice he decided, or was persuaded, that he could be more useful by continuing as a secret agent.

> Your Ldpp [Harley was now Earl of Oxford] knows and I Presume Remembers That when your Ldpp Honord me with your Recommendation to The Late Ld Treasurer [i.e. Godolphin], My Lord Offred Me a Very Good Post in Scotland and afterward Offred me to be a Commisioner of the Customes There, and That I did Not Refuse Those Offers, but it being your Opinion as well as his Ldpps That I Might be More Servicable in a Private Capascity, I Chose

Rather to Depend Upon her Majties Goodness That I Might be
Most Servicable, Than to Secure My Family a Maintenance and be
Rendred Uncapable to serve Her Majties Intrest.[24]

No doubt he was regretting this in the ensuing months, for his personal situation in Scotland grew more and more difficult. He
continued his regular reports to Harley, painting a somewhat depress-
ing picture of Scotland in the aftermath of the Union: the
recriminations of merchants, whose ships had been seized by the Customs officials for Customs fraud; the complaints of the brewers, who
were 'Goeing Mad' over the operations of the Malt Tax; and the rage
of the citizenry in general over the cheat (as they called it) of the English Government, in paying three-quarters of the 'Equivalent' (see
p. 67) not in gold but in exchequer bills, a form of currency difficult,
or sometimes impossible, to cash north of the Border.[25] He also,
presciently, noted signs of a coming Jacobite rising. The Duke of
Atholl, a leader of the anti-Union party, had announced the date of his
'Great Hunting', and 'Ld Sinclear & sevll Other of the popish and
Jacobite Gentlemen on Fife Side where I Now Am Are allready Gone
to it, who are known to be no sports men Nor Ever Used to Go'. The
Jacobites were declaring that their King James VIII would soon be on
the scene, and according to some he had already arrived incognito. All
agreed, Defoe wrote, that there was some mischief afoot. It was said
there was a plan to seize the 'Equivalent' on its way to Edinburgh, and
the Government forces were quite inadequate to cope. He offered to
go to the Highlands to make himself 'Master of as Much of these
Mysteries of Iniquity as Can be Obtaind'.[26] It was a gloomy story he
had to tell.[27]

In the *Review* meanwhile, he had been conducting a running critique
of the doings of the '*great* Gothick *Hero*', Charles XII of Sweden.[28]
Charles had been on the verge of declaring war on the Emperor, on
behalf of the Emperor's persecuted Protestant subjects – a mad step,
according to Defoe, seeing that he had left his own Protestant subjects in Livonia abandoned to the mercies of the Tsar (see above,
p. 36). But now he learned that John Dyer, in his influential *News-letter*,
had reported that a complaint had been brought against Defoe for his
aspersions by the Swedish envoy 'Lyencroon' (Christoffer Leijon-
crona, 1662–1710) and that he was to be arrested by the Queen's
Messenger. He responded robustly, taking his stand upon the justice

of a free country. He could, he said, see no offence in anything he had written. If he had said that King Charles was a bastard or a whore-master, his Majesty would have been at liberty to sue him, but he had never heard there was any law by which a king could have reparation on behalf of his government.[29] In one of two pamphlets he published in response to Dyer, he declared: 'The King of *Sweden* ... has carried it with so high a Hand in some parts of the World, that their Princes deliver up their Subjects bound Hand and Foot for him to use his Pleasure with them. – But *GOD* be Praised, the Queen of England is none of those.'[30] He offered to return to London to face his accusers, but also to make such amends to the King as seemed proper, and this he did handsomely enough, in the *Review* for 6 November, without eating his words.

Concurrently it was reported by the annalist Narcissus Luttrell that the Russian ambassador had complained of a remark by Defoe in the *Review* for 16 October about Charles XII's enemy Peter the Great.[31] It came in an address to Money: 'Thou makest Christians fight for the *Turks*, Thou hirest Servants to the Devil, nay, to the very Czar of Mus-covy'. It is not clear if any action followed this complaint, but it would by no means be the only time that Defoe would denounce the barbar-ity of the Russian regime.

Apart from this, we may suppose, his main preoccupation was with his *History of the Union*. The main body of this vast work consists of a transcript of the minutes of the day-to-day transactions of the Com-missioners for the Treaty in Whitehall and the lengthy debates in the Scottish Parliament, followed by Defoe's own 'Observations'. (Since the minutes were printed for the Government by his own publisher, Mrs Anderson, she was no doubt printing them for him simultane-ously.) The book begins, however, with several substantial historical and polemical chapters, beginning with a lengthy and admirable 'Gen-eral History of Unions in Britain'. Defoe evidently read widely for this,[32] very likely having obtained admission to the Edinburgh Univer-sity library or the Advocates' library, and among his sources are George Buchanan's *Rerum Scoticarum Historia*, James Tyrell's Whiggish *General History of England*, the Tory Robert Brady's *History of England*, Rymer's *Foedera*, Spottiswoode's *History of the Church of Scotland*, William Prynne's *Collections* and the unpublished manuscript of Sir Thomas Craig's 'De Unione Regnorum Britanniae Tractatus'.[33]

There had been many earlier attempts at a union between England and Scotland. Defoe relates the efforts of Edward I to secure one by marrying his son, the future Edward II, to Margaret, the heiress to the Scottish throne; the proposal by Henry VIII to marry his daughter Mary, and then his son Edward, into the royal house of Scotland; the projected marriage of the infant Edward VI to Mary, the infant queen of Scotland; the union of crowns in the person of James I and VI; the full parliamentary and commercial union under Cromwell; and the ill-fated Treaty of Union of 1670. (How the Scots should bless themselves that this latter failed, he remarks, for it could have crushed the prospects of the Kirk for ever.[34])

Then in the following chapter, 'Of Affairs in Both Kingdoms', he describes the tension and crisis between the two countries, which steadily grew fiercer through the reign of King William and eventually nearly led to war, prompting an abortive attempt at a union in the first year of the reign of Queen Anne. Its ill-success he puts down to the covert wrecking tactics of the Tory ministry and, above all, the failure to face the all-important issue of religion: the imperative need to preserve independence between the two countries' national churches.

Finally, in 'Of the Last Treaty, Properly Called the Union', he comes to the great and successful measure of 1707. This is to be the subject of the rest of his huge treatise, but he seizes the occasion to make a very bold, and characteristically provocative, political statement. Let us suppose, he says, that Oliver Cromwell was the murderous usurper and tyrant that people say; nevertheless, if we look for wisdom regarding an Anglo-Scottish union, it is above all in him that we find it. He may have conquered Scotland with the utmost ruthlessness, but he was not less 'Politick in Keeping, than Terrible in Obtaining', and the union he proceeded to create was 'the best Concerted, the best Executed, the best Approved, that ever this Island saw till now'. If ever a nation gained by being conquered, it was then.

> And what was the Foundation of all this? Nothing but the Natural Product of Common Reasoning; he [Cromwell] found that the only way to preserve the Conquest he had made on the Powers of the Nations, was to make a Conquest of their Affections; That the only way to do this, was to let them see their Interest and Happiness in his Government; and that this could only be brought to pass, by Uniting and intirely Incorporating the Nations into one; Communicating

Peace, Privileges, and all possible Advantages to them; And thereby letting them see the true way to their prosperity.[35]

*   *   *   *   *   *

Defoe's situation regarding his employers in England was becoming steadily worse, and at last his letters grew altogether piteous. Godolphin, at the time of Defoe's turning down the offer of a Government post, had promised him an allowance, but none came. 'If you were to See Me Now', he wrote to Harley (11 September), 'Entertaind of Courtisy, without Subsistence, allmost Grown shabby in Cloths, Dejected &c, what I Care Not to Mention; you wou'd be Mov'd to hasten My Relief, in a Manner Suitable to that Regard you were Allways pleased to show for me'. Having Godolphin's letter in his pocket, promising him 'Comfortable Things', it was a 'Very Mortifying Thought that I have Not One friend in the World to Support me Till his Ldship shall think Fitt to begin That allowance'.[36] On 29 September he humbly entreated Harley, as a last favour, to 'send [him] Out of This Torture'.

> Give me your Ordr to Come Away: Ile Ever be your faithfull and Sincere Servt whether Subsisted Or Not. Ile be the Constant Friend of your Family and Intrest, in Meer Remembrance of your past Care of me; It is Sir my Aversion to quit a post I am plac'd in by your Ordr and which without your Ordr I Ought not to abandonne; but Sir the Bravest Garrison May be starv'd Out, and It is my Duty to Tell you when I Am Not able to hold out Any Longer.[37]

Eventually, on 31 October, he received a letter from Godolphin suggesting he could draw on his allowance through his brother-in-law Robert Davis. Infuriatingly, however, even then it told him neither when he could draw, nor for how much.[38] Not till the end of another month did he actually receive any money, when Bell the postmaster sent him an order for £100. It gave 'New life to my Affaires', he wrote; and a few days later he set off on the road to London.[39]

*   *   *   *   *   *

Arriving home on 1 January 1708, he for the moment remained incognito, sending his brother-in-law to ask for an interview with

Godolphin. He had returned, as he would soon discover, at a very tense moment, for the power-struggle between Harley and Godolphin was reaching its dénouement. There had already been a further crisis back in September, when Harley was formally told by Lord Chancellor Cowper that his colleagues considered him a disturber of public business. Upon this, though earnestly protesting his innocence, he had asked Godolphin's leave 'to go into the country' – evidently as a prelude to resignation, though the resignation did not in fact take place.[40]

Godolphin's own position at this time was very painful. He had lost the favour of the Queen, who was by now taking her directions from Harley and Abigail Masham, yet at the same time he was under ruthless pressure to force further Junto lords on the Queen's Cabinet. The choice was clear. He must either give in to the Junto and dismiss Harley or reconstruct his government along Harleyite and 'non-party' lines. But the first seemed to him impossible, considering the Queen's rooted hatred of the Junto, so he opted for the second.

Negotiations to this end went on busily over the Christmas recess, and on 14 January 1708 an agreement was reached on a 'moderate scheme' on the Harleyite pattern. But very soon after, this plan fell to pieces, for it became clear (oddly, it does not seem to have been so before) that it would mean Godolphin himself stepping down.[41] The only remaining course, therefore, was to get rid of Harley, and on 29 January the Attorney-General told him officially that he no longer enjoyed the confidence of the Lord High Treasurer. The Queen, in turn, attempted to dismiss Godolphin, though hoping to retain his close friend and ally the Duke of Marlborough, but in response both ministers resigned.

Thus the stage was set for a celebrated scene, the fall of Harley. On 9 February 1708, at the usual Sunday meeting of the Cabinet Council, neither Godolphin nor Marlborough were in their places. Harley opened proceedings briskly but was met only by angry mutterings; whereupon, after a few minutes, the Duke of Somerset declared, 'I do not see how we can deliberate, when the commander-in-chief and the lord treasurer are absent'.[42] The Queen left the room in great distress and the meeting broke up in confusion. Two days later Harley resigned, and Godolphin and Marlborough were back in office.

The news spread quickly, and Defoe wrote to Harley next day saying he did not know whether to congratulate him or condole with him, but he believed he might have left a 'Tottering' party just in time. At all events he wanted Harley to know he himself was loyal.

> My Bussiness Sir was Onely in Duty and Gratitude to Offer my Self to you Against all your Enemies. My sphere is Low, but I Distinguish No body when I am speaking of The ill Treatmt of One I am Engag'd to as to you in The Bonds of an Inviolable Duty. I Entreat you Sir to Use me in Any Thing in which I may Serve you, and that More Freely Than when I might be Supposed following your Riseing Fortunes. Tis also my Opinion you are still Riseing – I wish you as Successful as I believ you Unshaken by This storm.[43]

*   *   *   *   *   *

Meanwhile Defoe was faced with an alarming question, how would this turn of events affect his relations with the Lord Treasurer Godolphin? Godolphin was a hardworking, responsible-minded but aristocratic and aloof man, not someone with whom Defoe could ever expect a personal intimacy; and, out of loyalty to his ousted patron, he had (so he would write later) decided not to approach Godolphin about future employment. However Harley, when he heard this, told him he was quite wrong: the Lord Treasurer would only employ him in what was honourable, and as for himself, he would not be the least offended. So Defoe asked for an interview, and upon meeting Godolphin his anxiety was soon set at rest. Some years later, in *An Appeal to Honour and Justice* (1715), he would give an account, perhaps somewhat rose-tinted, of the meeting. He told Godolphin he feared his obligations to Harley must count against him, for when great men fell it was usual for all their dependents to fall with them. '*Not at all Mr*. De Foe', Godolphin had replied, smilingly. '*I always think a Man honest, till I find to the contrary.*' He let it be known that the Government had plans for Defoe, and he even obtained him an audience with the Queen, who graciously praised his earlier services and told him she had appointed him for another mission, which was 'something Nice'. The Lord Treasurer would tell him more. It emerged that he was to be sent to Scotland again, on business that was 'far from being unfit for a Sovereign to direct, or an honest Man to perform' (though what it was, we are not told), and indeed he only had three days to prepare.[44]

One of the reasons for sending him there was that Scotland had just suffered an attempted invasion. A French fleet, carrying the Pretender and his followers with 6,000 infantry, had set sail for Scotland on 6 March, being immediately pursued by a naval force under Admiral Byng. The French had intended to enter the Firth of Forth and to capture Edinburgh, with the aid of local Jacobites; but they overshot the Firth, and Byng's arrival made it too late to retrieve the error. In the ensuing sea-battle they lost a ship, whereupon they abandoned their enterprise and made for home, taking the long route round Ireland and suffering grievous casualties along the way. By the time Defoe arrived in Edinburgh the castle was full of Jacobite prisoners.

The *Review*, however, did not give readers any sort of eye-witness account of the scene, and this leads us on to something important. During his previous stay in Scotland Defoe had confessedly written the *Review* as from that country, but during his present stay, which was to last nine months, he was careful to give no impression that he was writing from anywhere but England. On two occasions, for special reasons, he would admit to having been in Scotland recently, but even then with the implication that he was no longer there.

The explanation becomes clear when we read the first of three letters from Defoe to Godolphin (dated 26 and 29 June and 3 July 1708) which have only recently come to light.[45] As we saw, when, previously, Godolphin had offered him a Government post in Scotland, Defoe had refused, on the grounds that he was would be more serviceable as a secret agent, but the thought now entered his mind: could he not accept such a post, which would mean settling in Scotland, yet also go on with his secret service work? With this in mind he had recently asked for a post in the Customs, and on 26 June 1708 he wrote to Godolphin again.

> When I look Farther into This Case here, and See how Easily I may Enjoy this place Under your Ldpps Favour, and be Entirely Concealed from the wholl world, How it will Enable me to be allwayes Serving her Majtie both in Public, and private – Nay how I might even officiat Myself, and give very Little Umbrage here, but by a Deputy might have it entirely Concealed in England, and so be Free to be Disposed as her Majties Pleasure should think fitt – when I see this, and look back on the many Occasions in which your Ldpp has

done me Good, I Flatter My Self, that your Ldpp will Think of me in this affair.[46]

The cunning of the scheme, it will be seen, was that, if he were to appoint a deputy, it would be assumed he himself was remaining in England, which would be an effective disguise for his actual presence in Scotland, as a secret agent. But for this purpose he would need to maintain a strict incognito, and it would be essential that the *Review* should give no clue, or better still give a false clue, as to his whereabouts. In this and other respects, the atmosphere of espionage was thickening round Defoe. He was anxious not to be suspected of conducting a secret correspondence,[47] but a secret correspondence is what he would soon be drawn into.

It was the eve of the first 'British' election, and in the *Review* Defoe, in a series of articles, offered electors preposterous ironic reasons for voting for Tories and high-flyers. If they did so he wrote (18 May) '*We should have PEACE*, and who can put too much Value upon PEACE'.

> O Peace, Peace, who would not purchase Peace? What signifies Truth or Liberty, if we have but Peace, you cannot give too much for Peace? what if you had no Trade, *you should have Peace*; what if you had no Manufactures, yet *you should have Peace*; what signifies it to us, who has *Spain*, or who has *America*; what signifies Collonies or Plantations abroad, Merchants Ships or Men of War? *we should have Peace*, invalluable PEACE, inexpressible *Peace*, Peace that no Body could value, few understand, and no Man alive be able to tell how long it should last.

He would grant, he said (22 May) with nicely-contrived sarcasm, that in the last two Parliaments 'we had some weighty Affairs upon the Wheel, which might require a Kind of thinking, plodding, sedate Fellows, such as the *Whigs* generally sent up to the House'. But now there were only a few 'Trifles' to be dealt with, like detecting traitors, repelling foreign invasions and settling a Peace, and thus it was an excellent moment to elect a Tory parliament. 'These ill-natur'd *Whigs* will get us a Peace, *the Lord knows when*, they are so haughty with their *Hockstets* [i.e. Blenheims] and *Ramellies*, and so puff'd up with every Advantage they get, that they will not hear of a Peace *forsooth*, without the senseless Epithets of *Durable*, *Lasting*, *Firm*, and an odd Word *of a mighty Sound but altogether useless Signification*, a Thing they call HONOURABLE.'

Meanwhile Defoe brought to bear his whole repertoire of satire, genre-painting and solemn adjuration on the voting scene itself. He drew Hogarthian pictures of electioneering up and down England, scenes which he (untruthfully) claimed to have been witnessing in person. Here is Sir Thomas, a great local landlord, sitting in the public house all through market day, having come to a very expensive understanding with the innkeeper. The rooms are full. In one there are two or three butchers and half a dozen farmers, in another some townsmen, and 'a Parcel of their Wives' upstairs. Sir Thomas goes into one room after another. 'Here a drunken Butcher, gorg'd with his Ale, spues in his Worships Presence, there a Clown belches in his Face.' Farmer Q—'s wife quarrels with his steward, because 'Sir *Thomas* was not civil to her', that is to say he asked for her husband's vote but did not squeeze two guineas into her hand. Also an old woman is leaving in a huff, though nobody knows why. It is, so the neighbourhood gossips establish later, because when Sir Thomas spoke to her in the street he did not 'salute her Gentlewomanship' (i.e. kiss her), whereas he had 'kissed all the Goodies and Gammars in the upper Room'. Meanwhile, across the square at the Greyhound Sir William ('a jolly, frank, open handed Gentleman', whether a Whig or a Tory is not to the purpose) is having an even worse time. He salutes his constituents genially from the inn-gallery but they cry 'won't your Worship come and drink one Cup with your honest Freeholders?'. He says he does not care for it, but this will not do for them. 'If Sir *W.* won't drink with us', they tell his steward, '*that is*, thinks himself, *d'ye see*, too good to drink … with poor Country Folks … why then I'll tell ye, that Sir, *d'ye see*, we'll vote none, *that is*, come *Tom*, we'll be gone'. 'Could I but give you a Picture now of the Baronet among the *Boors*', writes Mr. *Review*: 'on one hand of him sits a Butcher greasie as the Master of the Company, fat as a Bullock of 12 *l.* Price, drunk as a Drum, drivelling like a Boar, foaming at Mouth with a Pipe in his Jaws, and being in the open Yard, holds it so that the Wind carries the Smoak directly in Sir *William's* Face; on the other hand sits a Tanner, not so fat, but twice as drunk as t'other, every now and then he lets a great Fart, and first drinks his Worship's health, then spues upon his Stockings'. A third dead drunk freeholder, bowing too low to Sir William, manages to overturn him, chair and all. Another countryman sells the Baronet a sow and a pig, at twice their proper price, and leaves, without positively promising to vote for him. He goes over the way to see what can be made of Sir Thomas, and keeps faith with both Baronets by voting for nobody.[48]

Mr. *Review* has a story for electors. A certain Lord (no matter who, where or when) owned a large shock-dog, of whom he thought very highly, and he was anxious to find some way of honouring him. It so happened that it was election-time, and a friend suggested the dog might run as the Town's representative. 'I know *Shock is rich*', he says, 'and if your Lordship will but come among us a little, and spend a litle Money, we'll make a good Party for him'. 'What, whether they see him or no?' asks the nobleman. 'Ay, ay, if it be said it is but a Dog of your Lordship's sending, we'll drink them into the rest.' But what about the other candidates, asks the Lord; 'they are both very honest Gentlemen, I doubt, *Shock* will never carry it'. 'They are honest Gentlemen enough', replies his friend, 'but they won't spend their Money'. Moreover, as he explains, he and his friends work on a sound principle. 'We judge by our Sences of seeing, feeling and tasting, all which are affected by our Way of choosing; whereas those that pretend to choose by Men's Vertues and Quallifications, take them unsight, unseen, and at best they do hear of them at a Distance, and when they come to make Trial of them, your Lordships *Shock Dog* would have done every Jot as much Service in Publick Affairs.'[49]

Now, Mr. *Review* hastens to say, however sagacious and far-seeing a dog were to be in question, nothing like this could happen in England. Perhaps sometimes, as at Tiverton or Coventry, 'Men have *cry'd in* and *cry'd out* without Sence of Persons, and being pass'd Sence of Characters, as the Golden Gale blew, or according as the Balmy Stream from the Tap has inflam'd their Understandings'. Still, this was no shock dog. 'We hardly ever had a Shock Dog sat in the *H—* of *C—*, since I can remember.' But curiously, when he was visiting the moon a little while ago, he was told that something of this kind had taken place at a lunar election. He offers this to his readers as '*a Word to the Wise*'.[50]

On another day, more earnestly, Mr. *Review* reminds misguided electors of their immortal souls. He asks them if they realize what a 'blind and unaccountable Thing' it is to 'swallow down your Country's prosperity in the Glass, and gorge your selves with the Life Blood of your Children's Happiness'.

Do ye know honest, blind and foolish Freeholders, do ye know what ye are doing, when ye are taking Money, or taking Drink from your shamefully submissive, cringing Candidates? Do you know that you Exchange Liberty for Gold and Posterity for Drink? Do you know that for ten shillings you are selling the inestimable Priviledge of a free born Subject, and putting your All in the hand of a mercenary? Do you know this, or do ye not consider it? – If ye do not know it, I'll put you in Mind of the horrid Absurdity as well as I can; and if I do draw the Picture of your brutish Practice, with a little more Gall than pleases you, I presume, you will see Cause to thank your selves, and not blame me.[51]

During this election Defoe renewed contact with his generous patron the Earl of Sunderland. The Earl evidently took a self-important and *de haut en bas* line towards him, instructing him to get in touch with him through a third party, a 'Mr. Shute', and causing him to write more than usually humbly and self-abasingly.[52] In a letter of 20 May he reported to Sunderland on the success of the Jacobites in misleading the 'poor honest but ill-natured imposed-upon' Presbyterians, who had reacted to the abortive invasion as if it had nothing to do with them, being merely a struggle between two foreign nations. About this, he told Sunderland, he could say more – evidently meaning that he could reveal some names. 'I think your Lordshipp, who I kno will make a prudent use of it, ought to be informed of the most exact and nicest part of this affair, and to kno who are the friends of Her Majesty's interest, and who the friend of her prosperity only.'[53]

He had been puzzled, or so he said, by what he saw of the election in Scotland, where there were 'some perfect novelties of conduct, *mysteria politica*, that are hard to understand'. There was a new party, the Squadrone, who were opposing 'Court' candidates for Parliament and making bargains with Tories, or, as he would later put it in the *Review*, 'Both sides set up *Whigs*, and both sides set up *Tories*; they that would be called the *Whig* Party vote for profess'd *Jacobites*, *Whigs* set up *Tories* against *Whigs* ... and *Tories* set up *Whigs* against *Tories*'.[54] It was a strange business, but he was cautious of saying more unless he could be sure his letter would reach Sunderland's hands. He had, he told him, written on the same subject to Lord Treasurer Godolphin, but he hoped Sunderland would not let Godolphin hear of their correspondence and the generous 'favours' he had been receiving. The burden of this letter is secrecy and the further things he could divulge, for Sunderland's ear alone.[55]

Receiving no reply, he held this letter back, not despatching it until 25 May, when he enclosed it in a second letter. For on re-reading it, he said, he felt that his urging secrecy upon Sunderland sounded shocking – 'as if Something Clandestine was acting', or as if he were serving two masters and 'keeping a Foul and False Correspondence between this part and England', a thing he had always abhorred. But really, he said, his reason was quite different. It was not (he declared piously) that he pictured any disagreement between Sunderland and the Lord Treasurer, for he was sure they were firmly in the same interest, the 'Intrest of England'. He requested secrecy simply because he feared that, if Godolphin heard of Sunderland's bounty to him, it might cool his own inclination to 'do something' for him, as he had promised.[56]

If Defoe was, at first, truly puzzled by the *mysteria politica* he was observing, he had good reason because, for the purposes of the 1708 election, the Junto Whigs had entered into a temporary alliance with the Squadrone, and not only that, had even made a pact with the Jacobites. Much here turns on the Jacobite leader the Duke of Hamilton. He had been imprisoned following the French invasion attempt, and the Junto had secured his release on the understanding that he used his influence to support their Parliamentary candidates. In these arrangements the leading activist had, in fact, been the Earl of Sunderland, who, in a widely-circulated letter to the Squadrone leader the Duke of Roxburgh, had claimed that the Queen was losing patience with the 'Court' Whigs (i.e. Godolphin's Government). '*I would not have you be bullied by the Court Party*', he had written, '*for the Queen herself cannot support that Faction long*'.[57]

These cynical manoeuvres would become, for Defoe, a memorable warning and a key to the disaster soon to overtake the Whigs. He came to speak of it as a fatal struggle between the 'Old Whigs' (that is to say the Junto) and the 'Modern Whigs' (in other words the Court party led by Godolphin and Marlborough), and he would often hark back to this theme. 'The Mischiefs which have happened since', he would write later, 'have all had their Rise and Spring from this corrupted Fountain'.[58]

The three recently-discovered letters from Defoe to Godolphin are illuminating here. In that of 3 July 1708 he comes down severely on the intrigues of the Squadrone and their Whig supporters in England. He quotes the laments of a 'Poor Depending Gentleman', Lord Forbes,[59] about the dominance of the new party. 'What can such a man as I do', he reports Lord Forbes as saying. 'They pretend they are sure of Kings, They show me Letters from Noblemen, that I kno' the Queen Trusts – I kno' my own Circumstances; if I appear against Them and they prevail I am undone.'[60]

Secrecy is to the fore in these letters to Godolphin, as in those to his rival Sunderland. Defoe sends Godolphin a brief paper he has written, as by a Scotsman, attacking the Squadrone, and he asks Godolphin to approve his distributing it all over Britain. Godolphin will notice, he says, that he has disguised his style, and he feels sure nobody will guess he is the author.[61] He has been sending Godolphin copies of extracts from letters he has received, and he anxiously begs him to ensure there is no danger of their writers seeing his transcripts (and perhaps recognizing his handwriting). This would wreck his plans, and it could also damage his reputation: it might look like his 'Maintaining a Counter Correspondence'.[62] We can safely assume that high among those he wanted his letters and transcripts concealed from was Sunderland.

*   *   *   *   *   *

It was at this moment of political paradoxes and mysteries that Defoe brought a new character into the *Review*, as an interlocutor, on the lines of the *Observator*'s 'Countryman'. He is 'Madman'. Mr. *Review* was walking near Westminster Hall when a man accosted him, asking him if he were 'D. F.', the author of *The True-Born Englishman*, and upon his admitting so, the man offered him the key of his lodgings. What sort of lodgings, asks Mr. *Review*? 'A very good Chamber, Sir, in *Bethlehem* [i.e. Bedlam]', the stranger replies. 'I assure you, it is one of the best in the House.' But might he not want it for himself, asks Mr. R. 'As much as any man alive', he replies, except for Mr. R., who is much madder. But, says Mr. R., do people not say that madmen think all the world mad but themselves. 'Ay, Sir', the Madman replies, 'that is your Case exactly ... I thought I should catch you now – And are not you a right mad Man, for do you not tell all the World they are mad? To day the *High-Flyers* are mad, to morrow the *Whigs* are mad; then the *French* are mad, and every Body has their Turns of Lunacy *with you*.' What could be madder than to expect them, being mad, to listen? 'Come, Brother mad Man, you had better for the Future talk with me; who knows what two mad Men may do.' 'With all my heart', says Mr. R.[63]

'Madman' becomes a standby for Defoe for the next five months. 'None but mad Men, you know, will speak Truth at such a Time of Day as this', 'Madman' tells Mr. *Review*. The world is mad – 'mad Projects, mad Parties, mad Methods, mad War, mad Peace, mad Trade' – the mad butchery of the Northern War, and the madness of saying so.[64] The polemical advantage of 'Madman' is that he can incarnate the madness of high-flyers, but equally the sanity of thinkers, like Mr. R., who are regarded by fools or knaves as madmen. He is a protection, enabling Defoe or Mr. R. to be more outspoken, since, by laying claim to his name ('Madman'), he gives a reversible or self-cancelling quality to anything he may say.

It is in defiance of one who is, after all, only a madman that Mr. *Review*, at this time, writes with especial boldness about Charles XII of Sweden and the Russian Tsar (see above, p. 82). With the aid of the outlook of 'Madman', again, Defoe is able to be equivocal in his praise of the much-vaunted Marlborough. 'Madman' pays Marlborough 'the greatest Panegyrick on him a mad Man can make': i.e. that he is madder than his opponent, the Duke of Vendome, and accordingly a better general, as Caesar was a better general than Pompey. He sings:

> Pompey was a mad Man, a mad Man, a mad Man,
> Pompey was a mad Man, a mad Man was he;
> *But* Cæsar *in* Pharsalia *routed his Batalia,*
> *Because he was a madder Man, a madder far than he.*[65]

The 'Madman' ploy works most effectively of all on the subjects of English education, and the English nobility. It is one of Defoe's most cunning and pungent pieces of satire in the *True-Born Englishman* vein. 'Madman' tells Mr. R. that when journalists blame the engineers for England's incompetent showing at the recent siege of Lille (which took vastly too long), they are being most unfair. For the engineers must nearly all have been killed – at least, he supposes so, from their disappearance – which at least is evidence of their commitment. Further, he can produce certificates from the army that these English engineers were 'the most accurate and exquisite People in the whole

Camp, and not one Engineer ever miscarry'd or misbehav'd, but the *Dutch*, *Germans*, or *French* refugees'. Mr. R. says he is very glad to hear it, for the honour of his country. And did they all behave so well? 'Ay, all', says 'Madman', 'every one of them'. And how many were there of them, asks Mr. R. 'NOT ONE' replies 'Madman'. 'Good Truth, to the immortal Honour of our Art-improving, Ingenuity-encouraging Age, not one *English* Engineer in the whole Army.' For England has always despised such useful people.[66] But then she may have had good reason, for Engineers are not an English breed. 'Every Clime and every Soil has its proper Produce; *Yorkshire* for Horses, *Essex* for Calves, *France* for Engineers, and *England* for Fools.' But surely, says Mr. R., England has 'a great many very skilful Artists, great Mathematicians, and compleat Masters now in Being'. 'Compleat Masters!' exclaims 'Madman'. 'Pray, what do you call compleat Masters? … These are the Men of Lines and Angles, the *So-so*'s of the Age, that study to know but not to serve'. Not that he despises learning:

> We have a great many learned People in our College of *Bedlam*, especially of your poring, Language-driving, Nothing-acting Scholars – But these Sort of useless Scholars, that are doing nothing, ever learning, knowing and informing themselves, but never practising; these I think the most useless People in the World, and such are all the Pretenders to Engineering in *England*, that ever I saw.[67]

'Madman' proceeds, a few issues later, to apply similar logic to the English nobility. He mentions a foreign rumour that why the siege of Lille went so slowly was because five English noblemen in the attacking force betrayed their country's plans to the French. But this, he says, must be a foul slander; for the truth is, there were no English noblemen there. In England the nobility, in contrast to the French, have no love for trenches or sieges. They 'make their Campaigns in Chocolate and cold Tea, they fight at home, and talk of Things abroad … challenge every Man's Conduct, and find fault with what they cannot mend'. But as for campaigns: 'ask an *English* Nobleman, *my Lord*, where did your Lordship make your last Campaign? Campaign, Sir, d—n ye Sir, I never make Campaigns, *I am a Person of Quality*, Sir, it's below my Dignity to make Campaigns, let the Mercenaries go abroad that fight for Pay, I scorn the Drudgery of the War'.[68]

* * * * * *

By November Defoe had returned to England and, among other things, to his quarrels with Charles Leslie. In the *Review* for 14 December 1708 he told Leslie, with relish, that he had returned from Scotland well furnished with details of clerical scandals, and in the issue for 15 January 1709 he reported the story of a certain High Church prebend of Durham cathedral ('*the same who formerly would have no Drink in his House brew'd with* Presbyterian Malt'). The parish of St. Nicholas in the city, so his story ran, had asked whether they might have a Lecturer to preach to them, and the dean and chapter, upon discussing it, were much inclined to encourage them, till the furious prebend rose and exclaimed 'G–d D—m them, what occasion was there for it, when they might come to the cathedral'. It was explained to him that the weaker members of the congregation, though they were anxious to hear a sermon, might not be able to manage the long walk to the cathedral; at which '*our pious and good Doctor answer'd with another* G–d D—m them, if they would not go to the Cathedral, they might go the Devil'. Leslie claimed that the story was a monstrous fabrication and warned Defoe that the Bishop of Durham might be bringing an action for *scandalum magnatum*. The story, off and on, provided them both with copy for several weeks.

The spring of 1709 looked like being a turning-point in the war. The French, after their losses of the previous autumn – the fall of the citadel of Lille and the capture of Ghent and Bruges – and with the appalling winter which followed bringing famine and bread-riots, were desperate for peace, and they were making numerous approaches to Britain and her allies. The fact was generally known, and in the *Review* for 19 March Defoe set out both what, ideally, he wished might be obtained by a peace, and what at least would be the minimum to insist on, in preference to returning to arms. He had always argued that the war would have to end with a partition and held that the Allies would be lucky to make peace on better terms, or even such good ones, as those devised by King William in his so-called 'felonious' Treaty.

The initial demands, he thought, ought to be sweeping: France should be required to restore the whole of the Spanish monarchy as it was at the death of King Charles II, and all countries and possessions belonging to Spain taken since the Treaty of the Pyrenees (1659). She should acknowledge the archduke Charles of Austria as King of Spain and enter into an alliance with him against Louis XIV's grandson

Philip V. She should recognize Anne as legitimate monarch of Britain and should support the Protestant succession. But if anyone should ask Mr. *Review* the 'ill-natur'd Question', whether he would be ready to settle for less than this, he had to admit that, rather than spend more blood and treasure, he would be.

Shortly afterwards, in a series of *Review* articles (9 to 23 April), he embarked on a history of 'exorbitant power': its long career from the earliest monarchies to the world-empire of Charles V, and then its migration to France. That it should have found its home in France, a country so long distracted by religious faction, was hardly to have been predicted, he wrote, and much of the blame lay with England. It was the weakness of the English and the Dutch, and their betrayal of the Rochellers, that had led to the crushing of the French Protestants.[69] Yet even then, and with the portentous advent of Louis XIV, Europe was too blind to perceive what lay beyond – no less than an attempt at universal monarchy. If England had realized this and played her proper part, the attempt would have had less chance of success.

> But drowned in Luxury, secure and supine, *England* fell in with all her [France's] Measures; our Court was acted by *French* influence; our Prince [i.e. Charles II] slept in the Arms of *French* Strumpets; was doz'd with the Arts of *French* Sycophants, Brib'd by the Power of *French* Pensions, and Debauch'd by the Plague of *French* Principles.[70]

He was in the middle of this history when the news came that peace negotiations were to begin at the Hague; and this prompted him to spell out the wider implications of his own proposals. Consistently with his unmoralistic attitude over power[71] he wrote: 'We do not fight against *France* as a Kingdom, or against the King of *France* as a King, no nor as a Tyrant insulting the Liberties of his own Subjects; but we fight against *France* as a Kingdom grown too great for her Neighbours, and against the King of *France* as an Invader of other Nation's Rights'. Moreover, though it might be feared that reduction of French exorbitance could encourage equal or worse exorbitance on the part of Austria, in fact the opposite might be true.

> *France* reduc'd to a Pitch of safe Equallity, is the best Trump you can play upon *Spain*, if ever they should come to lead the Game of Power again in the World … THE CHASE is *Exorbitant Power*; all the Powers of *Europe* are the Hounds; bring but *France* to run true, she will be the best and most stanch Hound in the Pack.[72]

Ought the Allies to attempt to arm the French Protestants and attempt to restore them? Ought they perhaps to try to re-establish the French Estates-General, and insist on negotiating with them rather than with Louis XIV? He thought this unrealistic.

> The *French* seem to be a peculiar Nation in that Respect, that they seem to have no Tast of Liberty, but to have made Bondage their Choice; GOD and their great Monarch seem to go Halfs in their Adoration, and it is great Pity to set a Nation free against their Will.[73]

On the other hand he asks – imagining something on the lines of the League of Nations or the United Nations – could not the Confederacy as a whole be form'd into a permanent body, 'a politick Frame or Constitution', which would act against any future breach of the peace?[74]

The peace talks were inconclusive, and it was decided to renew them the following year, this time at Gertruydenberg. In the end, however, they would come to nothing, being wrecked, in Defoe's opinion, by British unrealism and intransigence. He would often hark back to this as a great chance lost.

In the early part of the present year, 1709, an issue arose which could not have been better calculated to distinguish Whigs from Tories. Parliament had passed a bill permitting the naturalization of foreign Protestants, on condition that they took the oaths to Government and received the sacrament in any Protestant church. The fact became known in the Rhine Palatinate, where Protestants suffered much intolerance from their Catholic Elector, and within no more than three weeks there began a mass exodus to Britain of Palatine refugees. (It was encouraged by British merchants, who planned to send the Palatines on to the plantations.) Of those who arrived, 2,000 or so were discovered to be Roman Catholics and were sent back to Germany; but the remainder (by July amounting to some 10,000), mostly almost destitute, had to be housed in tent cities in Blackheath and Camberwell. The Queen made them welcome and contributed handsomely to their subsistence. On the other hand High Churchmen, who wanted only to admit such as would embrace Anglicanism, were strongly hostile, and so were many of the English labouring poor, complaining that the strangers would take the bread out of their mouths.[75]

Defoe regarded the measure itself as 'one of the best Bills … that has been brought into the Parliament this Session', and the situation it led to was one to which several of his most cherished principles seemed to apply. It was a favourite principle of his that the sheer number of Inhabitants is 'the Wealth, the Strength, and the Glory of a Nation'.[76] But this tied in inextricably with the arguments of *The True-Born Englishman*, i.e. that it was wonderfully absurd of the English to claim to be racially pure, and that, if they would only acknowledge it, they owed half of their most precious blessings to foreigners. Did they not owe their Glorious Revolution to a Dutchman? Had not providence, for its own mysterious purposes, turned the sufferings of the Flemings under the Spanish into a heaven-sent boon for the English?

The truth was, he argued, that, with all its wealth and flourishing industry, England was underpopulated. It had millions of acres of land, left 'just where the General Deluge left them' for want of people. The problem, he said, was not there being too much land but there being too few to exploit it. There was hardly a limit to the numbers a piece of land, if properly 'improved', would sustain, and planting it with corn might well not be the best solution. The wealthy Dutch hardly used the plough; nor did the ancient Romans, who aspired to that 'highest Improvement of Land in the World', the garden. 'The stately Palaces, their vast Aquæducts, their prodigious Pavements, and their mighty Theatres, Temples, and publick Edifices, of which the Ruins remain, shew the Multitudes that were entertain'd in that little Spot of Ground.'[77]

So if the nation would welcome these strangers from Germany, as it ought to, it remained to decide what to do with them; and he had a proposal. They should be settled in small townships, 'like little Colonies', perhaps of 50 to 100 families, in forests and wastes. (It would be best that the groups should not be larger, for fear of their clinging too long to their own language and customs.) They should be assigned a suitable selection of tradesmen and artisans, chosen from among their own number, and thus they would be made a 'publick good'.

> For their Numbers will increase the Consumption of our Wool, their Improvement of our Land will increase the publick Wealth, and yet their Manufacturers and Artificers shall not rob our Poor of one Days Work, for they shall work only for themselves.[78]

Admittedly, he wrote, it might be objected that such enclosure of wastes as he is proposing is forbidden by manorial tenures and laws of commonage. But a Court of Claims could be set up with the power to offer an 'equivalent' for those legal rights. Considering that the devastation and depopulation caused by William the Conqueror, in creating New Forest for his hunting, had gone down to history as a crime, it would be an irony, said Defoe, if cultivating and 'improving' forests and waste grounds should be thought a crime likewise. 'How, Gentlemen, can it be a Crime to make Forrests, and a Crime to unmake them too?'[79]

He filled the pages of the *Review* with thoughts and plans regarding the Palatines. An anonymous set of verses, *Canary-Birds Naturaliz'd in Utopia*, took note of his new enthusiasm.

> Where's *Daniel Foe*, that grand Canary ...
> Lately it was his dear Opinion,
> That Property was 'fore Dominion;
> A sacred Thing no Pow'r could alter,
> And Kings that did, deserv'd a Halter.
> But now the contradictious Rover
> Is turn'd *Canary-Bird* all over.[80]

However his scheme was not taken up; and in September he had to report that the Palatines were to be dispersed to parishes up and down the country, with a bounty of £5 a head. It was, he complained indignantly, the worst possible solution and would result in their being mere cottagers, hewers of wood and drawers of water, with no hope of self-improvement, or even (till they learned English) of enjoying organized religion. (The scheme, he said witheringly, was rather like the time-honoured English method of disposing of bastards.[81])

Eventually several thousands of the Palatines were shipped off to America, settling in New York, the Carolinas and particularly Pennsylvania, where they became known as the 'Pennsylvania Dutch'. The lost opportunity stayed in Defoe's mind, however, and many years later, in his *Tour*, he related how he had drawn up a scheme for re-peopling the New Forest and had argued it before Godolphin, the Lord Treasurer, and others. It was 'a Thing in it self Commendable, but as it was manag'd, made scandalous to *England*, and Miserable to those poor People'.[82]

In August Defoe set off with his son Benjamin on a private 'perambulation' to Scotland, where Benjamin was to be enrolled at Edinburgh University, and where he himself could attend to various business affairs (and, no doubt, renew his contacts with his many friends among the clergy). A High Church agent reported to his superiors at this time, one does not know how truthfully, that Defoe was being paid at least ten shillings *per annum* by every Presbyterian minister 'for his good services by the Review'.[83] During this visit to Edinburgh he signed a contract with John Ochiltree for a partnership for the manufacture of linen tablecloths, and he bought a share in the *Scots Post-Man*, though it is not clear that he ever wrote for it.[84] There would have been other business matters to attend to as well. He was dealing in horses and wine and was concerned, with his brother-in-law Robert Davis, in plans for building a new quay at Leith. He would have had matters to discuss with Mrs Anderson, who was publishing a separate Edinburgh edition (slightly modified) of the *Review*; and it was his last chance to make corrections to his *History of the Union*. His activities in Edinburgh seem to have earned him some public reputation, for in October the Town Council voted him an honorarium of fifteen guineas.[85]

It was while he was in Edinburgh that, in early November, there was a stir in England over a Guy Fawkes day sermon delivered in St Paul's Cathedral by Defoe's old antagonist, the high-flying Henry Sacheverell. Its text, taken from chapter 11 of 2 Corinthians, was 'In peril of false brethren'. According to Sacheverell the 'false bethren' within the church were the propagators of heteredoxy and heresy, such as Unitarians, Lockean rationalists, but also Latitudinarians; and within the state they were all those who, like the Dissenters, did not admit the obligation to absolute obedience to the supreme power and the illegality of resistance to authority. In its furious language and ferocious delivery, the sermon was a wild affair. A fellow clergyman said subsequently 'I could not have imagined if I had not actually heard it myself, that so much heat, passion, violence and scurrilous language, to say no worse of it, could have come from a Protestant pulpit, much less from one that pretends to be a member of the Church of England'.[86] Defoe, writing in the *Review* on 8 December 1709, recommended a 'moderate' attitude, telling the Dissenters not to be so angry at this turbulent priest but to let him run and rage.

See how he flies, champs, foams, and stinks; let him go, clap him on the Back; he began with the *Dissenters*; do but spur him, he'll run over every Body that stands in his Way, Bishops, Magistrates, Parliament, QUEEN, Hedge and Ditch, till he'd run himself out of Breath.

The invitation to Sacheverell to preach had come from the Lord Mayor, the Tory Sir Samuel Garrard; and it would have been usual for the preacher to be formally thanked and encouraged to print his sermon, but the Court of Aldermen, when it met a few days later, condemned the sermon as seditious. Nonetheless, Sacheverell had it printed, and, to the alarm of the Government, it became a runaway bestseller. Among the 'false brethren' of his sermon he had evidently had in mind the Godolphin ministry – it was said that Godolphin had been especially riled at being mocked under the nickname of 'Volpone'[87] – and eventually the Government decided to retaliate. On 14 December Sacheverell was summoned to the Bar of the House, and a committee was appointed to draw up articles of impeachment. The outcome of his trial would evidently be highly significant for the Whig cause, and the news of it (together perhaps with a summons from Godolphin) gave Defoe the feeling he ought to be closer to the scene. Accordingly he cut short his stay in Scotland and hurried back to London.

CHAPTER 6

1710: THE FATEFUL STEP

Sacheverell's trial was not at first expected to be a large-scale affair, but public interest proved very great, and it soon became plain that there would not be room in the Lords' chamber for all the spectators. Thus it was decided to stage it in Westminster Hall, and Sir Christopher Wren was commissioned to design the *mise-en-scène* and to arrange extra seating.

'Nothing is so much talked of as he [Sacheverell] all over the Town', wrote a fellow clergyman. 'I suppose we shall have him very speedily the subject of de Foe's Review, in which he has formerly had the honour of being substantially abused.'[1] He was right, and from late December onwards, for many weeks, Defoe filled the pages of the *Review* with the Sacheverell affair. He deliberately maintained his 'moderate' line in print. Indeed he began by arguing (22 December) that Sacheverell's sermon could be salutary. 'For my Part, *I really think*, these Ecclesiastick Faggot-Sticks, when they are thus lighted at both Ends, do no Harm – But as they flame and stink about the Town, they awaken the People, and bring them to their Senses.' But in any case, he said, it was unbefitting to kick a man when he was down. What called for punishment, he wrote (12 January 1710), was not so much Sacheverell as Sacheverell's crime. 'It is not necessary, that the *House* should push at this or that Person, but it is absolutely necessary that the Principles of absolute Government, the Doctrine of Non-Resistance, and the scandalous Jest of the Divine Right of Personal Hereditary Succession to the Government should be condemn'd and exploded by Parliament, and so bury'd in this Nation, as never to be brought to Light again among us.' Sacheverell, he reflected (14 January), had sworn loyalty to Queen Anne and yet preached such doctrines, which is as if he had renounced his baptism, burned his Bible, circumcised himself and preached the gospel of Mahomet rather than Christ, yet kept his gown and cassock, and called himself a Fellow of Magdalen College in Oxford. As regards the promised trial, he wrote (17 January) that the high-flyers were saying that the House of Commons '*dare not go on with it*', but Mr. *Review*'s humble opinion was that '*they dare not BUT go on with it*'.

Sacheverell meanwhile had become the hero of the day. On his various summonses to Westminster, his coach was followed by a milling crowd of supporters, some of them armed with clubs or staves; and during the night of 1 March a Sacheverellite mob rampaged through the City, systematically destroying Dissenting meeting houses. The rioters, chanting 'Sacheverell and High Church', piled up doors, floorboards, gallery rails and wainscotting on a giant bonfire in Lincoln's Inn Fields and another in Holborn, the carriers performing a sort of ritual dance around the blaze. The situation was soon more or less out of hand, and Sunderland, who had been at work in his office in Whitehall, was in a quandary. He knew he needed to send troops, but the only ones immediately on hand were the Queen's own household Guards, and it terrified him to think of leaving her unprotected. However, when he went to consult with her, she insisted that the soldiers must be sent, declaring that 'God would be her Guard'.[2] Thus towards morning order in the City was at last restored.

Defoe's tone about the rioters, in the *Review* (4 March), was pacificatory. These 'poor innocent Criminals', he wrote, must be made to see what they are doing, 'for nothing is so certain, as that they know not what they are about'. Were they to know what Sacheverell was to be impeached for they would 'more chearfully huzza him to the Gallows'. These riots, nevertheless, he said (16 March) had something special and unprecedented about them.

> We have had Mobbs formerly upon various Occasions – And I have some Thoughts of giving the World a short Tract I have had long by me, Entitled, *A History of the Mob* – But it was observ'd, those Mobbs always aim'd at pulling down some real Grievance – Such as Bawdy-houses, Mass-houses, sham Gaols for wrongfully impress'd Men, Nests of Kid-nappers, and the like.

'Captain TOM'[3] had not often been in the wrong, he wrote, but this Sacheverellite rabble was different. It 'mobb'd the very Constitution, and rabbled the Government', it was 'a direct mobbing the QUEEN and Parliament' – an attempt not 'suitable to the Temper of the People of England'.[4] Fortunately this 'strange, new-fashion'd Creature' was not destined to thrive and multiply. It 'just liv'd to Hiss and Grin, to denote its true Original, and then Dy'd'.[5] The issue was for him, in a sense, a matter of naming, and he would play cleverly with the meanings of the words 'rabble', 'mob' and 'People'. Thus a week or so after the great riot of 1 March he published *A Letter from Captain Tom to the Mobb, now raised for Dr. Sacheverell*, in which Captain Tom reviles the High Church rioters for not being a true mob. 'You a Mobb! You are the Scum and Dregs, the Tools and Vassals of the Romish Brood ... You Thieves, you everlasting Blot and Disgrace to the Honour of the Mobility!'[6]

The trial opened on 27 February, both sides having assembled a brilliant team of lawyers. The charges against Sacheverell had been summarized in four articles: (1) that, with 'wicked, malicious and seditious intention' he had aspersed the memory of King William and insulted the Revolution; (2) that he had vilified the Toleration; (3) that, in violation of a statute specifically prohibiting it, he had declared the Church to be in danger;[7] (4) that he had accused the ministry of disloyalty to the Constitution and the Queen of maladministration.

The manager of the prosecution was Sir Thomas Parker (shortly afterwards to become Lord Chief Justice), and his concluding speech, a withering analysis of Sacheverell's hypocrisies and a damning exposure of his Jacobitism, was regarded as a triumph. But equally eloquent was the great speech for the defence by Sir Simon Harcourt, which asked how it could be criminal for a clergyman to preach 'nonresistance' doctrines, when (seeing that they were affirmed in the Homilies, and endorsed by many Fathers of the Church) it was his legal duty to affirm them. Harcourt had been an inquisitor at Defoe's own trial seven years before, and his closing words plainly alluded to Defoe and his witticism which had so enraged Charles Leslie, the one comparing the 'wet martyrdom' of Charles I with the 'dry martyrdom' of James II. 'He [Sacheverell] is not the person he has been represented', Harcourt said.

> He hath no disloyal thoughts about him. Sure I am he would rather die in her Majesty's defence. We shall show your Lordships that there are such as run most vile comparisons between the Revolution

and the most execrable murder of King Charles the First, and can find no better difference between them than this abominable distinction, of a *Wet Martyrdom* and a *Dry One*.[8]

This was a foretaste of the proceedings on 6 March, when, in answer to article 3, i.e. as proof that the Church was indeed in danger, Sacheverell's lawyers read out some fourteen insults to the Church and irreverent reflections on the Queen they had dug out of Defoe's *Review* (as well as some from the *Observator*). Here were Defoe's animadversions on the high-flying clergy, who, with their scandalous lives and furious persecution of their brethren the Dissenters, would, he had written (12 March 1706), 'appear the most wretched, provoking, abominable Crew, that ever God suffer'd to live unpunish'd, since He destroy'd *Sodom* and *Gomorrah* by Fire from Heaven'. Here was his complaint (7 January 1710) that 'non-resistance' doctrines tended to 'unravel the Constitution' and 'invalidate the Queen's title to the crown', also his irreverent assertion (6 September 1705) that 'if *Jure Divino* comes upon the stage, the Queen has no more title to the Crown than my Lord Mayor's Horse'.[9] Here, too, was his audacious warning, given (19 June 1705) at the time of the general election of that year, that 'If the next Parliament should pursue the Steps of the last, the Nation ... will be so much nearer that Crisis of Time, when *English* Liberty being brought to the last Extremity, must open the Magazine of Original Power' (presumably implying a revolution).

In the *Review* for 9 March Defoe reprinted the whole series of extracts, saying that he saw no reason to be ashamed of them; and in the next issue he challenged his readers to show him a word in them, or in any of his writings, attacking the Church *per se*. The real danger for the Church lay, he said, not in Dissent or schism or heresies but in neglect of discipline and 'permitting those to open Heaven Gates to others, who carefully and avowedly shut themselves out'.[10]

Meanwhile on 7 March Sacheverell made a speech in his own defence. He was doing so somewhat against the wishes of his lawyers, but he was helped by friends in drafting his oration, and for the occasion he shrewdly abandoned his usual fire-breathing style. His pitch was that he, personally, was of no importance and his accusers might be right in regarding him as '*an insignificant tool of a party, not worth regarding*'. But in his person the Church was in dire danger. The Government wished to impose 'an eternal and indelible brand of infamy' on an essential tenet of the Church's teaching, the doctrine of non-resistance, and this amounted to telling the clergy what Christian doctrines they should, or should not, preach. How could he, as a humble but earnest Christian, not spring to the defence? What injustice it was 'to be punished in this world for doing that which, if we do not, we shall be more heavily punished in the next'! With the specific charges against him, in the four articles, he dealt skilfully, and he concluded with a personal apologia, in which his melodious voice and impassioned tones worked to amazing effect. The Earl of Nottingham wept.[11]

The Lords, afer lengthy and bitter debate, delivered their verdict on 23 March. They found Sacheverell guilty but merely suspended him from preaching the Gospel for three years and ordered that his sermon should be burnt by the common hangman. It was a surprisingly mild sentence (many had predicted a prison sentence, if not a defrocking) and it was widely interpreted as a victory not only for Sacheverell but for the High Church party as a whole.

His next few months were to be a dreamlike triumph. As soon as his trial was over, a wealthy former pupil of his presented him to a handsome living, the rectory of Selattyn on the border with Wales, and his long and rambling journey there, in the company of supporters, and likewise his return journey to Oxford, became a sort of royal progress.

Defoe, in the *Review* for 28 March, did his best to represent Sacheverell's lenient sentence as an exemplary piece of 'moderation'; and on 1 April, with neat sarcasm, he declared himself puzzled by the suspension of Sacheverell from preaching the Gospel. For, so far as he had heard, he wrote, Sacheverell had never preached the Gospel in his life. Such point-scoring, however, hardly measured up to the magnitude of his employers' disaster. For it soon became evident that the Godolphin ministry was in great peril. High-flying addresses to the Queen were flooding in from all quarters, some hinting broadly that she should dissolve Parliament and call a new election; and in mid-April, Parliament having been prorogued, she appointed Harley's ally the Duke of Shrewsbury, a moderate Tory, to the post of Lord Chamberlain – a strong indication that she might be contemplating a change of ministry. It led Defoe, ever more vocal on behalf of the present Government, to fantasize grotesquely about the men – or rather, the

'Old Women' – with whom the Tories, were they to come to power, might want to fill Government places. The Sacheverell trial, he said, had shown the 'Sympathick Influence of the Clergy upon the Sex, and the near Affinity between the Gown and the Petticoat'; and this had a connection with the '*Effeminate Counsellors*' that the high-flyers would impose on the nation, 'Who, tho' they appear under *Coronets*, and *Garters*, upright in Step, can Grin with Majesty, and look awkward like Lords; yet are mere *Goody*'s and *Gammar*'s in Matters of Counsel, *Stoop* in the Shoulders of Government, see through Nine pair of Spectacles apiece; Walk with State Crutches, go lame on the Honour Leg, have lost their Tast of Liberty, and Property, have befoul'd themselves with Tyranny, Walk as if they stunk of it, and look as if they smelt it'.[12]

Then, on 14 June, the Queen, victim for so long of the bullying of the Junto, dismissed the hated Sunderland, replacing him with a moderate Tory, Lord Dartmouth, as Secretary of State. Defoe's response to the news, in the pages of the *Review*, was double-edged. His view of the approaching mischiefs a 'desperate Party' would bring on the nation, and the ravages they would make on the nation's liberties, was, he wrote, as melancholy as anyone's; and – his mind evidently dwelling on the events of 1708 (see p. 92 above) – he laid the blame on 'the Folly, the Divisions, the selfish Principles, the Pride' of the Junto Whigs. Nevertheless, he said, it must never be forgotten that the record of the Godolphin ministry, its zeal and good judgement in the Queen's service and its success in raising her glory abroad, was remarkable, indeed unequalled. Moreover, it was a mystery why the Earl of Sunderland should have been removed. Who could bring against him the least accusation of corruption, neglect of business or disloyalty to his monarch? 'Not a Dog of the Party can Bark at him.' Nor indeed was it clear why the 'Party' were demanding the removal of several other ministers. 'Where's the Charge? Where is the Complaint – Where the Treasure misapply'd? Where the Law inverted and perverted?'[13] Defoe's eagerness in the cause of his patron, or erstwhile patron, Sunderland led him to write a further encomium of him in the next issue of the *Review*. 'My Lord *S—d*', he wrote there, 'leaves the Office with the most unblemish'd Character that ever I read of any Statesman in the World'. Was it not a remarkable tribute to Sunderland's honour, he asked, that when the Queen offered him a pension of £3,000 a year he refused it, saying '*He was glad her Majesty was Satisfy'd he had done his Duty; But if he could not have the Honour to SERVE his Countrey, he would not PLUNDER IT*.[14] He even returned to the theme of Sunderland's virtues in the following issue, though combining it with praise for Godolphin, quoting the opinion of 'the mighty *Bickerstaff* [i.e. Richard Steele]' that he was 'sparing of the Publick Money, and lavish of his own'.[15]

Two months later, after some agonizing, the Queen went further and dismissed Godolphin, her patient and loyal head of Government, doing so in somewhat brutal fashion ('as a squire would discharge a cheating bailiff', writes G. M. Trevelyan[16]). Her long-term intentions were now clear and were confirmed when, two days later, she appointed her adviser Robert Harley (whose plans to form a new administration were now ripe) as Chancellor of the Exchequer.

*   *   *   *   *   *

But meanwhile Defoe had taken a fateful step. He had sent a letter to Harley on 17 July 1710, presuming to 'Renew the Liberty of writing to [him] which was Once My honour and Advantage' and suggesting that Harley might like Defoe to work for him again. He made this approach, he said, in the name of their shared devotion to 'moderation' and with a hope that Heaven had preserved Harley to be the restorer of his country, bringing 'Exasperated Parties and the Respective Madmen' to their senses. It would be a privilege to be allowed to help in this good work, and he asked if they might meet.[17]

This step was evidently prompted by Godolphin's falling fortunes and Harley's rising ones, nevertheless it was very understandable. It is hard to gauge the tone of Defoe's relations with Godolphin at this time, but it is not to be supposed that Godolphin was deeply dependent on him; and what he wrote to Harley, about their shared devotion to 'moderate' views, was not untrue. All the same, it was a step which would lead him into a disastrous snare.

The two duly met, Harley evidently as always receiving Defoe graciously; and on 28 July Defoe wrote again. He had had some success, he told Harley, in persuading people that a change in the ministry would not mean they would be 'Devoured, and Eaten up' and that Harley and Shrewsbury, though they might be Tories, were not members of the 'Old Mad Party'. Moreover, he had some suggestions to make regarding Harley's present preoccupation, the conspiracy of the Whigs to 'run down' credit, as a way of blocking change. Rumours of a dissolution of Parliament had caused losses of several millions in bank and East India Company stocks, and on 3 August the Bank of England refused to lend money to the Government 'by reason of the sinking of credit'. The proper treatment of the 'shy virgin' Credit was a favourite topic of Defoe's, and he could see, as Harley could, that here was a matter over which he could give valuable help. Thus it was agreed that he should re-enter his old employer's service, and Harley promised to press the Queen to grant him a regular pension. This, Defoe stressed, would enable him to keep up the intelligence network he had created for Harley's use.[18]

Defoe wrote with a good deal of apparent openness in the *Review* about the consequences a change of regime might have for himself, a lifelong Whig. 'If I have had any Friends, Gentlemen', he said, 'it is among them you have turn'd out – If I had any Panegyricks to Write, it would be of those you think are out of Fashion; if I had Power to lead, perhaps I would lead them all in again'. The change, he said, had put the country in a state of alarm; 'Trade stops, Credit suffers a terrible Shock, every thing runs down in Value, and fears encrease, of its growing worse every Day'. So what were people like him to do? To cry out that the country was undone would be the way to make it so; to break the bank and tear oneself to pieces would be to ruin the nation and 'give our selves up to *France*'.[19] On the other hand, to appear contented would be to strengthen the hand of those who wanted to push things to extremity. It was not for him to question the Queen's justice or prudence in the present changes (and what good would it be if he did?). He would be very sorry to see a Tory administration, but he would rather see even that than a country totally ruined and become the prey of France and the Pretender. The nation, after all, belonged to the Whigs as much as to the Tories.

> The *Whiggs* have as great a Share in the publick Vessel, the Goverment, as any Body has; they are Embark'd in the same Ship (the Nation) with you all – Tho' the Managing the *Helm* is taken from them, and they are not pleased; yet shall they refuse to Hand the Sails, or Work the Pumps? *No, no* … When she [the vessel] Springs a Leak, every Man's Life is in equal Danger; the Sea, if it comes in, will Devour all alike; shall any Man say to the Com-

mander, you took me from the Steerage, or me from the Great
Cabbin, and have turn'd me afore the Mast, among the common
Sailors, and therefore Sink, or Swim, *I'll not Pump*?[20]

Moreover, he added, even if there were to be high-flyers or Jacobites
in the Queen's new ministry, the nature of the Constitution and the
'settled Stream' of the Government was such that they would all be
'*Whiggs* in the Management'. He listed some items essential to a Whig:
support of the legal right of the Queen to the crown and of the Protestant succession, respect for the rights of Parliament, heartiness in
opposing French exorbitance, vigilant protection of the Union and
inviolable loyalty to Toleration. 'Now if these are Things which
denominate a *Whigg*, then the present Government, and all the Ministers of State that are, or shall be, put into the Administration of the
Publick Affairs, if they will not overturn the Constitution, and overthrow the Foundations we now stand upon, must be *Whiggs*.' Let one
imagine someone impudently questioning one of the incoming statesmen: was he determined to carry on the war till France was reduced,
the Queen's title recognized, the Pretender banished from France and
the Spanish monarchy restored? If he answered yes, '*Why then*, my
Lord', the questioner would say, '*you are a Whigg*'.[21] Defoe grew fond
of this ploy and would make play with it in many subsequent *Reviews*.

He also began a long series of articles about 'Credit' and on 12
August was able to show Harley the finished sheets of an *Essay upon
Publick Credit*.[22] Its drift was that credit was not dependent on the
complexion of ministries but merely on the punctual and honourable
handling of funds, taxes and loans, and that the present slump in
credit arose from an inexplicable notion that the new ministry would
not be so scrupulous in these matters as the old one. The work made
a stir and was widely supposed to have been written by Harley,
prompting Defoe to say to him tactfully: 'The Town does me too
much Honour, in Supposeing it well Enough done to be your Own'.[23]
He followed it by *An Essay upon Loans*, which argued that it was a delusion to think that a political faction, by boycotting Government loans
and running down credit, could manipulate public policy. In the early
days of the war with France tempting inducements had had to be
offered to investors, but by now lenders were just as much in need of
loans to invest in as the Government was of investors.[24]

Harley's desire to form a 'moderate' administration was certainly genuine. He made no approaches to the Earl of Nottingham, to the Earl's intense resentment, considering him too implacable a High Tory;[25] and he tried hard to persuade certain leading Whigs – Cowper, Boyle, Newcastle and even Somers, the Father of the Junto – to remain in the Cabinet. However, apart from Newcastle, they were not to be tempted. Their price was that Parliament should be allowed to continue for the rest of its statutory term; and when, in September, the Queen announced a dissolution, they resigned more or less *en bloc*. The general election in October – the most furious of all those in Anne's reign – resulted in a massive influx of Tories, including a considerable number of declared Jacobites. Thus already even before assuming power Harley had experienced, as he was to do increasingly, the fatal slide towards party extremism.

*   *   *   *   *   *

It was agreed that Defoe should go to Scotland for a month or two, to help reassure the people there about the new Government and to quiet the fears of the clergy for the safety of the Kirk. He arrived on 9 November, the day before the election of the sixteen representative peers,[26] and on 18 November he related an extraordinary story about the conduct, on the occasion of this election, of the Duke of Argyll and the Jacobite Earl of Mar. The erratic Argyll, as Defoe well knew, was one of the peers Harley had recently won over to his interest (and who, as his reward, was soon to be appointed Commander-in-Chief in Spain). Nevertheless his behaviour, and the Earl of Mar's, as reported by Defoe, had been outrageous. They had pretended, in dictatorial fashion, to have firm instructions from the Queen as to who must be chosen (the list included several known Jacobites) and also that any candidate must pass a certain test, i.e. agree to the impeaching of Godolphin and Marlborough.[27]

There ensued a curious episode, very revealing as to Defoe's relations with his employer. He wrote to Harley that there had fallen into his hands the manuscripts of 'Two Vile Ill Natur'd Pamphlets', aimed at the Government, and that he hoped to be able to prevent their being published. One of them was called 'the Scots atalantis', and the other was entitled '*Atalantis Major*', being a 'Bitter Invective' against the Duke of Argyll and the Earl of Mar over the conduct already reported on by Defoe.[28] Six days later he wrote again with the good news that he had, though 'with Some Difficulty', succeeded in getting *Atalantis Major* suppressed.[29] Nevertheless six months later *Atalantis Major* was in fact published – with the facetious imprint 'Printed in *Olreeky*, the Chief City of the North Part of *Atalantis Major*' – and the author, undoubtedly, was Defoe himself.[30]

Defoe's visit to Scotland followed the familiar pattern. He wrote repeatedly to Harley, reporting on the temper of the nation and asking for definite instructions, but received no word of reply. Early in February, however, there arrived a long-awaited remittance of £50, whereupon he decided to come home. His stay had at least borne one solid fruit, for the Presbyterian ministers had appointed Defoe their agent in England.[31]

Meanwhile in London a new phenomenon had made itself felt, the 'October Club', a pressure-group of the more extreme Tory MPs, named after their partiality to 'October ale'. The Club appears to have existed as far back as King William's reign, but its numbers now swelled to something like 150, many of them 'young gentlemen of estates', and it had developed an agreed policy.[32] It wanted all Whigs, and not just ministers, to be turned out of office; Godolphin and Sunderland to be impeached; the rights of the landed gentry to be reaffirmed, at the expense of the moneyed interest and the military; and the signing of a peace with France. Harley was hopeful of curbing the Club, but his friend Henry St John, now Secretary of State, saw its great potential usefulness to his own career. Here was one important reason why, in this year of Tory success, these two politicians began to fall apart.

Defoe, eager to find ways to help the new regime without discrediting the Whigs, lampooned the 'October men' in the *Review* for 15 March 1711 as the same furious, irresponsible Jacobites the nation had suffered from for many years – with the implication that no-one should suppose they were favoured by Harley. He even, in this opening skirmish, mischievously pretended, quite falsely, that none of them were actually in Parliament. A month later he followed this with an entertaining and much longer piece of make-believe, *The Secret History of the October Club*, intended to convey the Club's hopeless imbecility. His point was that the agents of the ministry were making 'meer

Tools' of the Club. They (the agents) had no more intention of letting the October men, with all their 'mad Principles', into the administration, than they had to continue the Whigs in it; nor had the Club any real hope of destroying the Whigs as a party.[33]

It was essential to Defoe's strategy that the members should be visibly 'mad' high-flyers, and he gives an engaging, if apochryphal, account of the meeting, in 1710, of Picolomin, 'a northern Hero of *Gothic* Original', with an old Saxon friend of his named Edgar, who, though 'about a thousand times remov'd from King *Edgar*', still bears King Edgar's coat of arms. (Ancestral Tories indeed!) The pair, upon meeting, are quite overcome with emotion.

> After mutual Embraces, a By-Stander would have expected they should have spoke, but broken words interrupted with the strong firmentation of their Spirits, stifled one another; and they stood grinning and making signs to one another like Two Mutes. At last, Dam 'em says *Pico*; Confound them says *Edgar*; – Shall we – says *Pico*? No says *Edgar*, Plague says *Edgar*; Devil, says *Pico* … Will you meet us says *Edgar*? Where says *Pico*? At the *Bell* says *Edgar*. How strong are you says *Pico*? Twenty, and Increasing says *Edgar*. Have you any Members yet [i.e. of Parliament] says *Pico*? Pox! *Devil!* says *Edgar, and shakes his head; we shall* – what's the word says *Pico*? OCTO-BER says *Edgar*, and so they part.[34]

We are then privileged to attend their meeting. The Club is very bitter about being so let down by the new ministry. Were they not promised a treaty of Peace with France? Was not Marlborough to have been dismissed? Was it not expected that the Queen would abdicate in favour of her brother? Were the Whig leaders not going to be impeached? Was the Toleration not to have been rescinded? (In a word, no sooner had the managers of the new ministry got the administration out of the hands of the Whigs, but – according to Defoe's cherished formula – 'they turn'd Whiggs themselves'.)

It was beginning to seem to the Club, so they complained, that they had been the sport of cunning anglers, who had baited their hook with a 'roasted Priest' and had 'play'd with them as you do with a Trout'. The truth was, Harley was their worst enemy. 'He has been the only, or most material obstacle to all the true measures of High Church, and the great Cause of all their Grievances.'[35]

It was disappointing for them also not to have been as successful as they had hoped in attracting MPs to their Club, leaving them, as a second best, to elect members of the Queen's 'black divan'.[36] At all events, their present course was clear: they must cease exercising their invaluable talent for 'clamour, noise and raillery' on the Whigs and turn the stream of it on to the new ministry.

*   *   *   *   *   *

Harley's neglect of Defoe in Scotland, though it seems to have become a habit, may have had a new explanation, in the person of Jonathan Swift. Though Swift's name was well known to Harley, the two had only met for the first time in October 1710, but they had quickly struck up a strong friendship, and by the next month Swift had been engaged to write for the Tory *Examiner*. Their friendship, unlike Defoe's relations with Harley, was as between social equals. It no doubt caused Defoe some jealousy and alarm; moreover Swift and he were poles apart politically. He was struggling, in the teeth of increasing difficulties, to maintain his reputation as a Whig, whilst Swift was fashioning and purveying new-Tory attitudes. Swift, by his own admission, had hardly been political at all, or troubled himself 'with the difference between the principles of Whig and Tory', until the year 1702, when, on a visit to England, he had got to know some of the Whig leaders.[37] We might describe the outlook he now, with great brilliance, devised for the *Examiner* as a system of temptational Toryism. (One detects here the influence of Henry St John rather than of Harley.) It was tempting for a Tory, and appealing to his vanity, to be told he was socially superior to his adversaries, who 'by their Birth, Education and Merit could pretend no higher than to wear our Liveries'.[38] It was tempting to consider xenophobia as an appurtenance of national grandeur, as against those who, according to Swift, foolishly invited the Palatine refugees to Britain in 1709, in the belief 'that Trade can never flourish unless the Country becomes a common Receptacle for all Nations, Religions and Languages'. Equally it was tempting to be encouraged to despise the trading and financial elements in the community, who, as Swift sarcastically puts it, 'come with the Spirit of *Shop-keepers* to frame Rules for the Administration of Kingdoms ... as if they thought the whole Art of Government consisted in the Importation of *Nutmegs*, and the curing of *Herrings*'.[39]

The moneyed men, Swift argued, had only risen to influence because of the new mode of financing war by Government loans. But their funds and stocks were only an 'artificial' wealth, not a genuine addition to the country's riches, and they knew very well that their hold on power depended on the war, which therefore they had every reason for striving to prolong. This being so, there could be no better reason for wanting peace.

In his writing style, Swift cultivated the art of unspoken flattery. Often he would give no source, not even the author's name, for the classical epigraphs at the head of his essays – a mischievous hint that the chosen few, the ones whose influence in the nation really counted, would not need to be told. He put down Defoe and Ridpath (now editing the *Observator*) as 'two stupid, illiterate Scribblers' and claimed in general not to read them or their like.[40] This may have been true,[41] though the scorn he was to level at Whig allegories of the 'shy virgin Credit' ('To hear some of these worthy Reasoners talking of *Credit*, that she is so nice, so squeamish, so capricious; you would think they were describing a Lady troubl'd with Vapors or the Cholick'[42]) sounds like a dig at Defoe, and his quizzing of the slogan 'a good peace'[43] brings to mind Defoe's play with this phrase in the *Review* for 30 October 1711 and his *Essay at a Plain Exposition of that Difficult Phrase A Good Peace* (1711).

Defoe's response was breezy but cogent. 'It is true', he wrote – taking up Swift's remark that land was a '*Fund of Wealth*' – 'Land is a Fund' but it was foolish of the *Examiner* 'to bestow so much Wit on so dull an Argument'.

> *What makes Land a Fund?* Let any Man go back and Enquire what was Land in the Days of *Henry I*? The Ground stood just where it does now; the sweet Dews of Heaven, the refreshing Showers, the warm Beams of the Sun, all invigorated the Earth as much, as constantly, and as seasonably as they do now – But where was the Fund? – What was the Rent? Where the Improvement? ...
>
> Wretched Folly! Land despise Trade! and Trade set up against Land! – Can any Thing be more absurd? Is not Trade the Nurse of Land? And is not Land the Nourishment of Trade? Does not Land supply the Materials of Trade? And does not Trade enable the Land

to supply these Materials? Land produces Wool, Corn, Cattle, Timber, Hemp, Metals, and Minerals; Trade produces a Market for all
these, gives a Price to them, brings Home Silver to Circulate that
Trade, and feeds the People who take off these Provisions at a Price,
and by this, Land lives – What would Land be without it?[44]

*   *   *   *   *   *

By this time, Defoe's old enemies had come to suspect, or know of,
his return to Harley's service; and, despite his efforts to maintain a
Whig identity, they accused him of selling out to the Tories and plotting to help them secure a dishonourable peace. This, at least as
regards the Peace, was unjust, for his attitude had never been the
extreme Whiggish one of demanding total victory for the Archduke
Charles.[45] The war, he had consistently argued, must inevitably end in
a partition. The supreme aim of English foreign policy, he held, must
be to preserve the balance of Europe. If Spain were to remain under
French domination, and even more if the crowns of France and Spain
were ever joined, it would be giving 'Exorbitant Power' to France,
unsettling the balance of Europe and striking a fatal blow at the Protestant interest. But equally, no other European power (e.g. the Holy
Roman Empire) should be allowed to acquire 'Exorbitant Power'.
Indeed, he reasoned audaciously, if France could be reduced to a 'safe
Equallity' she could be an admirable defence against 'Exorbitant
Power'.[46]

But in April 1711 there came momentous news: the Holy Roman
Emperor Joseph had died of smallpox. It seemed very probable he
would be succeeded by his younger brother, the Archduke Charles, on
behalf of whose claims to the Spanish throne the war was ostensibly
being fought; and this, of course, greatly reinforced Defoe's convic-
tions about a peace. For the prospect of Spain and its American
possessions being added to the already huge Hapsburg dominions,
thus creating an empire vaster than the one of Charles V two centuries
before, spelled 'exorbitance' indeed. To refuse, after this, to entertain
the idea of a partition, he argued in the *Review* (28 April 1711), would
be tantamount to deciding never to make peace.

By this time, however, drama had overtaken the new ministry. A
French military adventurer, the marquis de Guiscard, employed for

some years by the Goverment in various minor capacities, was discovered to be have been spying on behalf of France. He was arrested, and on 8 March 1711 he was brought before the Committee of the Privy Council for interrogation. But suddenly, in the middle of the proceedings, he leaned across the table and stabbed Harley in the breast with a pen-knife. In horror, St John and others fell on him with their swords, giving him wounds he was to die of in a few weeks. Meanwhile Harley, so all the witnesses would report, behaved with extraordinary coolness and courage. His own injuries, though serious, turned out not to be mortal. During the weeks of his convalescence he was fêted as a national hero; and on his recovery the Queen raised him to the peerage, as Earl of Oxford, and appointed him Lord Treasurer. The incident, for the moment, greatly strengthened his position.

It coincided, however, with the first hints of something very different and which would eventually prove fatal to the ministry: a falling-out between Harley and his close friend Henry St John, now Secretary of State. St John put it about that Harley was idle, that he was dilatory, that he was divided in his purposes and did not have the best interests of the Tory party at heart. (It was St John's ambition that the administration should be entirely cleared of Whigs, even down to the most minor posts, and this was against Harley's intentions.) St John himself was certainly very far from idle, indeed he was an obsessive worker, and he complained that he did not get sufficient credit for it; Harley never thought to praise him to the Queen. (It would be a bitter grievance to him that Harley received an earldom, but when he himself was raised to the peerage it was only as a viscount.) Typically, he would claim to friends that it was he (St John) whom the assassin Guiscard had originally planned to kill – thus proving the importance the French attached to him as an enemy. It was only because Guiscard could not reach him that he turned his knife on Harley.

Defoe, who knew very well what was being said about Harley, saw it as the moment to come to his defence, and in May 1711 he took it upon himself to publish *Eleven Opinions about Mr. H[arle]y*, a (pretendedly) impartial analysis of his employer's character. The present age, it argued, was more noted for 'opinion' (or, rather, obstinate prejudice) in both religion and in politics than any previous one, and the Harley enigma was a prime example of it. 'Mr. *H—y* shall be with some the best, and with others the worst Man of the kind that ever lived in the

World'.[47] The eleven opinions he discussed included those of the Queen, the 'Old Ministry', the Whigs, the Dissenters, the October Club, the Jacobites and French, the Confederates, and 'moderate men'. The Harley so portrayed was a mystery man, a statesman fated to be misunderstood for the good reason that he was that rare thing, a 'moderate'. The rage of the October Club against him was, precisely, a proof of that; and in so far as the new ministry had fallen in with the 'hot' men of the Tory party, it was because the Junto Whigs, with their rooted personal aversion to Harley, drove them to it.

It is a clever pamphlet, but it illustrates all too vividly the danger of Defoe's position and the trouble he was storing up for himself. Speaking about the Dissenters and their reaction to the change of ministry, he wrote, sanguinely: 'There is no more to be seen now upon their Countenances of that Chagrin and Resentment that they entertained at first; the Fright they were in for their Tolleration, for their Academies, and for their Security against the Rabbles and Tumults of the Streets, is abated'.[48] In 1711 it was very possibly true; but by two years later, when those precious treasures of the Dissenters were in the direst danger or had actually been lost, it would make embarrassing reading.

*   *   *   *   *   *

One of the strongest Tory accusations against the late Whig ministry was that it had created an enormous national debt, mortgaging the country's income from taxation for decades or centuries to come; and as a remedy to this, on returning to Parliament after his recovery, Harley announced a plan for a new South Sea Company. It was to be based on the assumption of Britain's gaining the right to trade direct with South America (and in particular to secure the *Asiento* or slave trade, at present in French hands). By dint of this the Company would be able to take over much of the national debt. Harley asked Defoe to expound his views on it on paper, and he did so at length, both in the *Review* and privately to Harley himself, trying to scotch what he thought to be false ideas and rumours. It was, he argued, absurd to suppose that the Spanish would ever agree to free trade between Britain and Spanish America. It would be 'just as if *England* should make peace with *France*, upon Condition that the *French* should come over hither, and lie with our wives'.[49] The way to make the new Company prosper was, rather, to make a peaceful colonial settlement in southernmost America, from which the settlers would be able to conduct trade, with the tacit approval of the Spanish authorities.[50] Such a settlement in 'Valdivia' in Chile – a thinly populated area with a climate reputedly rather like Britain's – was a favourite project of his, which he had urged before and would eventually realize in fictional terms in *A New Voyage Round the World* (1725).[51]

Unquestionably the task for which the new Parliament had, in 1710, been elected was to secure a peace, and in the *Review* for 8 September 1711 Defoe took up the debate about peace in a pungent and two-edged satirical article. Since everyone seems to regard 'Credit' as quite dead, never to come to life again, he writes, 'The Question is short – WHAT'S NEXT?'. The high-flyers said Britain should sue for peace; but why, Defoe asks, being triumphant victors in the field, should we humbly beg France to grant us a peace? No, no, we must continue with the war, he says ironically, and show the French that we can go on with it 'to the End of the World, if need be'; and if no-one is ready to lend to the Government, the answer is simple, she must get money by taxes – beginning, maybe, with a tax on bread. There could be a swingeing tax on other necessities too, the sale of cattle and cheese and all kinds of cloth. The scheme would have at least one advantage, it would put an end to stock-jobbing – though not, perhaps, by 'the shortest Way', for it would call for an army of about a hundred thousand tax-gatherers.

This was merely fantasy, but throughout the autumn of 1711 Defoe was fertile in proposals as to what form a peace might take. He assumed that, in the present state of things, it would necessarily involve a partition, but over this the *Review* came into violent collision with the *Observator* – which now, after the death of Tutchin in 1707, was being conducted by George Ridpath.

It will be remembered that in January 1708 (see p. 28 above) Defoe had mildly reproached the new author of the *Observator* – who he was, he did not yet know – for reflecting adversely on King William, saying that the King had been bad at listening to advice. To this the *Observator*, to Defoe's indignation, had answered rudely, accusing him of ignorance of grammar. But, more importantly, he had cast doubt on Defoe's cherished claim to an intimacy with King William, and Defoe had been driven, no doubt painfully, to make a climb-down about it. Thus all hopes that these two Whiggish journalists might work in amity died almost at once and for ever, and their debates in 1711 about the shaping of a peace would be acrimonious. Defoe wrote in the *Review* for 1 September 1711, a little recklessly, that 'To give up *Spain* to the House of Bourbon, is a Thing so absurd, so ridiculous, you ought as soon to think of giving up *Ireland* to them'. Ridpath wanted to make out that Defoe, the advocate of a partition, had here contradicted himself, and Defoe strove, in vain, to convince him that he had done nothing of the sort: that by 'Spain' he had meant, not just Old Spain, but the entire and enormous Spanish empire, a very different matter.

Defoe next came out with a direct and powerful plea for peace, in the pamphlet *Reasons Why this Nation Ought to Put a Speedy End to this Expensive War*. Published on 6 October 1711, it is one of his most notable tracts. The opening, evoking the plight of the nation after nine years of war, is incisive and grim. 'In our Land Armies, we expend mighty Sums to perform trifling Exploits, and please our selves with a few Inches of Enemy Ground, bought too dear, and paid for with a double Price of Money and Blood.'[52] How many 'glorious' victories like the late one of Malplaquet, which cost twenty thousand men, can the country afford? When it was announced that this year's campaign would begin with the siege of Ypres and St Omer, did not 10,000 Allied troops desert to the enemy, leading the King of Prussia to threaten the most inhuman penalties against deserters? The author, so he makes plain, is not joining the vicious campaign against Marlborough and his fellow generals, 'of whose Conduct and Bravery the World speaks such Glorious Things'. It is merely that they have done all that men could possibly do, and now some other way of thinking is called for. We need to enquire 'what Reasons we have, which are drawn from within our selves, and turn upon the great Hinge of our own Affairs only, and which move, and press, and call upon us to put an End to this war upon the best Conditions we can'.[53]

The need, he writes, is visible to all. If the reader should walk from Ludgate to Temple Bar he would find more than fifty shops shut up or to let, and something of the same would be true in other trading towns up and down Britain. The number of bankrupts listed in the *Gazette* grows astonishing. Every necessary import or produce, corn and cattle excepted, is taxed to the highest possible pitch, so that if more money is required for the war the only remaining alternatives are a general excise on food and clothing – a measure Parliament has always avoided till the very last extremity – or that ruinous last resort, a stop on the Funds.

Defoe drops a remark or two into this pamphlet designed to disguise, or pretend to disguise, his authorship. He writes, for instance, 'Discourses of Trade are not the particular Talent of the Author of this' (whereas, of course, they were well known to be Defoe's passion), and praising a certain Whiggish author (meaning himself) for his downright advice to his fellow Whigs, warning them of their folly in risking 'sinking the Ship'.[54] This favourite ruse of Defoe's was one he probably expected some at least of his readers to see through and relish as amusing irony, but in this instance the deception seems to have succeeded. Abel Boyer, referring to *Reasons Why this Nation* in his monthly journal *The Political State*, surmised that it might be by Swift, and the Whig propagandist Arthur Maynwaring said he would never suspect the author to be a pensioner to the ministry, 'notwithstanding all those airs he is pleas'd to give himself of a familiar Correspondence with them'.[55]

Reasons Why this Nation made a considerable impression, almost as great as Swift's dazzling and xenophobic *The Conduct of the Allies* which came out about a month later: in a short time Defoe's tract sold some twenty thousand copies. But what Defoe did not know was that, at the very moment he was writing it, Harley and St John, in Whitehall, were conducting secret peace negotiations with a French agent, Nicolas Mesnager, and that on 27 September Mesnager had committed his country to a number of 'preliminaries'. There had long been rumours of secret peace talks and feelers, but nothing approaching the definiteness of this; and the fact soon became known, for the Imperial envoy Count Gallas got wind of it and leaked the 'preliminaries' to Abel Roper's *Post-Boy*.[56] The news must undoubtedly have alarmed Defoe. The affair would evidently cause a furious rift within the Confederacy, but it had a further significance for Defoe himself: it would make him wonder how many more secrets the ministry might be harbouring. Were some of these concerned with the Pretender? Might the ministry be in correspondence with St Germain? In a word, it brought home to him the true danger of his own position. To be a critic of the Tory high-flyers, but at the same time a critic of his fellow Whigs, provided a strong debating position, but it also earned him a double number of enemies, some of whom would be plotting to do him personal mischief, for instance by 'Raiseing Creditors, Reviveing old prosecutions, and Open Endeavours to Ruine and Distress me'.[57] In his letters during this period he lays great stress on his 'dependence' on Harley, giving the word a new meaning. On 30 November 1711, for instance, he speaks of his duty to speak out against Harley's enemies, who are also his own, and therefore of his 'Entire Dependence' that he will not be left unsupported in pursuing that duty; and again, on the 19th of the following August, he writes of being 'Driven by the Torrent Upon a More Entire Dependance On your Ldpp'. In the summer of 1712, in the course of a brief journey north, he reports to Harley (20 September) on the terrible rumours circulating, 'Such as, That The queen is For The Pretender, The Ministry Under the Protection of France, That Popery is to be Tollerated, That as Soon as a Peace is declared The War with the Dutch will be proclaimed'.[58] One seems to detect, in his alarmist tones, the hint of a challenge to Harley: *it had better none of it be true.*

Events now moved quickly. The revelation of the secret peace negotiations, which violated the treaty of the Grand Alliance, aroused the resentment both of the States General and of the Emperor and brought on a crisis among the Allies. The ministry managed to persuade the Dutch to agree, though very reluctantly, to an international peace conference on their soil; and in her speech upon opening Parliament on 7 December the Queen announced that, 'notwithstanding the arts of those who delight in war' (a cruel hit at Marlborough) such a congress should take place at Utrecht, beginning on the first of January 1712 (O.S.).[59]

This was a supreme challenge for the Whigs, and it prompted the Earl of Nottingham, furious at his exclusion from power, to perform a remarkable volte-face. He struck a bargain with his old enemies the Whigs, agreeing to help them in thwarting the Tory peace policy, in exchange for their support for (the thing he most of all cherished) a new bill against Occasional Conformity. In the Lords, where the Whigs still enjoyed a majority, he succeeded in adding a clause to their address of thanks to the Queen, to the effect that no peace would be acceptable which left Spain and the American Indies in Bourbon

hands; and on 15 December he introduced his new Occasional Conformity Bill, which, unlike its predecessors, passed without difficulty
and in a matter of days. Lord Oxford, meanwhile, was bringing his
own plans to a head. On 31 December 1711, at his instigation, the
Queen dismissed the great Duke of Marlborough from all his posts;
and on the following day she let it be known that she had created
twelve new peers (among them Abigail Masham's husband), thereby
giving Oxford his required majority in the Lords.

*   *   *   *   *   *

It was an extraordinary succession of events, and one gains the
impression that this, the beginning of 1712, was a moment of no
return for Defoe.[60] We have entitled the present chapter '1710: the
fateful step' – having in mind Defoe's return into his erstwhile
employer's service – and its ill-fatedness now grows all too visible. As
a would-be Whig and praiser of the old ministry, now serving the
Tories and being swept along with them he did not know whither,
Defoe's position was becoming hopelessly false, and the strains were
beginning to tell.

For one thing, a habit of concessions and surrenders to party
requirements was fast growing on him. There was, for instance, something too eager in his readiness, as a one-time panegyrist of
Marlborough, to justify the great man's dismissal, referring to it dis-
dainfully as 'This Most Necessary step of Deposeing The Idol Man'.[61]
Again, when in May 1712, secret instructions are issued to the Duke
of Ormonde, Marlborough's successor as Commander-in-Chief in
Flanders, ordering him not to fight except in self-defence (evidently a
somewhat shameful manoeuvre[62]), Defoe writes to Harley in terms
which strike one as remarkably, even barefacedly, venal. He tells his
employer that the rumour of these orders, reported by the *Flying Post*,
has raised a great deal of clamour, and if the report is not true, the
Government should show its stern 'Resentmt' towards the journal.
But if, on the other hand, the report *were* to be true, there were plenty
of 'justifyable Reasons' the Government could appeal to. If Harley
would give him 'The least Remote hint', he would gladly write something to 'Take off all the Edge of The popular Surprize'. Harley has
only to leave a message with his porter, saying '*yes*' or '*No*'.[63]

Moreover Defoe seems more and more tempted, deliberately blurring the distinction between his own personal enemies and the Government's, to act the informer and to encourage Harley, or through him the Secretary of State St John, in vengeful punitiveness – a vengefulness by proxy. Through much of 1712 and early 1713 his rival and long-time enemy George Ridpath made furious attacks on Defoe in the Whig *Flying Post* as a deserter from the Whig cause, as well as jeering at his private misfortunes (his troubles with his creditors and so on), and Defoe's language about him begins to grow hysterical. 'Their [the Whigs'] Incendiary The Flyeing post', he writes to Harley (19 January 1713), 'goes on with Such a kind of Unsufferable Insolence, and They Triumph So in The Ministrys Forbearance, That Really he does a Very great Deal of Mischief'. He is all for the Government's suppressing the *Flying Post*. 'I Never was forward to prompt any Mans Fate or Dissaster. I Believ your Ldpp knows it is Not My Temper', he writes, not very convincingly. 'But Never Governmt was Insulted in Such a Manner, and Never Cause was So kept alive by The Scandall and Ribaldry of So Insolent an Author.'[64] It was not long, moreover, before Ridpath was in fact prosecuted and found guilty of writing libels and was forced to jump bail and escape into exile. How much, if at all, this was Defoe's doing is impossible to say; but certainly his farewell to his rival in the *Review* for 7 May 1713 is exceedingly uncharitable.

It is important not to overstate things here. One is not convicting Defoe of entire moral dereliction. When Nottingham's Occasional Conformity Bill was going through Parliament in December 1711 he made urgent protests to Harley, who seemed not to concern himself much about it, pressing him to persuade the Queen to refuse her assent. He also stoutly condemned the same bill in three successive issues of the *Review* (20, 22, 25 December) as well as in an ironic squib, *A Speech from a Stone Chimney-Piece*. His message about the Dissenters was, as always, a tough one, but loyal. They had damaged their reputation by, precisely, the practice of Occasional Conformity; they were fools to have relied on the Whigs as their true friends; nevertheless, he argued, this bill was a shameful and intolerable invasion of their civil and religious liberties. 'Never was People thus Betray'd; never was a Party-Interest form'd at such a Price.'[65]

He also continued faithful to another cherished principle, the all-importance of the Protestant cause and, by corollary, of the nation's alliance with its great Protestant ally the Dutch. Swift's anti-Dutch propaganda in *The Conduct of the Allies* had done its work. Like his mentor St John, Swift saw advantage in representing the wily Dutch as the chief defector on their quotas and the weakest link in the Grand Alliance – for here was an argument, if need be, that could be used to justify Britain in making a separate peace. In February there was a debate in Parliament about the conduct of the Dutch, and Defoe's response in the *Review* (21 February), was solemn and uncompromising. He was far from thinking, he said, that Britain was obliged to carry on the European war upon 'unequal Conditions', with the Dutch deceiving her and not performing their proper share. But on the other hand,

> if any Man should ask me, whether I would rather wish to this Nation, a *Dutch War*, or a second Fire of *London*, as in 66, I profess I know not which I should answer, I should only say, *God forbid we should see either.*
>
> I have always said, and say it still, that on a good Understanding between *Britain* and *Holland*, depends the Safety of the Protestant Interest in *Europe*, and of *Britain* also ... No Man can desire a Breach between us, but he desires to open a Gap in the Protestant Interest, at which Popery may break in, and devour us all.[66]

By a month or two later a war with the Dutch became a real possibility, and some Whiggish critics were even accusing Defoe of advocating one. Whereas, he wrote, 'I ... would sooner thrust my Hand into the Fire than prompt such a Thing'. Nevertheless in the end there might be no alternative, and those who wanted the Dutch to reject the Queen's peace proposals were, he argued, precisely working for that appalling outcome.[67]

*　*　*　*　*　*

As we have seen, Defoe often complained of his political enemies 'Raiseing Creditors, Reviving old prosecutions' and endeavouring to 'Ruine and Distress' him. There was an example of this, or so at least he claimed, early in 1713. He was returning from an evening visit to Lord Oxford when he was arrested, at the instance of a Yarmouth creditor, and taken off to a debtors' prison, where he was held for eleven days. The warrant was for £1,500, though by some means he managed to persuade the creditor to accept £150, and only £25 in ready money.[68]

But then a few days later he was arrested again, at the instance of three Whig writers, William Benson, George Duckett and Thomas Burnet (the son of Bishop Burnet), on a charge that a sequence of three pamphlets he had recently written about the Succession were seditious. (The three were heard to complain that they themselves had all of them suffered prosecution for things they had written, whereas the *Review* spread its poison without fear.) Benson, who was an MP, managed to suborn a printer to give him the original manuscripts of the articles, in Defoe's handwriting, and on the strength of this he made a formal complaint to the Lord Chief Justice. As a result, on Saturday 11 April, a tipstaff, accompanied by a posse of constables and a crowd of onlookers, arrived at Defoe's home in Newington with a warrant for his arrest. They had to break in, so Ridpath reported in the *Flying Post*, for Defoe had fortified the house, and everything was done to achieve the maximum publicity.[69] He was taken to Newgate, and on the Monday he was brought before the Lord Chief Justice Parker.

The pamphlets, or at least the first two of them, were ironic parodies of Jacobite attitudes; but, as in the case of the *Shortest Way*, the legal mind had no patience with irony,[70] and Parker wrote to Bolingbroke suggesting that Defoe should be prosecuted.[71] Fortunately for Defoe, Lord Oxford, not for the first time, came to his rescue and sent the Solicitor to the Treasury, William Borrett, to secure his release under bail. In a letter to Oxford, recounting his adventures, he said that the arrest had really been aimed at Oxford himself, as a way of bringing to light Defoe's connection with him; and he audaciously suggested a ruse to counter it. The Government should begin bogus proceedings against him, which could in due course be quietly dropped, and meanwhile he would 'complain Loudly of the Oppression'.[72] But matters then grew more complicated. For he published two indignant articles about the arrest in the *Review*; and when Parker saw these he decided they were an insult to himself and to the laws of England and called for condign punishment.[73]

The two satirical pamphlets were, in fact, sparkling and well-sustained exercises in irony – witness the seductive tones of the following, proposing that Britain should make fast friends with Louis XIV.

> How strange it is that none of our People have yet thought of this Way of securing their Native Country from the Insults of *France*? Were but the Pretender once received as our King, we have no more Disputes with the King of *France*, he has no Pretence to Invade or Disturb us … As to the terrible Things which some People fright us and themselves with, from the Influence which *French* Councils may have upon us, and of *French* Methods of Government being introduced among us; these we ought to esteem only Clamours and Noise, raised by a Party to amuse and affright us; for pray let us enquire a little into them, and see if there be any Reason for us to be so terrified at them; suppose they were really what is alledged, which we hope they are not; *for Example*, the absolute Dominion of the King of *France* over his Subjects, is such, say our People, as makes them Miserable; well, but let us examine then, are we not already miserable for Want of this Absolute Dominion? Are we not miserably divided? Is not our Government miserably weak?[74]

But Defoe's caricature of Jacobite reasoning, could not, and was not meant to, silence a disturbing question: was the ministry loyal to the Hanover succession?[75] In the pages of the *Review* Defoe professed ignorance about this, though he asserted his personal faith in the ministers' loyalty. The best reason he could find for this faith, however, was the lame one that it was not *in their interest* to be treasonable.

Defoe's ingenious scheme to avoid trial went ahead, or so at least he believed, and the proceedings against him were duly set in motion – only for him to discover some months later, to his dismay, that they were in earnest and that a grave indictment for high crimes and misdemeanors had been prepared against him. It was altogether a serious crisis for him, and he came to the conclusion that his best hope was to throw himself on the Queen's mercy and ask her for a pardon – which fortunately, no doubt on Oxford's advice, she granted.[76]

At the beginning of April 1713 the news came that peace had at last arrived, and a peace treaty had been signed at Utrecht, though the Emperor refused to come into it. Defoe was highly critical of the terms of the treaty. In *An Appeal to Honour and Justice* (1715), he would write, 'No Man can say that ever I once said in my Life, that I approv'd of the Peace';[77] and in broad terms this is true and bears out his claims to independence. In the *Review* he harked back to the folly of the Confederates, three years before, in rejecting the markedly more favourable terms offered by the French at Gertruydenberg. This, in his view, was to have thrown away a great chance of securing the Protestant interest, perhaps for ever. 'The refusing that Peace', he wrote, '*was the Ruin of Europe*'. But, the Peace being now a fact, his line was that Britain should ask herself 'what good use we may make of it, whether we like it or no'. 'Whether the Peace be happy or no in its CONDITION', he wrote, 'it may be made to be happy in its CONSEQUENCES'. He listed the benefits it could bring, like the abatement of taxes and reduction of the national debt, and he described the glorious possibilities it opened up for British trade. The theory that Britain had lost, beyond retrieval, her all-important commerce with Spain he dismissed as absurd.[78]

Associated with the Treaty of Utrecht was a projected Treaty of Commerce with France, with whom trading relations had been cut off during the war; and here was a chance for Defoe, as a specialist on trade, to be of real service. By the ninth article of the Treaty the British Parliament would commit itself, within two months of signing, to repeal all prohibitions of French goods imposed since 1664 and to enact that no French goods imported into Britain should pay higher duties than similar imports from other European countries. In return, the French should repeal all prohibitions of English goods imposed since 1664 and restore the tariff of that year. (There were to be some exemptions to this, and commissioners would be appointed to discuss the finer details.)

In effect the treaty would more or less abolish the celebrated Methuen Treaty with Portugal of 1703, by which Portuguese wines were allowed into Britain at one-third of the duty paid by French wines and a complementary favoured-nation arrangement was granted for English woollens. Such a breach of faith with the Portuguese would no doubt be regarded as dishonourable; and an influx of silken goods, in which the French excelled, would probably bring hardship upon British silk-weavers. Thus the question, as it presented itself to Defoe, was whether these disadvantages would, or would not, be outweighed by the re-opening of the huge French market to the English wool trade.

About this he had no doubt. The woollen industry was 'the Life and Soul of the English Trade', and however other trades suffered it would make abundant amends.[79]

The Treaty of Commerce came up for debate in May 1713, and he set to work to defend it. He had in the past often condemned the ban on trade between England and France in time of war as absurd. According to him, the balance of trade between the two countries, which at first was to England's disadvantage, had taken a turn in England's favour at the time of King William's war – the very moment at which it had been decided to prohibit it. 'Thus has *England* been always kept Poor and Honest, and has always taken Care to have a Principal Hand in her own Misfortunes.'[80] Nor, he argued, would the balance be any less favourable to Britain if the trade were now renewed. The argument that, as a result of the war, the French had learnt to do without British wool, was ridiculous: 'It was never heard that the *French* ever went about to make a Piece of Bays in this World'.[81]

Such was the importance of the treaty to the Government that it even commissioned Defoe to start a new periodical in support of it. It was named *Mercator*, and the first number appeared on 29 May 1713, overlapping with the last few issues of the *Review*. Its central thesis was a bold paradox: that the belief, which up to now Defoe had certainly shared, that in its earlier days the trade with France had been to Britain's disadvantage, was actually false. He had been given privileged access to Customs House records and, so he claimed, had made there a curious discovery. In the year 1674 Charles II had appointed Commissioners to draft a treaty of commerce with France, whereupon the merchants consulted by the commission had, for party-political purposes, produced a fraudulent 'Scheme' or analysis, according to which the French gained over Britain every year by something like a million pounds sterling. But by re-examining the figures and correcting the merchants' calculations it could be shown that the trade with France had *always* been to Britain's advantage. (It has to be said that Defoe's thesis, though he pursued it with considerable zeal, was never very convincing, and some years later he admitted he had rather overstretched matters on behalf of his client.[82]) Before long, a Whig counterblast to *Mercator*, the *British Merchant*, was launched, and the two journals would debate and bicker for many months.

There was strong opposition to the Treaty of Commerce at West-minster – partly, simply, out of prejudice against dealings with a Popish and persecuting nation. The attack on the bill was led, rather unexpectedly, by Sir Thomas Hanmer, a 'Whimsical' or 'Hanoverian' Tory, and on 18 June 1713 it was defeated in the Commons. It was a rare and notable victory for the Whigs. Bolingbroke, who had been the principal inspirer of the treaty, blamed the defeat on Oxford's lukewarmness, and it marked a further stage in their falling-out.

An impression was left that the Treaty of Commerce might be re-introduced at a later date, and to encourage this, Defoe, in August, published the entertaining *Memoirs of Count Tariff*, a 'secret history' of the unholy alliance between the Dutch and the Whigs to which the bill (supposedly) owed its defeat.[83] (It is to be remembered that, though regarding friendship with the Dutch as all-important politically, Defoe thought them cunning and avaricious rivals when it came to trade.) 'Count Tariff' had made his first appearance in a satirical tract by Addison, *The Late Tryal and Conviction of Count Tariff* (1713). At his trial described there, the first witness against him was 'a Man with a Hat drawn over his Eyes in such a manner, that it was impossible to see his Face'. 'Being ask'd his Name, he said the World call'd him MERCA-TOR.'[84] His evidence was rejected as untrustworthy.

Defoe's pamphlet tells more of the history of this Count Tariff, an honest French gentleman, who, back in 1699, entered into a business partnership with Mynheer van Coopmanschap, 'a cunning, tricky, cir-cumventing, sharping' Dutch broker.[85] Over the years, it has been borne in on him that Coopmanschap, a mere 'pedlar' or carrier of other people's goods, has been defrauding him, and recently he has been cultivating the friendship of Alderman Traffick of London and the famous country clothier Harry Woolpack. He holds out to them the possibility of a really large-scale importation of English woollens into France, in exchange for a lowering of the duty on French wines and a few other French goods.

The news of this greatly alarms Coopmanschap, who hastens to England to discuss it with his friends there. They are, to a man, ene-mies of Tariff, and have founded a Club upon this basis; and Sir Politick Falshood, the chairman, invites Coopmanschap to address its members. His speech is very winning.

First, he gave them thanks for the great Services they had done him upon all Occasions in time past, and the great Obligations which they had laid upon him; *for That*, not regarding their Country, their Liberty, their present Advantages, or their Posterity, they had, with a steady and unshaken Zeal, always preferred his *Interest* to THEIR OWN.

He cannot but be grateful too, he says, that when, a few years ago, they were in a business partnership with him, they had never insisted on his paying his agreed proportion of the joint stock and had had the friendliness not to examine his accounts. Further, when several of his principal British friends 'were in danger of being turned out of their Shops and Employments by their LANDLADY', Coopmanschap's friends had been so good as to tell her flatly she must not do this. How kind it was, too, that when they were planning to run down credit in England, they gave him enough time to rescue his own money first.[86]

Coopmanschap then proceeds to describe the dangerous association, now developing, between Alderman Traffick and Count Tariff, and tells them what a scandalous character Tariff is: a Frenchman and a Papist, a 'tricking false Fellow that never kept his word with any Body', and a bankrupt, not able to make good what he has promised. He would load Britain with his 'Wine, Brandy, Silk, Linnen, Paper, &c.', but in return would give her no more than 'large Promises and good Words'.[87]

Sir Politick, in his reply, tells Coopmanschap that his gratitude is much appreciated, and he assures him that, though some of the Club's members have left to join a partnership with 'Merchant *Moderation*', he can still depend on its assistance in anything he may desire. Thus he hopes that Coopmanschap will remain their friend; and since (as he will well understand) some of them may occasionally have a little trouble with the law, they would be glad to know that if so – whether they be 'felonious-Bankrupts, Murtherers of Nobility, Duellers, Scots Libellers, Traytors, or what kind of Offenders soever' – his country will offer them hospitality.[88]

As to Count Tariff's British associates, Sir Politick confesses that the knowledgeable Alderman Traffick is a difficult customer. But Woolpack, he says, is a well-meaning country fellow, very passionate and ignorant, and it should be easy to shake his confidence in Tariff. It is only necessary to tell him that all those ready to trade with the French are Jacobites. Moreover, he (Sir Politick) has discovered a good reason why Count Tariff would never keep his promises to British manufacturers. For the French have found ways of making fine cloth from coarse wool; nay, they have discovered how to make woollen goods 'WITHOUT WOOLL'. The club members are awestruck. 'LAURD!', cries an elderly member, '*What will become of poor England! This will ruin us all with a Witness!*'.[89]

When Count Tariff comes to his trial, the Club, aided by the Whig coffee houses and Ridpath's '*Lying Post*', and by dint of raising the mob, secure his condemnation. The French wool-manufacturers had been terrified at the prospect of British competition, but their under-cover agents in England can now send them a cheering letter. They can look forward to another year's prosperity, and the Club has acquired for them a present of fine English wool, all ready for their smugglers to collect it.

*   *   *   *   *   *

Among the Government's Whig critics at this period the most vocifer-ous and best known was Richard Steele, who kept up the attack in a succession of periodicals and then in a fiery pamphlet, published in 1714, *The Crisis*. At the time of the *Tatler* Defoe had been a warm admirer of Steele, speaking of him as 'that Universally and indeed Deservedly approv'd Author' and as 'that happy Genius';[90] and replying to a letter by Steele in the *Guardian*, attacking the Treaty of Commerce, he was still courteous, saying that Steele was 'a Man whose Sense and good Manners qualifies him to be a Match for any Man, provided his Cause be good' (which, as he implies, it was not here).[91] But as Steele pressed his attacks, all changed, and Defoe developed a hostility towards him which eventually grew quite savage. Steele denounced the Government for its failure to compel the French to demolish Dunkirk (as they were required to do under the Treaty of Utrecht) and accused it of putting the Hanoverian succes-sion in danger. In the general election of August–September 1713 he was elected as MP for Stockbridge and, even before he had taken his seat, there was talk among Tories of having him expelled from Parliament. Defoe complained bitterly about him to Lord Oxford, saying that his *Englishman* was practically treasonable, and urged retribution.

> Sure my Lord, Justice Vested with Legall Power will not allwayes Suffer; If the Government Never Exerts it Self The Friends of the Government will not be Protected ... If my Lord The Virulent writeings of this Man May Not be Voted Seditious, None Ever May, and if Thereupon he May be Expell'd, it would Suppress and Discourage the Party and break all Their New Measures.[92]

Oxford may have been of the same opinion, for in March 1714, no doubt at his request, Defoe sent him a long 'Collection of Scandal' from Steele's writings. It cited Steele's insolence in saying that the people of Britain 'expected' the Queen to have Dunkirk demolished; also in saying he would like to hear the Elector of Hanover's reaction to the Queen's recent claim to a 'perfect Good Understanding' with the Hanoverians. (The Elector's silence, Steele implied, spoke volumes.) It quoted Steele's reflections on how Britain had 'basely and Unrighteously' deserted their wartime ally the Catalans and his seditious account of Britain as 'Given up to France and bound hand and Foot, lyeing at the Mercy of The French King'.[93] On 18 March, only a month or so after taking his seat, Steele was in fact expelled from the House, for asserting in print that the succession was in danger under Oxford's ministry, and no doubt Defoe has to be regarded as at least partly responsible.

Nor was this the end of the vendetta. On 22 April 1714 Defoe launched a new thrice-weekly journal, published by John Morphew, entitled the *Monitor*. (John Dunton, in *Queen Robin: or the Second Part of Neck or Nothing*, writes, one does not know how truly, that the *Examiner* was paid by Harley, and that '*The Mercator* and *Monitor* were in the pay of B[olingbro]ke'.[94]) There soon sprang up a running battle between the *Monitor* and Steele's current periodical the *Reader*. The *Monitor* recalls, with heavy sarcasm, how the Dutch Deputy Tugghe presented a Memorial to the Queen, asking that the harbour and mole at Dunkirk should be spared, and how this 'stirr'd up ALBION'S *Immortal Genius* (as the *Celebrated Author* of the Doggerel PROPHECY styles a late Rott–n Member of Parliament) to tell the Queen, in one of his *Immortal* Pamphlets that the British *Nation* expected *the Immediate Demolition* of the Fort and Harbour, giving her to understand that she was not to take her own time'.[95] In retaliation, the *Reader* for 26–8

April bracketed the *Monitor* with the *Examiner* as wishing to 'hurt and betray the Liberties of Man', and in its next issue it printed a 'CAVEAT' against the *Monitor* for suggesting things against the honour and duty of the Queen under pretence of vindicating her ministers. That Steele has guessed Defoe to be the author is clear from a letter he pictures himself sending to the Oxford ministry, reporting the disrespectful language – 'contemptible and destitute' – used recently by the *Monitor* about its friend and protégé the Pretender. 'I hope you will take the proper Methods for doing Justice in this Case', the imaginary letter begins, 'by sending the Bearer [i.e. the Monitor himself] to the Stocks: for being exalted to publick View and a higher Pedestal is a Distinction which he has known already'.[96]

The *Monitor*, in its first issue, claimed to be a non-party journal and a despiser of '*the Rabble of Authors, Hackney-Scriblers, News-Makers, &c.*'.[97] This, however, did not prevent it from mud-slinging, or from a violent attack on 'the *Wolf* of Mindel—m' (i.e. Marlborough[98]) and the danger of his coming over in wrath to 'reduce us' and dictate to the Queen.[99] It also began to drop alarming hints of coming repression. The freedom of the press was of course a very precious thing; nevertheless, it hinted, the Government might at last be forced to find some remedy against its abuse. Her Majesty might, perhaps, even have to resort to 'the Method of Former Reigns (*viz.*) STRETCHING and SHORTNING'.[100]

Nemesis, one might say, has overtaken Defoe. The tone of his journal, and especially its guilt-ridden anger in defence of the ministry, has grown rabid. For all his protestations of independence and his sometimes genuine demonstrations of it, Defoe has, for the moment, come to sound like a 'mad' Tory.

CHAPTER 7

DEFOE AND THE WHIG SPLIT

The story of the very last days of the Tory ministry is well known. The unfortunate Queen, seriously unwell and continually harassed by Abigail Masham (now very much Harley's enemy) as well as by Bolingbroke, at last gave in and announced, at the Privy Council in Kensington on 27 July 1714, that she was dismissing Oxford and putting the Treasury in commission. There ensued a tempestuous altercation within the Council, the usually impassive Oxford furiously denouncing Bolingbroke for financial chicanery and later engaging in a shouting-match with Harcourt in the Long Gallery, audible enough to disturb the Queen in her private apartments. In the evening he went to surrender the White Staff to the Queen. She had for some time been complaining of his rude and inconsiderate, and sometimes drunken, behaviour; but it still disturbed her to part from him, the more so that she did not trust Bolingbroke, and she granted him a long farewell audience.

The stress of the day's events was really too much for her, and it soon became plain that she was dying. The news left the Bolingbroke–Harcourt–Atterbury cabal bewildered and unprepared. Over the last four years Bolingbroke had made great efforts to purge the armed forces and the magistracy of Whigs, no doubt with some ultimate intention of bringing in the Pretender. But the risk of precipitating a civil war, even with French help – but very likely with Marlborough and his veterans as opponents – seemed too great. (Moreover the Pretender had recently lost much popularity by declaring he had no intention of changing his religion.) Bolingbroke therefore tried instead to make a power-sharing pact with the Whigs, but he was firmly rebuffed. Meanwhile by 30 July the Queen's condition had taken a turn for the worse, and at a Council meeting that day the ministers (reinforced by the unexpected arrival of the Dukes of Argyll and Somerset), gave it as their opinion that she should offer the White Staff to the Duke of Shrewsbury, a revered elder statesman and a moderate Whig. (Shrewsbury's friendship, they no doubt realized, might serve as a protection for them when the Elector of Hanover arrived.) The Queen, who may or may not have still known what she was doing, complied; express messages were sent all over the country; the Dutch, who were pledged to defend the Protestant succession, were alerted; and when, the following day, the Queen died, the Elector George was proclaimed King of Great Britain with little disturbance.

The position in which this left Defoe, bereft of his eminent protector and the butt of endless attacks as a turncoat and hireling of the disgraced Tories, was certainly grim. One might even be tempted to suppose it desperate, but this would come from thinking of him as essentially, if not solely, a political writer. This was not the case; and indeed at this very time he was writing a long non-political work, the religious treatise *The Family Instructor*, which was to be the most successful of all his publications apart from *Robinson Crusoe*. (Published in January 1715, it was still receiving new editions well into the nineteenth century.) It is worth noticing, none the less, that in the second edition of the *Family Instructor,* he describes how, at the time of its first appearance, he tried to conceal his authorship, so that readers might not be prejudiced by his tarnished reputation.[1]

What gives food for thought, though, is his occupation at the time of the Queen's death, or very soon after. He was writing for, indeed he was conceivably the main author of, a Whig journal! It was entitled *The Flying Post and Medley*, and one might for a moment be tempted to mistake it for the *Flying Post, or, the Post-Master*, the mouthpiece of Defoe's old enemy George Ridpath – for it had an identical format and employed the original 'cuts'.[2] How he came to be doing this is curious. Ridpath himself, in April of the previous year, had taken refuge from the law in Holland, keeping control of the *Flying Post* but leaving the day-to-day running to assistants in London; and some quarrel had broken out between him and his printer William Hurt, leading him to dismiss Hurt. The sham *Flying Post*, launched on 27 July, was Hurt's retaliation. The first number was extremely weak, but in his preamble Hurt announced that he had found a promising author for subsequent numbers and was '*not without Hopes that that Person's Performances may answer so far the publick Expectation, as to merit some part of the Correspondence with which he has been hitherto favour'd*'. This person was most probably Defoe, and at all events Defoe certainly worked for the periodical, as the Government soon had reason to know.

This sham *Flying Post*, the first outlet for Defoe's pen after the fall of the Tories, was a vigorous and trenchant Whiggish journal, highly censorious about the ousted ministry. It contained a libellous paragraph reporting how a certain great Tory duke had taken a bribe to relinquish his post; it related at length the treatment suffered by the great Roman general Camillus, whose envious rivals, like Marlborough's, got him dismissed because he won too many victories; and it made a swingeing attack on those Tory statesmen who would like it to be thought they had stayed in office for so long, resisting the yearning to retire to the country, out of a sense of patriotic duty. What is noticeable, however, is that the journal does not attack Lord Oxford personally.

Before long, the journal was in serious trouble. The issue for 19 August contained a letter (signed 'Dublin') plainly meant to accuse the Earl of Anglesey, recently sent to Ireland to help remodel the armed forces, of Jacobite activities. His task, the letter said, had been 'to break no less than 70 of the honest Officers of the Army, and to fill up their Places with the Tools and Creatures of Con— Phi—s [Sir Constantine Phipps, the High Tory Chancellor], and such a Rabble of Cut-throats as were fit for the Work that they had for them to do'. Anglesey, one of the Lords Regent in charge of Britain pending the arrival of King George, had taken violent exception, and upon his complaint William Hurt, the publisher John Baker and Defoe were arrested and interrogated, Hurt's premises were raided, and a copy of the offending letter, in Defoe's handwriting, was discovered. Here is how he reported the affair to Lord Oxford in a letter of 31 August 1714.

> I had not given your Ldpp The trouble of any of the Little Ruffles I meet with in The world, if it were not That I See allwayes Som little Stroaks of Malice (in Every Thing that pushes at me) pointing at your Ldpp who they would fain Think they affront when they fall upon me.

This makes it Necessay for me to Lay before your Ldpp a brief hystory of Fact on a Broil which I have just Now upon my hands, which would not be Otherwise worth your hearing.

It has been long That I have been Endeavouring to Take off the Virulence and Rage of the Flying Post. Mr. Moore[3] has been a wittness to the Design and to Some of the Measures I took for it, which were Unsuccessful.

After Some Time an Occasion Offred me which I Thought might be Improv'd Effectually to Overthrow it; the Old Author Redpath Quarrell'd with his Printer Hurt and Takes the Paper From him; Hurt Sets up for himself and applyes himself to a Certain Author to write it for him, but being Not Able to get any One to Publish it, he lost ground.

It Occurr'd to me That To Support Hurt would be the Onely Way to bring the paper it Self Out of Redpaths hand, and to this Intent I frequently at his Request Sent him paragraphs of forreign News but Declin'd Medling with home Matters.

The publisher Recd a letter Very Unhappily for me and finding it full of Reflections desir'd it to be Softn'd as he calld it, and Sends it to me. I left out indeed a great Deal of Scandalous Stuff that was in it but added Nothing and Sent it back. This they have printed from my hand, and I am Charg'd as the Author of the Letter, am Sent for by a warrant and held to Bail.

The use They make of this is that I have Insulted my Ld Anglesey and that your Ldpp has Employ'd me to do so.

God knows that all I did in it was to prevent their Printing Severall Scandalous Reflections on his Ldpp which I therefore struck quite out and Wrot the Rest Over again; I Humbly beg your Ldpps Intercession with my Ld Anglesey in this Matter, assureing his Ldpp I Never knew any thing in this Matter Other than the Above and did nothing in it but with Design to Serve his Ldpp.[4]

The 'little Ruffle' over the Lord Anglesey letter was actually very serious, and Defoe would come for trial over it in June 1715, escaping severe penalties only by great good fortune. His claim to have done no more than 'soften' the Anglesey letter is a line of defence he often resorted to in such situations and is not too convincing. But what is more to our purpose is the nature of Defoe's letter. One pores over it, trying to make out what it is actually saying, both about the Anglesey affair and about the spurious *Flying Post*. What exactly does Defoe mean by 'Endeavouring to Take off the Virulence and Rage of the

Flying Post', or by the 'Measures' he took towards this? (Would abusing Ridpath in the *Monitor* count as such a 'Measure'?) What was it that Arthur Moore could, reputedly, bear witness to? Certainly, it is not easy to understand what Defoe is telling Oxford, but then the thought arises, does he actually want to be understood? A dream-like feeling comes over us, as if we have read letters like this elsewhere, ones which depict Defoe as a spy in enemy territory, a patriotic fifth-columnist employed to disable and enervate the Opposition's polemics. And of course we have: he was to write similar letters to Charles Delafaye (the Undersecretary of State) in 1718, to explain his activities on the staff of *Mist's Journal* and *Mercurius Politicus*, a matter which we shall come on to.

*   *   *   *   *   *

Defoe made it plain from very early on that, despite his old employer's fall from power, he intended to be loyal to him, and it would be fair to say that he was as good as his word. Gratitude, it would seem, was the virtue which counted most for Defoe, and it was not just in jest that, in *The True-Born Englishman*, he declared ingratitude to be the favourite English sin. One remembers the touching moment in *Robinson Crusoe* when Crusoe tells Friday of his plan for them to separate, and Friday, whose intense attachment to Crusoe springs from gratitude, thrusts a hatchet into his hand, urging him to kill him instead.[5]

In a letter to Oxford of 3 August 1714, Defoe wrote that 'The Surprissing Turn given by The Immediate hand of Providence'[6] (meaning the Queen's death) had caused him to hold back the vindication of Oxford that he had proposed publishing. Presumably he meant the lengthy pamphlet, *The Secret History of the White-Staff*, which in fact came out in the following month (being followed by two further parts, in October 1714 and January 1715). The general line of the pamphlet is the (probably true) one that Harley originally hoped to employ only 'moderate' men and to conciliate some of the more moderate Whigs, but that, at the time of the election in October 1710, party fury rose to such a height that he and his colleagues were 'driven to make use both of Means and Hands which they never intended to make use of' – in particular, employing covert Jacobites.[7] It was, moreover, a path of no return and later led to rash and desperate measures: the creating of twelve new peers, to secure an immediate majority; the bringing in of an Occasional Conformity Bill, by an unholy bargain; and so on. On the other hand, at least during the first year or two of the administration – so the argument runs – Harley showed unrivalled finesse and was unfailingly triumphant: 'No Head but his could have extricated it self out of such Labyrinths, escap'd so many Snares, and brought himself out of so many Difficulties, as he had done'. He so completely refuted the accusation that Britain had betrayed her allies the Catalans in the late war that an Address of Thanks was made for the care the nation had shown towards them. He managed to show that the pensioning of certain Highland clan chieftains, which was held against him as a crime, was positively money well spent. We are told of the 'silent, quiet Steps' by which he outmanoeuvred and silenced the October Club, even recruiting the members for his own policies.[8] Further, a leading theme of Part II of the *Secret History* is the skill with which Harley outmanoeuvred the Scottish Jacobite nobles by having them sent up to the Union Parliament as representative peers; for almost the first thing they had to do, on arriving in Westminster, was – so they discovered to their dismay – to declare allegiance to the Queen and the Hanoverian succession! The suspicion always hanging over the administration was that it was plotting against the Protestant succession; but, so Defoe pictures Harley as reasoning, if the Jacobite 'tools' whom the ministry employed liked to feed themselves with such a hope, it might take them off from all their other mischievous projects. Of course in fact, he argued, nothing could be more absurd than 'this Phantome of the Jacobites, of believing the White-Staff was in their Interest'.[9]

Even when the ministry fell apart, the pamphlet says, and Harley's 'hot' colleagues conspired successfully against him, forcing on him a measure (the Schism Bill) to outlaw the Dissenters' schools, which everyone knew was a mine to blow him up, he succeeded in 'castrating' the bill, taking out 'all the malicious and persecuting Part'.[10]

Defoe moreover gives his pamphlet a telling conclusion. He depicts the amazement and fury of the ministers (as if 'Planet-struck') when they learn that the White Staff,[11] relinquished by Harley, is not to be given to one of themselves but to the Duke of Shrewsbury. Up to now Defoe has avoided personalities – for the good reason, as he says, that certain of the ministers are still in office and could make trouble for him. But for the purposes of his colourful dénouement he brings Bolingbroke, Bishop Atterbury and Harcourt, the Lord Chancellor, on to the scene in all their bewilderment and fury.

> The Blast of Hell and the Rage of a Million of Devils be on this Cursed *Staff, said He* [Harcourt], *flinging the Purse,* &c. *on the Ground*, IT IS HE that has ruin'd us, and broken all our Measures ...
>
> *Give away the Staff!* said the Bis—, By Lucifer I could not have believ'd she [the Queen] durst have done it! What can we do without it, We have but one way left, *France* and the Lawful Heir; it must, and shall be done, By G—d.[12]

It would take another volume, Defoe writes, to relate all their extravagant speeches on this occasion and the desperate and treasonable measures proposed by their 'Chief Leader' (i.e. Harcourt).

As will have been seen, Defoe depicts Harcourt, rather than Bolingbroke, as the leader of the cabal, and he presents him as a smooth-talking and self-seeking hypocrite, who did not care who was dismissed so long as it was not himself, and who eventually, and deservedly, 'fell unpity'd of every Side'.[13] By contrast, according to Defoe, Bolingbroke ('Lord John Bull') a man of 'old English Plainness', stood by his principles and kept his head. Defoe, however, somewhat undermines his apologia for Bolingbroke. For he remarks, apropos of a speech he attributes to him, urging his colleagues to strengthen their ties with the Elector: 'the Historian does not affirm that this Discourse was really spoken Word for Word by Lord *John Bull*, it is rather what he *wishes* were true.[14] This gives us a hint, but only a hint, as to Defoe's real assessment of Bolingbroke, which remains a puzzle. It is noticeable that whenever he alludes to Bolingbroke, who it seems may have been his paymaster on the *Monitor* (see p. 134), his language grows opaque and obscure.

The *Secret History* made a stir and provoked a host of attacks and answers. According to one of them, *The History of the Mitre and Purse* (1714), Harley was a cunning trickster in the pay of the French. He played a treacherous part towards James Drake (author of the high-flying *Memorial of the Church of England*) as he did towards Sacheverell, encouraging and then betraying them. He was really at heart, though he disguised it, a dangerous Dissenter, 'whose Father could whine and Cant most enormously, and had Stiffen'd his Son's Temper into very serious Bent'.[15] By contrast, the 'Mitre' (Atterbury) and the 'Purse'

(Harcourt) – though Harcourt was led by the nose by Harley – were honourable men. G. V. Bennett asserts this pamphlet to be by Atterbury,[16] but this seems unlikely in that it begins with an absolute paean of praise for the 'Mitre': 'a Bishop, who for Learning, Piety, Politeness, and Sagacity may be rendred equal to the Brightest Luminaries of the *Protestant* Church'.[17] This, if Atterbury's friends had come to know he was the author, would have made him look a fool. It seems more probable it was by William Pittis.

It was widely suspected that the *Secret History of the White-Staff* was by Defoe, and that he had written it under Oxford's instructions. The author of *Considerations upon the Secret History of the White Staff, Humbly Address'd to the E— of O—* (n.d.) addresses Oxford on the assumption that he was, in essence, the author, and he is slighting towards him about his achievements. He had got himself stabbed, had pensioned some Highland rebels and had found jobs for a number of his relatives: that was about the sum of it.

Oxford himself, despite Defoe's letter promising a vindication, thought the Whigs might have commissioned the *Secret History* in order to embarrass him. 'The policy is plain', he wrote to his friend Dr W. Stratford on 23 November 1714. 'He ought to be treated as a fool who had the staff, if he ever encouraged a vindication.'[18] But by this time he had realized that his political career was probably at an end. King George, when he landed at Greenwich on 18 September and held court there, had received him with the greatest frigidity, in fact had pointedly turned his back on him.

It seems probable that Defoe soon became aware that Oxford felt embarrassed by the *Secret History*; and certainly, if not quite an 'amazing tissue of lies' as G. V. Bennett calls it, it contains a good deal of clever invention.[19] For instance, far from the cabal being 'Planet-struck' at the Queen's giving the White Staff to the Duke of Shrewsbury, she did it, as we saw, at its own suggestion. One reflects that, whether or no Oxford was made uncomfortable by the *Secret History*, it was likely to have done him good rather than harm; but at all events Defoe now resorted to an amazing stratagem. He published, in January 1715, a pamphlet entitled *The Secret History of the Secret History*, 'Written by a Person of HONOUR', which argues that the *Secret History* was a baseless fabrication, with no real relation to fact and no political purpose, and the same was true of the attacks on it (such as

The History of the Mitre and Purse). Indeed they might well be by the same author or authors. The enemies of Lord Oxford were taken in by the seeming purpose of the *Secret History*, i.e. to clear Oxford's name, leaving the writers of the tracts, who caused 'the deceiv'd People to Dance in the Circles of their drawing', to enjoy the spectacle of mankind's credulity.[20]

The narrator tells how, on visiting a coffee house, he heard people discussing the authorship of the *Secret History*, and how one among the company, who seemed to be a Quaker, stood out against the general opinion. 'Don't you believe', he was asked, 'that he [Lord Oxford] has furnish'd Materials for this Book to *Daniel De Foe*, or some such other Scribler, as for Money he might get, to do such a Piece of Drudgery for him?'. To this the Quaker replies, in a mysteriously confident tone, that he does not believe Lord Oxford or anybody connected with him was responsible for the book. Pressed to give his reasons, he offers only what he says is by no means the chief of them, merely that the vindication is too weak to be by Oxford himself. The narrator is impressed by the Quaker's manner and follows him out of the coffee house to a nearby tavern to question him further. The Quaker tells him how, out of curiosity, he had actually gone in person to interrogate Lord Oxford, who denied any connection with the *Secret History* with the utmost indignation; and then how, through the good offices of a fellow Quaker, he had contrived a meeting with the person generally supposed to be the author, Daniel Defoe.[21]

The Quaker found Defoe a very sick man, having recently suffered an apoplectic fit. He nevertheless allowed himself to be questioned and told the Quaker that he did not write the *Secret History*, nor did he believe that Lord Oxford had anything to do with it. His own connection with the pamphlet, he said, amounted to no more than, having caught sight of some of the copy while it was in the press, he was asked by the printer to look at it and 'did Revise Two or Three Sheets of it, and mark'd some Things in them, which he dislik'd'. This declaration of Defoe's the Quaker feels he cannot question, being spoken by a man 'as it were stepping into the Grave'; and he is confirmed in his belief in it by what he is told by two other writers in the trade. There are, so he learned from them, several 'clubs' or sets of men kept in constant employment by a congeries of booksellers, writing on whatever subject they were asked to, regardless of political parties, and happy to devise answers to their own pamphlets. Indeed, the Quaker says, he can name one such hackney writer, a certain William Pittis, who wrote *The History of the Mitre and the Purse*. Apparently Pittis actually confessed his authorship and showed some of it in manuscript to the writer of the *Secret History of the Secret History*, and the latter knows who was Pittis's employer and how much he was paid.[22]

Defoe was perennially fascinated by credulity and the ease with which it could be played upon, and the fact is important to the present book. One recalls a discussion in the *Review* for 30 August 1712, where he writes that the growth of lying is related to, but in a way less dangerous than, the growth of credulity: lying is a private Crime, but 'believing Lies is a National Judgment, a Humour that taints the whole Blood of the People'. In his (largely fictitious) *Minutes of the Negotiations of Monsr. Mesnager at the Court of England* (1717) Defoe shares the glee of the French King's agent in England at the readiness of English hack writers to write in the French interest. 'Those Writers of Pamphlets in *England*, are the best People of the Kind that are any where to be found,' writes Mesnager, 'for they have so many Turns to impose upon their People, that nothing I have met with was ever like it; and the People of *England*, of all the People I have met with, are the fondest of such Writings'.[23] But the *Secret History of the Secret History* is Defoe's supreme essay in this genre. Here, to exculpate himself *vis-à-vis* Lord Oxford, he explores the possibilities of mendacity and credulity to their very limits – even hinting to his readers not to be in too much of a hurry to believe the very pamphlet they are reading.

This was by no means the end of Defoe's preoccupation with his old employer. In February 1715 he published the apologia for his own political conduct, *An Appeal to Honour and Justice*, from which we have several times quoted. It is obviously an important document, and we have reprinted it in its entirety as Appendix C (see below pp. 199–233). One reflects that many of the claims it makes are reasonable, and many of the facts that it asserts are genuine, whilst one or two of these latter are clearly false.

It was not absurd for Defoe to have pictured himself, at this moment, as a man suffering vilification almost beyond compare, the victim of 'infinite Clamours and Reproaches, causeless Curses, unusual Threatnings, and the most unjust and injurious Treatment in the World'.[24] The stream of printed attacks on him had not slackened, and he was for the time being without protection and defenceless against them. Equally, he had good cause for thinking he was, for whatever reason, the victim of false literary attributions on a scale unparalleled, a truth which has complicated his reputation ever since. He could fairly complain of it as one of the greatest pieces of injustice towards him,

> that whenever any Piece comes out which is not liked, I am immediately charg'd with being the Author, and very often the first Knowledge I have had of a Books being publish'd, has been from seeing my self abused for being the Author of it, in some other Pamphlet publish'd in Answer to it.[25]

As for his denial that he had written at Harley's direction, or 'taken the Materials from him, been dictated to, or instructed by him',[26] any reader of his letters knows, from his lamentations, that to extract specific directions from Harley was pretty well an insuperable task.

In the *Appeal* Defoe pleads for understanding of his attitude towards Oxford. In rescuing him from Newgate in 1703, Oxford, he wrote, had been his worldly salvation, and this had created unalterable obligations, which time could not weaken. He had had for ever afterwards a duty to adhere to Oxford, and eventually to his ministry; and if it should have happened (as it did) that things were done of which he disapproved, he could hardly be expected to have said so publicly: the most that decency would allow was silence. This is no doubt reasonable.

Similarly, it is the case that he was decidedly critical of the Utrecht peace settlement in print, and likewise that he frequently said in print that he regretted the fall of Godolphin, as 'a great Disaster to the Nation'.[27]

What was undoubtedly not true, on the other hand, is his assertion that he had written no book since the death of the Queen, and at most had revised two sheets *of The Secret History of the White-Staff*.[28] This was a particular form of fiction he was fond of as regards his own writing, and it was never very convincing. The same may be said of his reckless insistence that he never 'receiv'd of the late Lord Treasurer, or of any one else by his Order, Knowledge, or Direction, one Farthing, or the Value of a Farthing, during his whole Administration'.[29] It was certainly untrue, and Laurence Hanson has identified nine payments to him during this period, including one (for £100) for which he thanks

Oxford in a letter dated 26 July (almost Oxford's last day in office).[30] Of course he may have clung to the sophistry that the payments were, strictly speaking, not from Oxford but from the Queen. But the important point is: he must have known he would not be believed.

The *Appeal* has a strange 'Conclusion' by the publisher. Acccording to this, the Author suffered a 'violent Fit of an Apoplexy' before he could finish the pamphlet and since then had been languishing near to death, so that his friends had decided not to hold up publication any longer. This corresponds neatly to the Quaker's account in *The Secret History of the Secret History*, and one reflects that, if anyone ever had good reason to suffer a breakdown, it was Defoe at this moment. Thus it could even be true. Though, as his critics have often remarked, for a dying author he remained remarkably productive.

During the same month Defoe also published a tract written in pseudo-Quaker style entitled *A Friendly Epistle by Way of Reproof From One of the People called Quakers, to Thomas Bradbury, a Dealer in Many Words*. It is a rebuke to Bradbury, a celebrated Congregationalist preacher, for calling for blood and for vengeance against the late Queen's ministers. For, the tract argues, the Peace was God's work, even if He had to use some unworthy instruments to bring it about. Bradbury should have reserved his strictures for the great ones of the present regime and the flood of wickedness – the avarice, and those 'Houses of Abomination' the playhouses – they are bringing upon the land. The tract throws light on Defoe's political stance at this moment, for he is plainly making no bid for reconciliation with the Government and Court and indeed exploits the 'plain speaking' of Quakers to say some harsh things about them. 'Verily, Thomas, it appeareth unto me, That the Iniquity of the People aboundeth, even of their Rulers, in a much greater Manner, than in the Days when thou wer't aggrieved thereat.'[31] The pamphlet quite alarmed the genuine Quaker fraternity, who published a letter in the *London Gazette* for 1–5 March and the *Daily Courant* for 7 March vehemently denying any part in it or its 'Irreverent Expressions Reflecting upon the King, Princes and Rulers' and supposing it must be a 'Contrivance of some Adversary of Ours, whereby to vent his own Invectives against the Government in our Name'.

The pamphlet was published by Samuel Keimer, a printer and religious eccentric who had at one time been a member of the 'French

Prophets' – at which time, in the words of George Healey, he 'grew a beard, wore yard-lengths of green ribbon, and wrote his name on large apples'.[32] He felt bitterly disillusioned when a fellow 'Prophet' forced him into bankruptcy and the debtors' prison and for a time more or less lost all religious faith. In his autobiography he tells how he used to entertain his fellow prisoners with a take-off of the Quaker preaching style, 'mixing my Discourse with somewhat filthy'. Eventually, however, he felt seriously drawn to the Quakers, and though he did not formally join them, he felt his soul 'knit in Love to the truly sincere, humble bowed down Souls among them'.[33]

It was Keimer who had published *The Secret History of the Secret History of the White Staff* and it is significant that, though not written in 'Quaker' language, it has a truth-loving Quaker as its protagonist. In the course of 1715 Defoe would produce several more 'Quaker' pamphlets under Keimer's imprint – reprimands to Henry Sacheverell, to the Duke of Ormonde and to the Earl of Mar (*A Trumpet Blown in the North*) – and in January 1716 Keimer and Defoe seem to have begun a collaboration on a new weekly, the *London Post* (advertised as being 'the only Weekly Paper wrote in behalf of this present Government').[34] The second issue (13 January 1716) carries 'A Rebuke from one of the Lord's People called Quakers, to R— S— [i.e. Richard Steele] the reputed Author of a vain Pamphlet call'd the Town-Talk'. It is a reprimand to Steele for printing the full text of the Pretender's recent declaration, which contained some very offensive remarks about King George, and asks Steele, was he not 'afraid of his ears'? 'Verily Richard, for my part I cannot but think by thy way of writing, but thou art a disguis'd Jesuit.' It seems most probable that this is by Defoe.

In June 1715 Lord Oxford, together with Bolingbroke and Lord Ormonde, was impeached for high treason, and was sent to the Tower, and early the next month Defoe published *An Account of the Conduct of Robert Earl of Oxford*. It is unrelievedly eulogistic, making much of the fact that, whereas Bolingbroke had escaped to France, which must suggest an admission of guilt, Oxford had bravely determined to stand trial. His colleagues, so the *Account* said, had wished to bully and dictate to the Queen, but he had urged her to take a more active role in affairs and (contrary to common belief) had done his best to reduce the power of a 'prime minister'. It had been a happy day for him when he persuaded the Queen to release him from office, enabling him to disown the misdeeds of his colleagues. Of these Bolingbroke is represented as the most troublesome; and now that Bolingbroke is off the scene, Defoe is markedly rude about him. He cites Bolingbroke's vengeful rage at being denied an earldom as the sort of thing that had brought the ministry into contempt.

*   *   *   *   *   *

The first general election of the new reign was held in February 1715, returning a predominantly Whig House of Commons, and the Government set to work at once to rake over the crimes of the late ministry. The Whigs were enjoying the reward of their impressive party unity during the last four years, but they found it harder to restore unity within the nation. It was a problem for them that the King, who spoke no English and took very little interest in specifically British affairs, was not popular, and his ministers found themselves in a power-struggle with the King's German advisers, not to mention his rapacious German mistresses. There were anti-Government riots all through the summer, much as at the time of the Sacheverell trial, and eventually this led to the passing of a stern Riot Act, still on the statute-book today.[35]

It had been rumoured for some time that the Jacobites were planning a rising, and at last on 6 September 1715 the Earl of Mar raised the standard of rebellion at Braemar, being supported by a small force of gentry on the Border and an English force in Lancashire recruited by the Northumberland MP Thomas Forster. The rebellion soon proved an ill-managed affair, and it was crippled by the lack of help from France, Louis XIV having died in the previous month and the French Regent being eager for friendship with Britain. By 3 November Forster's troops had surrendered at Preston and on the same day Mar suffered defeat at Sherrifmuir. The Pretender arrived in Scotland just before Christmas but too late to redeem the situation, and early in February he and Mar, with their few troops, slipped away in despair. (An expedition to Devon, under the leadership of the Duke of Ormonde, never even managed to land.) Before long the prisoners taken at Preston were being marched to London, with their hands tied behind their backs.

Jacobite feeling remained strong in Britain, however, and Lord Townshend, Secretary of State for the Northern Department, instituted a fierce campaign of repression against anti-Government journals. Of these the most influential were *Robin's Last Shift* (which was launched in February 1716, changing its name in May to *The Shift Shifted*) and *Weekly Remarks*. Both were conducted by the Jacobite George Flint, who was frequently arrested and in and out of prison (as was his printer Isaac Dalton) and who for a time edited his journals from Newgate. According to Flint, Britain itself was a prison, as well as godless, and was given over to foreigners. Prisoners of war were being treated with inhuman cruelty, some of those left at Preston being chained together like dogs; a 'standing army and severities' were ruining British trade; and Parliament had three pernicious and tyrannous bills on hand. One (the Septennial Bill) was to extend the life of this and future Parliaments; one to continue the suspension of Habeas Corpus, begun the previous September; and one to give a vote for a religious Lecturer to all the 'Tag-rag and Bob-tail' of country parishes. It was known that the King was planning to revisit Hanover in July, greatly against the wishes of his ministers, and Flint reported the rumour that he would be smuggling more than two million pounds sterling out of Britain.[36]

It was at this period that, according to Defoe, an overture was made to him to be reconciled with the Whig Government. His trial over the Anglesey letter had come on in July 1715 and he had been found guilty, though sentencing had been postponed; and it seems that, fearing that he might be forced to flee the country, the inspiration came to him to write to Chief Justice Parker, begging him to reconsider his case. The result, according to Defoe's account, was that Parker not only generously put a stop to further proceedings but recommended him to Townshend as a Government agent. Townshend, convinced by his professions of attachment to the Whig interest, directed him to write a weekly journal in opposition to Flint's *The Shift Shifted*. But then the idea occurred to them, so Defoe relates, that he 'might be more Servicable in a kind of Disguise', i.e. masquerading as a Tory. Accordingly he gave up the weekly paper and 'engaged' in a monthly periodical called *Mercurius Politicus*, as well as taking over the management of *Dyer's Newsletter*, a Tory organ, with a view to taking the 'sting' out of it.[37]

Defoe's employment by Lord Townshend cannot have lasted much more than half a year, for on 12 December 1716 Townshend heard from the King at Hanover, to his great mortification, that he was dismissed from his post as Secretary of State. In compensation he was offered the Lord-Lieutenantship of Ireland, and after much irresolution he grudgingly accepted. But, as soon became known, a serious division was developing in the Whig party generally, of which this was only the beginning. It was a struggle for power not only within the party itself but also between it and the German 'junta' – that is to say the King's German advisers Count Bernsdorf and Baron Bothmar and his French secretary Jean Robethon. Defoe's career and affiliations during the next year or two have to be understood by reference to this split.

Bothmar had been the King's principal agent in England in the latter years of Queen Anne's reign, and Townshend largely owed to him his place as Secretary of State and head of the Administration. However, their friendship had cooled; and so had Townshend's relations with the King's mistresses, the Countess Schulenberg and Baroness Kielmansegge, who did not think him as helpful as he should have been in their money-making intrigues and quest for English titles. The King, moreover, came to suspect him of taking sides with the Prince of Wales, with whom he himself was on appallingly bad terms, and of trying to increase the latter's powers as Regent during his own absence in Hanover. Part of the King's purpose in going to Hanover was to conduct secret negotiations towards a treaty of alliance with France. He was accompanied there by Stanhope; and the Earl of Sunderland, on the pretext of visiting the Continent for his health, contrived to join in these discussions. Sunderland had been enraged that Townshend should have been given the Secretaryship of State, which he had coveted for himself, and he seized the present chance to strengthen his position. Bothmar and Bernsdorf hankered after English titles, and he promised to try to secure the repeal of the Act of Settlement, which made this impossible; and at the same time he sowed seeds of suspicion of Townshend in the King's mind. On the King's instructions he wrote Townshend a furious letter, reporting the King's resentment at receiving so little support from England; and at the same moment Stanhope wrote to Townshend (he was told the answer must be in French so that the King could read it) accusing him of wantonly holding up negotiation with France. Townshend's dismissal followed soon afterwards, his post being given to Stanhope.[38]

Defoe was not slow to react to the Whig split. In mid-January 1717 he published *The Danger of Court Differences*, in which he is ironic about both sides, though he pretends to think the division must be only a Jacobite fiction (for the fatal consequences of disunity were plain from history). He followed this a week or so later with *The Quarrel of the School-Boys at Athens, as lately acted at a School near Westminster*, a satirical allegory featuring a famous schoolmaster (George I), his usher (the Prince of Wales) and certain leading boys at a school in Athens, relating what they got up to when the headmaster was temporarily called away. It does not particularly favour either side (and is polite to the Prince of Wales), but it notes what 'good Boys' they have all been since the Master's return. It makes the point that the boyish 'Captain of the Cashkeepers' (i.e. Walpole) objected to the scheme of 'bringing in some *Foreign* Boys'.[39]

Meanwhile on 21 January an old adversary of Defoe's, John Toland, published a remarkable anonymous treatise entitled *The State-Anatomy of Great Britain*, evidently designed for the attention of the King, who had returned to England two days earlier after his long sojourn abroad. The *State-Anatomy* described itself as a 'memorial' sent by an English friend to a foreign ambassador, who was shortly to be sent to England, explaining various puzzling English words and phrases, such as 'Tory' and 'Whig', 'Commonwealth men', 'Danger of the Church' etc., and painting a eulogistic picture of the present state of Britain. The country had in George I a monarch of the utmost personal attraction, 'mild and gracious as goodness it self'[40] and with a grasp of financial matters which politicians might envy. Contrary to rumours, moreover, the Prince of Wales was 'as dutiful a son, as he's a most tender and loving husband'.[41] The nation, as now organized on wise Whig principles, said the friend, stood in the sharpest possible contrast to the recent scandalous Tory regime.

The State-Anatomist nevertheless takes it on himself to offer advice. He advocates a pugnacious foreign policy and recommends a peacetime army for Britain of a size sufficient to render her considerable abroad, though the nation ought also to keep brigades of soldiers in the service of other countries, to serve as a 'nursery of experienc'd

Officers'.[42] All this, however, he says, is not a proposal for a standing army, a thing which has always been fatal to the nation's liberties.

On religious matters, he argues for a complete freedom of conscience, though he commends Occasional Conformity as a 'noble' practice, fulfilling the behest of the Apostle Paul. He would have Roman Catholics excluded from the kingdom, not on confessional grounds but simply because they do not acknowledge the authority of the Government; and on the same principle he would also like to see non-jurors banished. He is, however, by no means a xenophobe and warmly praises the Whigs' readiness to welcome foreigners. Indeed he tells his correspondent that 'no good *Englishman* forgets … the great and important services' which Count Bernsdorf and Baron Bothmar have rendered to Britain and that he 'need not fear, but by a particular Act they'll be created Peers of this kingdom'.[43]

Toland's treatise proved a disaster for Defoe. It provoked him to publish a furious reply, *An Argument Proving that the Design of Employing and Ennobling Foreigners Is a Treasonable Conspiracy,* expressing amazement at the 'Arrogance' of the author of the *State-Anatomy* in 'dictating to the House of Lords' and plotting to 'prostitute the illustrious Blood of our Nobility' – as if unaware of the reproaches already earned by England's ancient nobility 'by their being so unhappily mix'd with spurious and Foreign Blood'.[44] This leads him into the windiest rhetoric about that most precious of bodies, the English peerage.

> It is not the receiving, or not receiving, of these Gentlemen into the House of Lords, which is the Case before us; but it is communicating the Peerage of Britain to Foreigners; this is what I am speaking to, *viz.* opening the Door to let in *Germany,* or *France,* or *Holland,* for *where one Nation enters, all Nations may* follow, into the Honour of Peerage, and, which is most astonishing, into the *LEGISLATURE* of *Great Britain: O most illustrious and august* Nobility, whose Veins are swelled with Royal Blood, and among whom is found all that now remains of the ancient Race of *British, Saxon,* and *Norman* Kings! How have you, *too often already,* been invaded, under the Pretence of rewarding Merit, and exalting Men of Fame?[45]

It would moreover, wrote Defoe, mean allowing strangers to form part of the judiciary.

> O venerable and awful *Judicature;* who can describe the Majesty of your Assembly! Untainted in Honour, calm and mature in deliberating,

impartial in judging; when in passing Sentence you lay your Hands upon your uncorrupted Hearts, how much superiour is it allowed to be, even to an Oath sworn by the *ETERNAL GOD!*[46]

He further attacked the State-Anatomist's proposal of a general religious toleration, saying that it amounted to a toleration not merely for every variety of the Christian religion but for any religion, Christian or not; and he condemned with horror his insidious design to introduce a standing army.

The whole *State-Anatomy* affair, he asserted, must be the conspiracy of a 'Sett of selfish and designing Men' who, fearing public exposure by 'some honest and loyal Patriots, who yet remain in the Administration', had made use of this hireling to test the temperature of the nation.[47] The phrase 'a Sett of selfish and designing Men' must, if obscurely, be aimed at Townshend's enemies Stanhope and Sunderland; and though Defoe piously disclaims any suggestion that the State-Anatomist's proposals could possibly derive from King George, he allows himself at one point a covert gibe at the King. He asks whether, if today we give peerages to two Germans, 'at length our Posterity may be offered two Turks' – a hit at King George's faithful Turkish pages, who were reputed to earn a fortune by backstairs influence. The inference one has to draw is that Defoe has sided with Townshend, as one of the few 'honest and loyal Patriots, who yet remain in the Administration', and who has, for the moment, lost his employment.

This *Argument* of Defoe's went a long way to ruin his reputation. Abel Boyer, no friend to Defoe, spotted him as the author, attributing the *Argument* to a 'mercenary Retainer' to Lord Oxford, 'A *Scribbler* (*Trium Litterarum*) famous for writing *upon, for and against* all manner of *Subjects, Persons* and *Parties*'.[48] This seems to have alerted Toland who, in a second part of his *State-Anatomy*, published at the end of March, seized gleefully on the gross inconsistency between the sentiments of the 'Arguer' about 'blood' and race and those in *The True-Born Englishman*. He mentions Defoe's 'venomous' joke at the expense of the King's two Turks and quotes his rancorous references to '*a covetous* Dutchman, *a mercenary* Frenchman, *a haughty insolent* Spaniard, and *a lewd assassinating* Italian', remarking:

> AND now what's pleasant enough, the author of this foul and rascally stuff, is the very man (my Lord) who wrote the *True-born*

Englishman, a Satyr against the whole *English* nation for their contempt of Foreigners. This is the man, who, in the Explanatory
Preface to that Satyr, says he's *of opinion, that had we been an unmixt
nation, it wou'd be to our disadvantage … An* Englishman *of all men*, says
he in the same Preface, *ought not to despise Foreigners as such; since what
they are to day we were yesterday, and to morrow they will be like us.*[49]

This is fair game, and it is hard to understand how Defoe came to
put himself in such an absurd position. No doubt he was feeling out
in the cold, for the dismissal of Townshend must have meant the dry-
ing-up of his secret service pay; and by contrast the *State-Anatomy* gave
the impression that its author might be basking in Government
favour. (Moreover he was intending to use it to injure Defoe's patron
Lord Oxford.) It is significant that Defoe wrote his *Argument* during
Stanhope's tenure as Secretary of State, which was to last only four
months, during which time there seems to have been no offer of
employment to him. His employment, however, was renewed by Stanhope's successor Lord Sunderland, who had been his patron some
years earlier, and this, evidently, would have made his *Argument*, with
its anti-Government polemics and its rudeness to the King, a serious
embarrassment. Thus when, in May, he brought out *A Farther Argument against Ennobling Foreigners*, an anonymous reply to Toland's *Second
Part*, Defoe took the line that he had had nothing whatever to do with
the *Argument*. Toland, Defoe claims, had adopted a quite new mode of
self-defence.

> This is, to find out an Author who he thinks fit for his encounter,
> and call him the Writer of the Book which he contends with, (it mat-
> ters not with him whether he is the Man or no) and thus having
> drest up this *Man of Straw*, he begins the fight. This he has done in
> the Case before me, where finding it greatly for his purpose, that *De
> Foe*, Author of the *True born Englishman*, should pass for the Author
> of the *Argument against enabling* [*sic*] *Foreigners*, &c. he has singled him
> out, and fallen upon him in a most merciless manner; for he has rec-
> ommended him to the Revenge of his Foreigners, (what mercy he
> will find there may be guess'd at.) He has also, as far as his good
> Wishes may have effect, recommended him to the Resentment of
> the Government. He has expos'd, ridicul'd, banter'd, and in a word,
> as far as in him lies, murther'd the Man; and yet all this while, this
> Man, as I find, was no more Author of this Book than the Man in

the Moon: Nay, *as I hear*, for I have no Knowledge of the Man, he has been sick in his Bed all the while.[50]

But then, the 'Arguer' adds, changing tack, say it *had* been Defoe who wrote the *Argument* as well as *The True-Born Englishman*, what would it matter? 'It had amounted to no more than this; either that he had been *wrong before*, and was now *better inform'd*; or *second*, that he had contradicted himself, and wrote one time one thing, and one time another, a fault which Modesty should have taught *Toland* to have pass'd over in silence, that it might not be retorted upon himself'.[51] It was no business of the present writer to salvage the reputation of a fellow (i.e. Defoe) he knew nothing about.

This defence, with its ruthless sacrificing of Defoe's own name, is an extraordinarily lame one, and not made more credible by the now stale rumour about his sickbed, but it perhaps seemed the best left open to him.

In April 1717 Lord Townshend was dismissed from the Government altogether, and the true dimensions of the Whig split became public knowledge. Walpole resigned in sympathy with Townshend, against the King's earnest pleading, and the two statesmen, with some twenty of their followers, set themselves up as an Opposition, and over the next few years they would often join forces with the Tories. They threw themselves into a power-struggle with the German junta and into resistance to the King's use of the British armed forces in what were essentially Hanoverian interests.

Noticeably, all Walpole's eagerness, as chairman of the Committee of Secrecy, to bring Lord Oxford to trial disappeared at the same moment. It was a point that Defoe made sardonic play with in a pamphlet of 1 August, *The Old Whig and Modern Whig Revived*, a tract caustic both towards the Government and the Walpolite Opposition. He writes there, as a saddened Whig, on the fatal capacity of politicians to ruin their own, and their country's, prosperity by their personal competitiveness, thinly disguised as 'patriotism'. It reminds him, he says, of the way the Whigs in 1708 threw away all their glorious success by splitting into 'Modern' Whigs and 'Old' Whigs, thereby letting in the Tories. (Though, he reflects, the Tories were probably capable of acting just as badly.)[52]

*   *   *   *   *   *

Lord Oxford's trial was at last imminent, and imprisonment had brought out his courage and insouciance. The Government had long hoped he would escape from the Tower, and the King was said to have sent an emissary to him, promising him his freedom if he only would retire to the country and meddle no more in politics. To this his response had been to clap on his hat, saying: 'My Lord, you see the cock of my hat on this side ... if the Court would but ask me to turn my hat to the other side, and assure me I should have my liberty for it, I would not do it'. It was his duty, he said, to vindicate the Constitution of England and the administration of the late Queen.[53]

It was partly to help Oxford that in June 1717 Defoe published the remarkable *Minutes of the Negotiations of Monsr. Mesnager at the Court of England.* Mesnager was a real person, an agent of Louis XIV who came to England in August 1711 to help form 'preliminaries' towards a peace treaty and who later served as a plenipotentiary at the Congress of Utrecht. However Defoe, for his own purposes, considerably extends the length of Mesnager's stay and re-arranges the facts of his career, as a way of posing the question, how the Tory 'Peace' of 1711–13 might have appeared to French eyes; and, more significant, how England itself might have appeared to Mesnager. (It was an aim already shadowed forth, years before, in the plan of the *Review.*) The work was an ingenious and complex fiction, scoring a number of cherished points for Defoe, such as the wonderful readiness of English hack-writers to promote any set of ideas one asked them to, and the low tone of English public life. It also allowed him to adopt an effective tactic on Lord Oxford's behalf – that of explaining the false rumours of his disloyalty to Queen and country by reference to his personal faults: his deviousness, secretiveness, proneness to indolence and fertility in false promises. Mesnager gains the impression that Oxford is a person of 'real great Capacities, general Knowledge, and polite Learning, a taking and very engaging Way of Conversation', but that he is a different man when it comes to public business; 'for there his Discourse is always reserved, communicating nothing, and allowing none to know the whole Event of what they are employed to do'. People tell Mesnager (and Defoe could have confirmed it from bitter experience) that 'he scarce ever sent any Person abroad, though on Matters of the greatest Importance, but that he left some of their Business to be sent after them'. In the main, it is Mesnager's impression

that he was regarded as well-intentioned, but he had 'taken such exot-
ick Measures to bring his own good Designs to pass, that his Good
would be as fatal as other People's Evil'. Mesnager suspects the Pretender's courtiers at St Germain of putting pathetic faith in the
assurances given by Harley and his ministers, not realizing that they
would 'give them Promises in Plenty, but not run the least Hazard for
them to do any Thing effectual'.[54]

Abel Boyer spotted the historical untruths in the *Minutes* and
guessed, from its '*loose Stile*, and *long-winded, spinning way of Writing*', that
Defoe was its 'forger', though Defoe, in his customary manner, loudly
denied this.[55] Boyer also rightly recognized the intention to help Lord
Oxford: thus he delivered his usual diatribe against Defoe, as a 'tool'
of the Tories and a performer of 'dirty Work'.[56] What he did not recognize was the work's artistic cleverness.

*   *   *   *   *   *

On 31 March 1717, in the midst of the conflict within the Whig party,
the Bishop of Bangor, Benjamin Hoadly, delivered a controversial sermon in the Chapel Royal on *The Nature of the Kingdom or Church of
Christ*. Hoadly (1676–1761) was a prominent Low Churchman and
Erastian, holding that the Gospels offered no warrant for Church
authority in the civil sphere, and his sermon was intended to help clear
the way for the repeal of the Test Act and the other laws against the
Dissenters. It was condemned as subversive by the high-flying Lower
House of Convocation, which appointed a committee to examine it,
and it was also bitterly attacked by Andrew Snape, the headmaster of
Eton, who claimed that, before publishing the sermon, Hoadly, on the
advice of a friend, had softened the wording to conceal his real meaning. Hoadly denied this and demanded to know the identity of the
alleged 'friend'. Snape said he had heard the story from the Bishop of
Carlisle (William Nicholson), who had identified the friend as the
Dean of Peterborough (White Kennett); Kennett vehemently denied
that he had told Nicolson any such thing, and a furious debate (the
'Bangorian controversy') broke out in the newspapers, excitement
running so high that for a day or two, so it was said, business in the
City was brought to a standstill. The ensuing pamphlet war would last
for a year or more.

Hoadly was a favourite of the Government and vaunted to the skies by pro-Government journalists such as Toland and Boyer, but Defoe distanced himself from him, treating him largely as a figure of fun. What he seized on with relish was the public name-calling and vituperation among Hoadly's friends and foes, taking it as a rich example of the degeneracy of the Anglican clergy.

His first contribution to the debate was a pseudo-Quaker *Declaration of Truth to Benjamin Hoadly*, an elegant piece of teasing, praising Hoadly for so clearly bearing witness to Quaker doctrines, and telling him that the only step he still needed to take was to abandon his lawn sleeves (those 'prophane Ensigns of Idolatry'[57]) and join the Quakers. He followed this in July with *The Conduct of Christians made the Sport of Infidels*, a fictitious letter from an Armenian merchant in Amsterdam, describing the shocking swearing, false oath-taking and factiousness of the British 'Nazarenes' (i.e. Christians); and in August he elaborated on the same theme – that the Turks may in some ways be better Christians than the Christians – in a *Continuation* of the famous *Letters Writ by a Turkish Spy*. The spy, a pious Muslim, reports with amazement the shocking contempt for religion he observes in Europe.[58]

*   *   *   *   *   *

How, then, shall we describe Defoe's political stance at this time? There is an important matter we have not yet discussed and which throws light on the question. In May 1716 a new monthly journal was launched, entitled *Mercurius Politicus*, edited – and written – by Defoe. To give one reason, among several, for thinking this was so, the journal made a point of praising his pamphlets as they appeared. In its issue for January 1717 it called *The Quarrel of the School-Boys at Athens* one of the 'merriest Pieces of Drollery ... that have been met with in this age' and it quoted some verses belonging to it which do not appear in the published text;[59] and in February 1717 it commended Defoe's *Argument* as a 'smart' reply to Toland.

Mercurius Politicus was distinctly successful, proving a serious rival to Abel Boyer's Whiggish monthly the *Political State*, and this led to a running battle between the two journals. Toland, in *The Second Part of the State Anatomy*, complained that *Mercurius Politicus*, despite its professed impartiality, was malicious towards the Government,[60] and in this he was right. In the second number, and again in July, when reporting on the surprising dismissal of the Duke of Argyll from all his posts, *Mercurius Politicus* hinted discreetly at the real reason for it, i.e. Argyll's friendship with that object of the King's wrath and detestation, the Prince of Wales. In the same July number the first item in the list of contents reads 'Of Stripping the Palaces, and sending the Furniture Abroad', an allusion to King George's rumoured plans to take untold wealth and valuables with him to Hanover. In the report itself Mercurius defended the monarch against these rumours, if not very warmly, but by then the contents-page listing would have done its work. In a later section of this issue the journal says it will now do what, for many reasons, it could not do earlier and print some of the speeches made against the Government's Septennial Bill. 'The Impartiality we have profess'd in this Work', writes the editor, 'obliges us to give Posterity a true Account [of] who appeared for their Liberties, and who against them'.[61] The nudge to the reader is hard to miss, and there follow full-length reports of four impassioned Tory speeches against the bill, including one by Shippen, in which he speaks of seizing 'perhaps our *last Struggle* for the *Liberties* of those we *represent*'.[62] Defoe later, in a letter to Charles Delafaye, the Undersecretary of State, would convey the impression that *Mercurius Politicus* was an already-existing Tory journal, which he had infiltrated so as to 'enervate' it, in the Government's interest, but all the evidence points against this.[63]

Thus it appears that, even before the crisis and split in the Whig party, Defoe had joined the ranks of the Government's critics; and in view of this it need not surprise us that during the spring or summer of 1717 he joined the staff of that notoriously High Church and covertly Jacobite organ, Nathaniel Mist's *Weekly Journal: or, Saturday's Post*. Mist had been a common seaman in the navy but had settled in London as a printer some time before June 1716, launching his journal near the end of the same year. It was to become the most popular of all the weekly journals and was much hated by the Government, who did their best to make Mist's life a misery. Defoe's connection with it soon became known. On 24 August 1717 *Read's Weekly Journal* spoke of 'Daniel Foe' as author of *Mist's Weekly Journal* and as espousing the illiterate Mist's cause, and on 7 September the *St. James's Weekly Journal*, edited by Abel Boyer, accused Defoe of 'writing against the Government in Disguise, to have the Advantage of defending it in Publick'.

Only last Saturday, says Boyer, Defoe had abused 'the greatest Character this age has produced on the side of Truth, Virtue and Religion' (i.e. Hoadly). The relationship between Defoe and Mist lasted, off and on, for several years, and William Lee, in his biography of Defoe, tells various highly-coloured stories about it.[64] But Lee, a knowledgeable and extremely decent but credulous man, is not to be trusted.

Defoe's own explanation, given later, was that, on the encouragement of Lord Townshend, he had insinuated himself into Mist's service as a translator of foreign news, with the aim of keeping Mist's *Weekly Journal* 'within the Circle of a Secret Mannagement'.[65] It was the same explanation as he would give as regards *Mercurius Politicus*. But before discussing this further we should examine his activities on the *Weekly Journal* during 1718. At the beginning of this year it appeared that the current quarrel between Philip V of Spain and the Emperor was near to plunging Europe into another war, and in the issue of Mist's *Weekly Journal* for 1 February 1718 there appeared a letter on this subject signed 'Sir Andrew Politick, Kt.'.[66] 'Sir Andrew' asks Mist whether the Spanish can really hope to win a land battle against Prince Eugene or a naval one against Britain and the Dutch? Will the Emperor, at present involved in a war with the Turks, be bold enough to take on both the Turks *and* the Spaniards? If the Emperor and Philip come to blows, what will Britain do? If Britain were to take the Emperor's side, what effect would that have on the stock exchange and the national credit?

The gist of this may be stated in few words: 'Sir Andrew' is suggesting to Mist, the editor of this popular Opposition journal, that the Whig Government shows signs of wanting to involve Britain in an unnecessary, and very likely ruinous, war. Mist welcomes the suggestion and answers at some length, saying it might be folly to underestimate the Spaniards' military strength; and as regards Britain becoming involved in a war on either side, all he can say is, '*We hope not*'.

One or two further communications from 'Sir Andrew Politick' followed during the year. In the issue for 1 March 1718, a letter signed 'Charles Ridpath' rebuked Mist for being biased in favour of the Spaniards: did this not put him in the position of wanting the Emperor, Spain's enemy, defeated by Turkish infidels? Mist replied that he suspected that this 'Ridpath' was really his old friend Sir Andrew Politick again, and the accusation was false; his dearest wish was for Britain to involve herself with neither of these monarchs. 'We have nothing to do, as Protestants, with the Quarrels of these Popish *Potsherds of the Earth*, one Way or other; let them dash themselves together in Pieces one against the other, as they please.'

In June 1718 the Spanish invaded Sicily, and in August a British fleet under Admiral Byng was sent to threaten reprisals, though Britain and Spain were not officially at war, and destroyed half the Spanish fleet off Cape Passaro. To this Spain, who complained bitterly about the breach of international law, responded by impounding the British merchant shipping in its harbours. War was evidently going to follow, and the issue of *Mist's Journal* for 25 October 1718 carried another long letter from Sir Andrew, this time more definitely inflammatory and anti-Government (it is printed in full below, pp. 194–8). It consisted of ten queries. 1. Whose quarrel was it? And what had Britain to do with it? 2. What would she be fighting for? 3. Why should Britain fight for the Emperor, seeing he had proved such an unhelpful ally during the War of the Spanish Succession? 4. Among the pretences for the war offered by the Government, the strongest seemed to be that Britain was bound by guarantee to help protect the Emperor's possessions in Italy. But according to the Spanish, this guarantee ended at Utrecht. 5. What condition was the country in to carry on a new war, and would the advantages be equal to the loss of its trade with Spain? 6. Would Britain's supposed new ally France be any real support in a war with Spain, seeing she had recently spilled so much blood and treasure to put Philip on the throne? 7. Would France not take the war as a chance to engross the trade with Spain? 8. What hope was there, even if Britain defeated Spain, of Spain's recompensing British merchants for her seizure of their vessels and effects? 9. Had not Spain already paid sufficiently by losing half her fleet? 10. Even if Britain should take rich spoils from Spain's plate fleets, did not four-fifths or more of the cargoes of her galleons belong to other European owners?

Mist had been in trouble with the Government all through this and the previous year, and he now found himself in worse straits.[67] The Sir Andrew letter was declared treasonable; Mist's offices were raided and searched and the staff taken into custody; and on 1 November Mist himself was made to appear for questioning before Lord Stan-

hope and James Craggs, the two Secretaries of State. His statement
was reported as follows:

> ... says that Daniel De Foe has usually written part of the paper
> entitled *The Weekly Journal or Saturday's Post* printed by the examinant,
> and that because it should not be known who was the author he
> always destroyed the copy; That the said De Foe did particularly
> write the letter inserted in the said *Weekly Journal* on Saturday, Octo-
> ber 25, 1718, and subscribed Sr Andrew Politick, to which the
> examinent made some few alterations in transcribing the same, not
> altering the substance; That the Answer to the Letter aforesaid
> inserted in the same paper was also written by the said De Foe and
> transcribed by the examinant in the same manner.[68]

On the same day, Thomas Warner, bookseller of Paternoster Row, tes-
tified before the Undersecretary Charles Delafaye that:

> ... by what he has heard in conversation and from other reasons he
> does believe Daniel Defoe to be the author of a great part of the
> said paper, and particularly of a letter ... subscribed Sir Andrew Pol-
> itick, for that he, this examinant, had some days before a
> conversation with the said Defoe, who, in discourse, talked to him
> to much the same purpose as what is mentioned in the said letter,
> and that since the printing thereof, the said Defoe has owned to the
> examinant that he had seen the said letter before it was printed; That
> Nathaniel Mist has also owned to this examinant that Daniel Defoe
> had given him a copy of the said letter, tho' at the same time pre-
> tended to give him a caution not to print it. The examinant further
> says, that he paid to the said Defoe after the rate of twenty shillings
> a week for his service in the writing of the said paper, that upon
> some difference that happened between them, money which the
> examinant believes was for the said Defoe's use has been paid by the
> examinant to the order of Samuel Moorland, Esq., and of late the
> examinant has paid money as formerly upon Mr. Mist's account and
> for the service above mentioned into the said Defoe's own hands at
> the rate of 40*s* a week. The examinant further says that the said
> Defoe has been daily with him for two or three days past, appearing
> much concerned at the proceedings against Mr. Mist, saying that he,
> Defoe, would not on any account be known to be the author, for if
> he thought he should be proved the author he would quit the
> nation, and that he was under an obligation from above not to med-
> dle with the paper above-mentioned, and desired the examinant to
> exhort Mr. Mist to stand by it and not declare the author, promising

in such a case to stand by him, and to use all his interest in his favour.[69]

Another document records that a certain Jonathan Marshall, being asked whom he received the offending letter from, said 'he believes it Mr. Defoe's hand, received from Jonathan a gardiner who is employed by Mr. Defoe, and believes it came from Mr. Defoe'.[70] Meanwhile, a fortnight earlier, it had been reported in *Read's Weekly Journal* that Defoe had obtained a security of £500 from Mist not to reveal that he wrote for *Mist's Journal*.[71]

It is surprising that Defoe's biographers have not made more of this incident, and curious, too, how they have interpreted it. George Aitken, who unearthed the official reports on Mist's interrogation, seems to have thought that Mist misled his examiners, and the Sir Andrew Politick letter was really written by himself. He moreover imagines the examination to have been in some sense a comedy, since Stanhope and Craggs 'were in Defoe's secret, and knew much more than Mist and his friends, who thought they were making revelations about Defoe'.[72] James Sutherland, by contrast, allows the scandalous letter to have been by Defoe, but he imagines it was merely that Defoe had overdone his impersonation of a Tory and Jacobite. 'If Defoe told him [Warner] that he was under an obligation from above not to meddle with Mist's Journal, he was telling him something that was very far from the truth: he was under an obligation, in fact, to meddle with it as much as possible.' Defoe had simply taken his masquerade too far.[73]

It is significant that Aitken does not discuss the content of the Sir Andrew Politick letter; and what one notices is that it is not some extreme and treasonable piece of Jacobitism but is broadly in line with the critique of the Government being made by Walpole and the other 'defectors' from the Whigs, and by the Tories. They were, for instance, arguing that the King's current support for the Emperor was given in the hope that, in return, the Emperor should invest him as ruler of the duchies of Bremen and Verden, which he had recently purchased from the Danes – an ambition of no particular interest to Britain. These are sentiments broadly similar to those of Sir Andrew's previous letters, and it seems reasonable to suppose that whoever wrote the letter of 25 October also wrote the earlier ones, and also the editorial replies, which were not in radical disagreement with them. (The effect aimed at is fairly plainly a Platonic dialogue, in which one speaker puts up an argument for the other to correct.)

Thus there is unusually strong external evidence and at least a modicum of internal evidence for Defoe being the author of these letters; and when one actually reads the letter of 25 October, an incisive and challenging piece of work, it becomes hard to go along with the idea that it was merely a 'slip' on Defoe's part, a matter of pretending too hard. Indeed, if we think him the author of all the 'Sir Andrew' letters and of the replies to them, such an idea becomes impossible: why should Defoe have been at quite such pains to further Mist's anti-Government cause?

It seems we need to read Defoe's relations with Nathaniel Mist in reverse. It was not Mist whom Defoe was deceiving, but rather Delafaye, and through him Delafaye's superiors. He was in some sort of collusion with Mist, which gave him an ideal disguise under which to propagate his own anti-Government views. His position on the *Weekly Journal* would have been a perfect concealment. His apparent extreme frankness to Delafaye, his sending him or Sunderland copies of treasonable pamphlets, with suitable expressions of horror, and his dutiful reports to him about his efforts to keep Mist in check would have been an excellent ploy. Twice at least he did indeed induce Mist to print an admission of past imprudences and a promise of better behaviour in future; and when the news of these efforts reached the rival press, this would also have been to his advantage. At one point it was reported in *Read's Journal* that Mist and he had fallen out, over an article which he had forced Mist to publish, against 'railing and insulting King George', and that Mist was threatening to sack him.[74] Such rumours would have suited him admirably. It meant that, for the time being at least, he was managing to hoodwink even the sharp-eyed Whig press.

The important business of the bond bears this interpretation out. The sum of £500 was a very considerable one, and its size implies that there was some very grave secret Defoe needed to prevent Mist from betraying. This could hardly have been the mere fact of his associating with a Tory journal, which was hardly a secret to the world and not at all to Delafaye. Much more likely, it was the fact that he was deluding his own Government employers. If Delafaye and Stanhope were to find out what he had really been up to, he would have been in terrible trouble and might well, as he told Warner, have had to take refuge abroad.

So now we need to turn our attention to the famous letters which Defoe wrote to Delafaye in 1718, purporting to describe how, two or three years before, he had been commissioned by Lord Townshend to insinuate himself into the management of Tory journals, to restrain and 'enervate' them. It is a fascinating story, which catches hold of the mind and has influenced all those writing about Defoe since the letters became known, but can we believe it? The more one thinks about it, the harder this becomes. On questions regarding his authorship Defoe never felt much compulsion to tell the truth, and the Delafaye letters may, more likely, have been one of his most accomplished fictions.

These six letters were discovered in the State Paper Office in 1864 and they had a momentous effect on Defoe's reputation. They were published for the first time that year in two numbers of the *London Review* with an anonymous commentary savagely hostile to Defoe – accusing him of 'baseness and dishonesty', 'rascality', 'dirty and disreputable work' and the like.[75] Defoe's admirers, who were numerous at this time, were greatly disturbed by the revelations, and especially William Lee, who set to work on an enormous reading programme to examine the journals with which Defoe said he had been involved, in the hope of wiping Defoe's reputation clean. In 1865 he published five extensive articles in *Notes and Queries* attacking the reviewer in the *London Review*, and eventually, in 1869, he published a three-volume *Life and Recently Discovered Writings* of Defoe, the first volume being a lengthy and panegyrical biography, including many new attributions, and the remaining two volumes reprinting a mass of anonymous journalism from *Mist's Weekly Journal*, *Applebee's Journal*, etc. which Lee, on the strength of internal evidence, proposed adding to the Defoe 'canon'. He, characteristically, accepted Defoe's account as true but argued that, though Defoe had been 'unwise' to put himself in such a questionable position, the letters showed him in an admirable light, and did nothing to sully Defoe's 'moral character as a man, a patriot, and a Christian'.[76] Defoe studies were profoundly influenced by Lee's book and to some extent are so still.

So let us examine the letters, and especially the one dated 26 April 1718, a little more closely, remembering that it was written at the moment when Lord Stanhope, who would hardly have known the details of any past arrangement between Townshend and Defoe, was resuming the office of Secretary of State for the Northern Department. The text reads as follows.[77]

Sir,

Though I doubt not but you have acquainted my Lord Stanhope with what humble sense of his Lordship's goodness I received the account you were pleased to give me, that my little services are accepted, and that his Lordship is satisfied to go on upon the foot of former capitulations etc., yet I confess Sir I have been anxious on many accounts, with respect as well to the service itself, as to my own safety, lest my Lord may think himself ill served by me, even when I may have best performed my duty.

I thought it therefore not only a debt to myself, but a duty to his Lordship that I should give his Lordship a short account as clear as I can, how far my former instructions empowered me to act, and in a word what this little piece of secret service is for which I am so much subject of his Lordship's present favour and bounty.

It was in the ministry of my Lord Townshend, when my Lord Chief Justice Parker to whom I stand obliged for the favour, was pleased so far to state my case, that notwithstanding the misrepresentations under which I had suffered, and notwithstanding some mistakes which I was the first to acknowledge, I was so happy as to be believed in the professsions I made of a sincere attachment to the interest of the present Government; and speaking with all possible humility, I hope I have not dishonoured my Lord Parker's recommendation.

In considering after this which way I might be rendered most useful to the Government, it was proposed by my Lord Townshend that I should still appear as if I were as before under the displeasure of the Government; and separated from the Whigs; and that I might be more serviceable in a kind of disguise, than if I appeared openly; and upon this foot a weekly paper which I was first directed to write, in opposition to a scandalous paper called *The Shift Shifted*, was laid aside; and the first thing I engaged in was a monthly book called *Mercurius Politicus* of which presently.

In the interval of this, Dyer the news-letter writer having been dead, and Dormer his successor being unable by his troubles to carry on that work, I had an offer of a share in the property as well as in the management of that work.

I immediately acquainted my Lord Townshend of it, who by Mr Buckley let me know, it would be a very acceptable piece of service; for that Letter was really very prejudicial to the public, and the most difficult to come at in a judicial way, in case of offence given; my Lord was pleased to add by Mr Buckley that he would consider my service in that case as he afterwards did.

Upon this I engaged in it, and that so far, that though the property was not wholly my own, yet the conduct, and government of the style and news, was so entirely in me, that I ventured to assure his Lordship the sting of that mischievous paper should be entirely taken out, though it was granted that the style should continue Tory, as it was, that the party might be amused, and not set up another, which would have destroyed the design, and this part I therefore take entirely on myself still.

This went on for a year, before my Lord Townshend went out of the office: and his Lordship in consideration of this service, made the appointment [agreed payment] which Mr. Buckley knows of, with promise of a further allowance as service presented.

My Lord Sunderland to whose goodness I had many years ago been obliged when I was in a secret commission sent to Scotland, was pleased to approve and continue this service, and the appointment annexed; and with his Lordship's approbation, I introduced myself in the disguise of a translator of the foreign news to be so far concerned in this weekly paper of *Mist's*, as to be able to keep it within the circle of a secret management, also, prevent the mischievous part of it, and yet neither Mist or any of those concerned with him have the least guess or suspicion by whose direction I do it.

But here it becomes necessary to acquaint my Lord (as I hinted to you Sir) that this paper called the *Journal* is not in myself in property, as the other; only in management; with this express difference, that if anything happens to be put in without my knowledge, which may give offence; or if anything slips my observation which may be ill taken; his Lordship shall be sure always to know, whether he has a servant to reprove, or a stranger to correct.

Upon the whole however, this is the consequence, that by this management the *Weekly Journal* and Dormer's Letter as also the *Mercurius Politicus*, which is in the same nature of management as the *Journal*, will be always kept (mistakes excepted) to pass as Tory papers, and yet be disabled and enervated, so as to do no mischief or give any offence to the Government.

I beg leave to observe, Sir, one thing more to his Lordship in my own behalf, and without which indeed I may one time or other run the hazard of fatal misconstructions: I am Sir for this service posted among papists, Jacobites, and enraged high Tories, a generation I profess my very soul abhors; I am obliged to hear traitorous expressions, and outrageous words against his Majesty's person, and government, and his most faithful servants, and smile at it all as if I approved it; I am obliged to take all the scandalous and indeed villainous papers that come, and keep them by me as if I would gather material from them to put them into the news; nay I often venture to let things pass which are a little shocking that I may not render myself suspected.

Thus I bow in the house of Rimmon; and must humbly recommend myself to his Lordship's protection, or I may be undone the sooner, by how much the more faithfully I execute the commands I am under.

I forbear to enlarge. I beg you, Sir, to represent these circumstances to his Lordship in behalf of a faithful servant that shall always endeavour to approve his fidelity by actions rather than words.

I am, Sir, your most humble servant
DE FOE

Newington, April 26. 1718

P.S. I send you here one of the letters stopped at the press as I mentioned to you. As to the manuscript of Sultan Galga, another villainous paper, I sent the copy to my Lord Sunderland; if the original be of any service it is ready at your first orders.

What Defoe says about Dormer's newsletter sounds plausible as far as it goes, for in October 1715 Dormer, a known papist, was in fact in serious trouble with the authorities; but unfortunately no copies of the newsletter from this period seem to have survived.

We have already described *Mercurius Politicus* as it was in its early days (pp. 159–60 above), and in the broadest terms this was how it continued till at least near the end of 1718,[78] though becoming rather more noticeably the champion of Defoe, puffing his writings as they came out. So how does this square with what he tells Delafaye about it? The question is as much one of logic as of fact. Are we to suppose that *Mecurius Politicus* had already been launched, by the enemies of the Whig Government, before Defoe joined its staff? Does he mean that he worked his way into this dangerous anti-Whig journal in order to tame it and take the sting out of it? Laurence Hanson, in *Government and the Press 1695–1763*, seems to suppose he means this and, moreover, that it was true – though, he says, 'He [Defoe] joined the staff of *Mercurius Politicus* so soon after the founding of the paper as to prevent adequate comparison of its tone under his influence with what had gone before'.[79] There is, though, a fatal objection to this theory. It is that the paper shows no sign of having been tampered with or emasculated, and indeed it got a shade more anti-Government in tone as time went on.

But perhaps Defoe did not mean to suggest any such thing. His language – 'the first thing I engaged in was a monthly book called *Mercurius Politicus*' – is at least ambiguous. Is perhaps to 'engage in' the same as to launch or to found? William Lee understood it so and takes it for granted that Defoe was the author right from the start.[80] It is possible indeed that Defoe meant to be ambiguous, but for another reason – the same reason as prompted him to insist that, unlike the case of Dormer's newsletter, he was not the proprietor of *Mercurius Politicus*, merely its author or editor. This would leave a certain vagueness as to the extent to which he was the sole or chief editor, a matter of importance if the paper were to run into trouble. 'If anything happens to be put in without my knowledge, which may give offence', he tells Delafaye, 'or if anything slips my observation which may be ill taken; his Lordship shall be sure alway to know, whether he has a servant to reprove, or a stranger to correct'. He will know this, that is to say, because Defoe will tell him, a convenient arrangement. When, in 1718, the publisher John Morphew is prosecuted for a passage printed in *Mercurius Politicus* two years earlier, Defoe hastens to write to Delafaye disclaiming responsibility. No-one, he says, can pretend to make him responsible, 'otherwise than It might be Said I Saw or Overlookt the book, nor indeed can they prove So Much as tha[t,] So that I can in No Wise be Said to have faild in my Duty on acccount of this Latent affair'.[81]

But let us hypothesize that Defoe was, and admitted being, the launcher or founder of *Mercurius Politicus*. It would then remain to ask what his purpose was. Paula Backscheider, in her *Daniel Defoe: His Life*, explains that this journal gave the ministry 'a steady, reliable Tory mouthpiece'. It defended the Church of England, but its statements about the Church 'contrasted sharply with those of true High Church writers'. It made comments with a Tory tinge on passing events, but 'these small touches, appearing comfortably after the event or made about events of relatively limited impact, give the paper its Tory bias without actually helping Tory causes'.[82]

One could cavil at this description, for it does not seem true that *Mercurius Politicus* only reported events of 'relatively limited impact', or that it was any less prompt in reporting them than, say, Boyer's *Political State*. But something more important clamours for one's attention. It is the question: why should Townshend, a Whig Secretary of State, have wanted a 'steady, reliable Tory mouthpiece'? He had enough to do, one would think, coping with *The Shift Shifted* and the revived *Examiner*, without going out of his way to sponsor a new anti-Government journal.

Which brings us back to Defoe's letter. For there is a deeper ambiguity in it than we have yet mentioned. Defoe, we suggest, is wanting – though without precisely saying so – to convey the impression that launching a new Tory Journal, under his management, would not be fundamentally different from taming or undermining an already existing one, like Mist's *Weekly Journal*. Now, looked at coldly, that is plainly ridiculous. That he should have proposed to infiltrate an already-existing Tory journal is plausible. It has no resemblance to his being encouraged to start a new Tory journal, thereby adding to the Government's troubles. If Defoe was the founder of *Mercurius Politicus*, which it seems fairly clear he was, it must have been because it was something he wanted to do, and the journal said things he wanted said. Its outlook is, after all, perfectly consonant with the one conveyed in 'Sir Andrew Politick's' letters, which there is such strong evidence that he wrote. The two taken together provide a clear picture of his political affiliations in 1717–18. But that their purpose was to advance the interests of the Whig administration (whether while Townshend was a part of it or after he joined the opposition) is a proposition that brute logic forbids one to swallow.

CHAPTER 8

THE RETURN OF THE PRODIGAL

On 18 September 1718 Defoe launched, or helped to launch, a new thrice-weekly journal, the *White-Hall Evening Post*,[1] and in its issue for 29 November there appeared a letter to the editor, signed 'SPANISH', which could very possibly be by Defoe himself, but anyway seems to throw light on him. The letter takes to task the 'Author' of the '*White-Hall Evening Post*' – no doubt meaning the writer of the 'Sir Andrew Politick' letters – for arguing against a war between Britain and Spain. For is not a war absolutely necessary to defend Britain's trade? If the writer of the present letter has guessed the identity of the 'Author' rightly, he has heard this man say he 'would be glad of an Opportunity to retrieve the good Opinion of his Friends, which he lost by being drawn into former Follies'. The editor should tell him that now is the time for him to rejoin his friends and 'let the World see, that whatever he might be formerly biass'd to say in a Case which he could not defend, like a Counsel pleading for his fee, and obliged to make the best of a bad Cause; yet that now he speaks from Inclination, and has a Cause that must go along with his Judgment, as well as with the duty of an Author'. He should know that it is expected of him to show the need for Great Britain to exert herself against Spanish 'Exorbitance', and he should be told (the words of 'Sir Andrew Politick' are repeated and rebutted) that ''tis Nonsense to talk of this War from Religious Amusements, that it is carried on between Popish Powers, who we ought to let fight with one another as long as they please, and look with pleasure to see them dash themselves to pieces one against another, that the Protestant Powers may see their Enemies weaken'd, and their own strength reserv'd to pull them all down at last'. If the *White-Hall Evening Post* author will listen, the letter says, 'he shall be forgiven all his former wrong steps; and honest men will begin to receive him again, and restore him to their good opinion, as a man return'd to himself, and inclined to make us (to use his own words) '*L'Amende honorable* for what is past'.

It is hard not to read this as Defoe, with the aid of a clever little make-believe, publicly announcing his return to his old allegiance, i.e. to the Whigs and to the Government side. The remarks about the Author's zealous stretchings of points on behalf of his clients ('like a Counsel pleading for his fee') would certainly fit Defoe, who would admit that, when writing *Mercator* on behalf of the Tories six years before, he 'had a bad Cause to handle' though he did his best for his clients.[2] *Read's Weekly Journal*, his most unrelenting critic at this time, would contain in its issue for 6 December a poem 'On *Daniel Foe's* turning Whig again'.

> As Rats do run from falling Houses,
> So *Dan* another Cause espouses:
> Leaves poor *Nat* sinking in the Mire,
> Writes *White-Hall Evening News* for hire;
> Deserts his Tory-Rory Prigs,
> And finds new fools among the Whigs ...

We do not know why Defoe might have chosen to make such an announcement at this moment but, obviously, it could have been under pressure from the Government. It is a loose end in the 'Sir Andrew Politick' story that we do not known how Delafaye and his superiors reacted to Mist's revelations. One can imagine them as enraged or thunderstruck, but they could hardly have risked bringing one of their own undercover agents to trial. Thus it could be that the intriguing item in the *White-Hall Evening Post* (if it really is by Defoe) was written at their dictation.

At all events, at the same moment, the tone of *Mercurius Politicus* changes and it drops its discreet anti-Government sniping. The issue for December 1718 gives its approval to a war policy ('The Pulse beat high for a War with *Spain*') and goes out of its way to compliment the Government and Parliament. The Commons are lauded for so promptly passing the necessary money bills, and it says that 'the Harmony between the King and his People seem'd not only Confirm'd, but even carried farther than it had been usually carried in the Reign of any of his Predecessors ... the House shew'd his Majesty, that as they had nothing to desire of their Sovereign, which was either unfit, or unlikely to be Granted, so they had no Doubt in their thoughts that His Majesty would deny them any thing which it was reasonable for them to ask'.[3] But to this we need to add something more important. For in 1719 Defoe turned novelist, and the enormous success of *Robinson Crusoe* may have caused him from now on to be less obsessed by party-politics. At all events, he would remain a placid supporter of the Government for the rest of his career.

*   *   *   *   *   *

This prompts us to digress a little about *Robinson Crusoe*. It is an engaging feature of Defoe's novel that, both during Crusoe's solitude on the island and after he has acquired companions, it amuses him to picture himself as a monarch or grand lord of the manor. He has furnished himself with the appurtenances of noble existence, not only a 'Castle' but a 'Bower' or 'Country Seat'; he has 'weighty Affairs' on his mind, even if it is only making a cage for his parrot; and he calls 'a Council', though it has no other member.[4]

But if this is the daydream of a man clad in shaggy goatskins, it is none the less true that he is a monarch in fact, which is an enjoyable situation. It gives Crusoe 'a secret Kind of Pleasure', on surveying a delightful valley, to think 'that this was all my own, that I was King and Lord of all this Country indefeasibly, and had a Right of Possession; and if I could convey it, I might have it in Inheritance, as compleatly as any Lord of a Mannor in *England*'. His companions at table are his parrot, a royal favourite and the only person allowed to talk to him; his dog, 'now grown very old and crazy'; and two cats, who look forward to marks of his princely favour. 'It would have made a Stoick smile to have seen me and my little Family sit down to Dinner; there was my Majesty the Prince and Lord of the whole Island; I had the Lives of all my Subjects at my absolute Command. I could hang, draw, give Liberty, and take it away, and no Rebels among all my Subjects.'[5]

In many respects these daydreams and actions of Crusoe are given support by Defoe's political philosophy, as expounded in his *Jure Divino* (1706).[6] That the island belongs to Crusoe since he is the first European to find it, and that this makes him both ruler and landlord, with the right to convey the property, or (as he later does) lease it to tenants, is perfectly in the spirit of the poem. As for his fantasy that he has the lives of all his subjects at his absolute command, it puts us in mind of these lines in Book V of *Jure Divino*.

> If any single Man possess this Land,
> And had the Right, he must have the Command;
> If once he was but *Landlord of the Isle,*
> He *must be King*, because he own'd the Soil;
> No Man his just Succession could dispute;
> He must both make the Laws, and execute;
> No Laws cou'd ever be on him impos'd,
> His Claim of Right, the Peoples Claim *fore-clos'd*;
> And he that wou'd not to his Rule submit,
> *Must quit the Place*, the Place was all his Right.[7]

It is important, nevertheless, that there is no hint in the novel that Crusoe is a tyrant, or even a budding one. He is a man of scruple, often troubled in his mind over the rights and wrongs of killing innocent savages; and in a paternalistic way he is a kind master and friend to Friday. Nor, it seems, are the oaths that he receives or imposes as a monarch meant to recall the oaths of 'passive obedience' so bitterly vilified in Book IV of *Jure Divino*. Tyranny, as depicted in *Jure Divino*, is inextricably bound up with 'divine-right' delusions and the pretence that kings are gods, and there is nothing of this in Crusoe.

It is here that two arguments in *Jure Divino* need distinguishing. It is asserted at the opening of the poem, in memorable words, that all fallen humankind are potential tyrants.

> Nature has left *this Tincture in the Blood,*
> That all Men *would be Tyrants* if they cou'd:
> If they forbear their Neighbours to devour,
> 'Tis not for want of *Will*, but want *of Power*.[8]

By definition, the poet himself and his readers are included in this charge. It is therefore not so much an accusation as the statement of a fact of life, though one very salutary to remember.

It is right, therefore, that we should find Crusoe's power fantasies innocent and even half appealing. They are fantasies that, it is implied, we might have had ourselves, in his shoes, and they have no direct connection (though of course they have an indirect one) with the crimes of a Nero or a Sardanapalus. Crusoe, in this, as in other respects, is the average or representative man.

The point is brought out clearly by a passage in *The Farther Adventures of Robinson Crusoe* in which Crusoe is looking back, years later, on his return visit to his island. During his brief stay he used his authority to make property arrangements, settle local rivalries and establish Christianity, but after a few weeks he had succumbed to his 'rambling' propensity and had set off with his nephew for the East Indies, leaving the island to its fate. Now he blames himself severely for this as self-indulgent and irresponsible. He ought, he tells himself, to have taken a patent from the English Government to secure his property; should have brought new settlers with him; should have settled there himself; and should have fortified the place in the name of England and introduced commerce.

> But I was possest with a wandring Spirit, scorn'd all Advantages, I pleased my self with being the Patron of those People I placed there, and doing for them in a kind of haughty majestick Way, like an old Patriarchal Monarch; providing for them, as if I had been Father of the whole Family, as well as of the Plantation.[9]

What Crusoe is accusing himself of here is not of anything in the nature of tyranny, but of the more venial offence of behaving like an 'old Patriarchal Monarch' – a ruler like one of those autocratic Highland clan chieftains satirized in Book II of *Jure Divino*.

> The Prince with *Whoop* and *Whistling Trumpet* shrill,
> Summons his Slaves from ev'ry Neighb'ring Hill,
> Tells them, his Enemy's *Bull* has stole *his Cow*,
> And *Dire Revenge* th'obedient Rabble Vow.[10]

Nor – and this is the important point – do readers instinctively go along with Crusoe in his belated self-recrimination, any more than with his sense of guilt at rejecting his father's advice and the 'Blessings attending the middle Station of Life':[11] at least, they will not simply regard them as the book's 'message'. Defoe's novel just does not work in that way, and perhaps no complex novel could. If *Robinson Crusoe* has a 'message', it is a very different one, the one that most readers since Rousseau have found in it. It is that Crusoe's career is a story that no *arrière pensée*, or belated qualm of political correctness – no knowledge that an 'old Patriarchal Monarch' is a plague and a scandalous anachronism – can make seem other than humanly triumphant. *Robinson Crusoe*, that is to say, is not a political novel, and even more not a party-political one, for all that it has roots in political theory.

*   *   *   *   *   *

It is true that Defoe did not at once cease after *Robinson Crusoe* to do battle with rival Whig journalists. In particular he continued his vendetta against Richard Steele. On the first day of the year 1720 he launched a new periodical, entitled *The Commentator*, which would appear twice weekly until the 16th of the following September. It seems to be a kind of imitation of Addison and Steele's *Spectator*, and the Commentator has this in mind when he says it is not proper for a British subject to be 'an idle Spectator' at this time of day. The Commentator is a youngish man, inexperienced in the ways of the world and a beginner in the literary profession. He is a warm admirer of the present Whig Government, led by General Stanhope, James Craggs and the Earl of Sunderland; and, judging from an incident mentioned later, he would appear to be a Church of England man – though one tolerant enough to stroll into a meeting house.

When we first meet him, he has taken it into his head to launch a new journal. A friend tells him this is the quickest way to starve, but the Commentator has 'too much the Spirit of an Author' to listen. In his opening number he deliberately, though light-heartedly, flouts one or two of the conventions expected on such an occasion. It is usual for a journal editor to claim to be above 'party', but the Commentator stoutly affirms that his *is* a party-paper. He will claim to be impartial, but not neutral. In fact, he confesses, he would like everybody to have the same opinions as himself; but if he can even 'confirm one Doubting Member of the Commonwealth', he will consider it a sufficient reward – so long as 'the small article of *Copy-Money* be annex'd to it'.[12] (This reference to money, it may be noticed, breaks another taboo.)

His role, he decides, is simple: it is to praise the ministry for its adept handling of the Spanish war and to stress the amazing good fortune of Britain in having so just, so competent, so long-suffering a set of governors. Indeed, he writes, the Government may be said to do justice to everybody but itself, and this may be a weakness.[13]

– 177 –

He has a high opinion of himself and goes a round of the coffee houses, trying to discover what people think of his paper. He receives some ugly snubs in the process. A group of clergymen at Child's Coffee-house say that the new author would better concern himself, not with politics, but the peril from sceptics and atheists. But perhaps, he timidly suggests, '*this Writer may be a Layman, and would not presume to invade a Province that does not so properly belong to him*'. 'Sir', says one of the clerics crushingly, '*'Tis every Man's Province, whether of the Clergy or Laity, to do as much as in him lies to vindicate the Christian Religion in general, and the Church of England in particular*'. But, replies the Commentator, could not a journal editor, by defending the Government from the loads of dirt and infamy daily thrown at it, do for the Government what Jeremy Collier has done so magnificently for the stage? His question is received in silence, and he guesses that they suspect him of being a friend of a pestilent critic of the Government, Richard Steele. Such blows are compensated for, however, by his warm reception at another coffee house. There too they guess, to his credit this time, that his paper may be by Steele, or perhaps by the poet Ambrose Philips, and they make him blush by the handsome things they say.[14]

Part of what we are offered by this new journal is a fresh look, as if by a neophyte, at the workings of the journalistic industry. 'It is incredible', writes the Commentator on 8 January, 'what Quantitites of Goods have been drawn off in a few Years from *This great Magazine of Intelligence*, which yet remains inexhaustible. What heaps of *Nonsense* and *Forgery*! What Reams of *Declarations, Manifesto's, Hymns, Ballads,* and other merry Conceits! And what Loads of Weekly Journals! These are, literally speaking, *Loads* of Scandal and Sedition, which have been pack'd up, like Bales of Cloth, and sent by the *Carriers* and *Waggoners* into all Parts of the King's Dominions, to be duly distributed by the Agents of the Party in the several respective Counties.'

In a nice little episode (28 March), the Commentator relates how, during a tour of the Western counties, he puts up at a noted inn on the Western road, where the landlord ('a Jolly Red-fac'd Fellow') asks if he would like to look at the newspapers, which have just arrived. It makes him inquisitive, and over supper he gets the Landlord tipsy on his own '*Poison-Port*' and broaches the subject of these journals. '*Why, Landlord*', he says, '*you take in a great Number of these Papers. Sure they must cost you the Devil and all for Postage*'. No, no problem there, replies the Landlord; for he is Postmaster himself, and moreover he has several customers who subscribe for most of them, '*and they take them off my Hands again after my Guests have read them*'. An excellent plan, remarks the Commentator; and perhaps that means they cost him very little? Well, rather better than that, replies the Landlord. It would never do if they were to cost him anything. It was a little the other way round; and 'in the Openness of his Heart' he shows the Commentator his subscription book, with its complicated and profitable scheme of lending fees and reading fees and copy-making fees. It includes, a Defoean touch, 'Whitehall Evening-Post *taken in to please the Two Surveyors of the Posthouse, a rascally Paper*'.

One asks oneself, however, what to make of the Commentator's politics. Given his youth, his incautious frankness and his naivety, could Defoe be expecting the Government to take them very seriously? It hardly seems likely, and if the journal has a more serious political purpose, it seems to concern Richard Steele.

Steele was making himself felt again as an opposition journalist and was unpopular with the Government on several counts. Not only had he, in his journal *The Plebeian*, attacked the Government's cherished Peerage Bill of 1719,[15] he was also involved in a long-running quarrel with the Lord Chamberlain, his onetime friend and benefactor the Duke of Newcastle. In 1714 he had been given a royal licence, and later a patent, to run Drury Lane Theatre, together with four actor-managers. It was specified as his duty to reform the stage along Jeremy Collier's lines; however, by 1720 it was being said, in the press and elsewhere, that he had achieved very little in the way of reform, indeed was still offering much the same repertoire as thirty years before. His occasional choice of new plays for Drury Lane was said to be inept, and the lowbrow afterpieces to be a disgrace. Eventually, on 23 January 1720, the King, at Newcastle's instigation, issued a warrant revoking his licence.

Meanwhile, on 2 January (the day after the first appearance of the *Commentator*), Steele himself had launched a periodical called *The Theatre*, partly to continue his quarrel with Newcastle. It purported to be written by an elderly gentleman, 'Sir John Edgar', whose first venture into literature this was; and in the opening issue it argued (as Steele had earlier done in the *Tatler*) that the stage, when well regulated, was 'a most liberal and ingenuous diversion', and the profession of actor most ujustly despised. But since the stage was a representation of the world, Sir John intended to employ his pen on other subjects too, when the service of his country required it.

We hardly need look further for the reason why Defoe, an entrenched enemy of the stage, makes his Commentator an enthusiast for it, holding that Jeremy Collier has so much improved the national taste that, nowadays, 'Plays *are, properly speaking, almost the only* Innocent Diversions'.[16] Defoe's plan in his new journal, in part at least, is plainly to tease and harass Steele; and the motive for this must be made to appear not Puritan disapproval of the stage, but Steele's shortcomings as a spokesman for it. Moreover when, in the pages of *The Theatre*, 'Sir John Edgar' attacks the Government on political issues, Defoe's Commentator can, in responding, capitalize on Steele's theatrical troubles. One sees this going on, with a good deal of cleverness, in the *Commentator* for 15 February 1720. By this time the critic and disappointed playwright John Dennis has joined the onslaught on Steele, publishing a swingeing pamphlet against him (*The Character and Conduct of Sir John Edgar*), and, under the pseudonym 'Sir John Falstaffe', launching a periodical entitled *The Anti-Theatre*. The Commentator, who has been studying the 'advertisements' of this feuding in the newspaper, finds it 'a very melancholy Prospect' for the Nation.

> What, Poet against Patriot! Player against Poet! And Poet against Poet! ... I was in hopes, these much-to-be-lamented Differences, as they arose from small Beginnings, might have been amicably composed; and indeed it were to be wish'd further, that they might have ended in the *Union* of the *Two Houses*;[17] But instead of that, it is too visible, that the Seeds of this *Theatrical Fury* are every Day ripening into an open War.

As a declared lover of plays, the Commentator says, his feelings are too much disturbed by the danger threatening them. However, fortunately, his eye was also caught by other advertisements, which were of a healing nature ('though they were very much upon the *Anti* too'). For instance '*Antivenereal Pills, Antiscorbuticks*, with a *Compendious Treatise of the Itch*; and several others, which seem to be calculated wholly for the Health, Ease and Benefit of Mankind'. There ran through them, he says, an admirable 'Air of Veracity, Candor and Disinterestedness, and such an universal Benevolence to our afflicted Fellow-Creatures'.[18]

By this time Steele was much in the news, campaigning against the Government's scheme by which the South Sea Company should take over the national debt. The scheme was recommended for acceptance by a Commons committee on 1 February 1720, and on the following day Steele attacked it in a tract, *The Crisis of Property*. It argued that any attempt to meddle with the existing rights of annuitants, as was contemplated under the scheme, would bring scandal and dishonour on the nation; and he followed this two weeks later with *A Nation a Family*, which proposed that the entire national debt should be paid in the form of annuities for life.

His campaign also spilled over into the *Theatre*, and in the issue for 16 February Steele (referred to as 'the injur'd Knight') tells 'Sir John Edgar' that a pamphlet he is now printing, about paying the nation's debts (*A Nation a Family*), is based on the principle that 'I would provide for my Family as if it belongs to the Nation, and not for the Nation as if it belonged to my Family. Let others serve the Nation by taking care only of themselves; I will serve it with contempt of any thing for myself, but what I will enjoy in common with others.' 'Sir John', half flatteringly, says that this is 'too old-fashioned [i.e. too high-mindedly moral] even for me'.

The point of the Commentator's teasing about the 'universal Benevolence' offered in advertisements for patent medicines becomes clear. It is a hit, and rather a neat one, at Steele, whose tone does indeed sometimes sound a little over self-righteous. Equally, when the Commentator, in the issue for 19 February, discusses the devices for self-praise employed by hack writers, the chief target – this time explicitly – is Steele. Writing in dialogue, says the Commentator, is a valuable device, authorized by Cicero and other ancients.

> But for a Man to publish Letters address'd to himself, full of his own Praise, and in his own Works, methinks it somewhat too gross; the World sees too easily through the Disguise, and is too apt to conclude the Author and his Correspondent to be one and the same Person. What! Sometimes Sir John Edgar! and sometimes Sir Richard Steele! and both at the same Time, and in the same Paper! This is so like the Rehearsal,
>
> Sometimes a Fisher's Son, sometimes a Prince[19]
>
> that he is lost between one and t'other.

Steele devotes the issue of the *Theatre* for 19–22 March to a further attack on the South Sea plan, and the Commentator, in the number for 25 March, grows even more merciless. The only two people in Britain not to be gambling in South Sea stock, he says, are 'Sir *John Edgar*' and himself. As for himself, it arises from no disapproval of moneymaking, only the misfortune of having nothing to gamble with; but with Sir John the motive will certainly be different. 'Sir *John*, I know, would not take a poor Player's Bread from him for the riches of both the *Indies*; much less would he shew any countenance to a Project, which he thought destructive to the Good of his Country.' It is another instance of his '*universal Benevolence*'. His trouble is that 'because he means well himself, he is too apt to suspect that Nobody else does so'.

One of the 'pleasing Reflections' prompted by the recent advent of peace, remarks the Commentator, is that it is precisely the agents of war who have succeeded in creating peace. By this, evidently, he intends a compliment to Stanhope, who distinguished himself as a general before he became the head of the Government, but he widens it into praise of professional soldiers in general. They are sometimes accused of wishing to prolong war, but this is quite unjust – though it is their good fortune that they have a master (i.e. George I) who will never let them starve. Of one reward, however, they might well complain of being deprived: a worthy history of the amazing series of victories won by them in Flanders a decade or so ago. It was widely understood that 'a very Great Man' (he means Steele) was going to undertake this task, all the more so since he took subscriptions for it, yet nothing has so far emerged.[20] But no doubt, says the Commentator mock-solemnly, this was a great deal to ask of a man who has taken responsibility for 'the *State*, the *Stage*, and the *Funds*, besides many useful Projects for the Advancement of his private affairs' (a dig at Steele's ill-starred project, the Fish Pool) 'and the general Good of Mankind'.[21]

The *Theatre* came to an end with the issue for 5 April; and one gains the impression that, as a result, Defoe began to lose interest in his Commentator, a persona mainly invented for the purpose of teasing Steele. His chief topic now, and increasingly, became the South Sea fever, about which he took the line that the South Sea Company was an altogether different affair from John Law's famous Mississipi

'System' in France. In the autumn of 1719, when Law's financial system was at the height of its success, he had published a powerful critique of it (*The Chimera: or the French way of Paying National Debts*), predicting that, despite Law's great talents, the whole enterprise would end in disaster, being 'an inconceivable Species of meer Air and Shadow' only made possible by the arbitrary character of the French monarchy.[22] The South Sea Company, and the sudden rise in its stocks, were, he argued, a quite different matter. The company was solidly based, and it paid a regular dividend; and so long as it continued to do the latter, the furious buying and selling and the soaring price of its stock should not affect its intrinsic value. Indeed, they could benefit the country. In the words of a letter to the *Commentator*, quoted in the issue for 8 April, 'The publick Stock of the Nation is not a Farthing the more or less for the Difference in the Price. 'Tis all among our selves.'

By May the Commentator, like his fellow journalists, has taken alarm at the spread of the South Sea mania, but rather as a social evil than a financial one. Some said the 'projecting' madness would be difficult to cure, but the Commentator is sure a British Parliament will be equal to the challenge. All one can say for 'bubble' mania, he reflects ironically (13 June), is that it has found out the great secret of reconciling Whig and Tory, and of making Britons all subjects of one government and one king – and for this it shall have his panegyricks 'as long as Sun and Moon endures; nay, and after it too, by Candlelight'.

It was not till October that the South Sea Bubble finally and unmistakably burst and the Government, like the whole country, was seized by panic; but by this time the *Commentator* had ceased publication. It was succeeded on 5 October by a twice-weekly half-sheet journal entitled *The Director*, entirely concerned with the South Sea débâcle. It was written, from its fifth number, by Defoe, and like the later pages of the *Commentator* it is defensive of the Government and the South Sea Company, blaming the 'bubble', not only on the directors but, even more, on despicable stockjobbers and sheep-like investors, who ruin themselves by panic selling – or as Defoe puts it, employing a favourite trope, 'dying for fear of death'.[23]

The journal's theme, insistently reiterated, is that the South Sea Company needs to be distinguished from the 'bubble' surrounding it.

The Company (in the launching of which in 1711 Defoe was of course involved) was, the *Director* says, 'the best Project in the World', though it has been managed 'in the worst Manner that was ever known'.[24] But if it will pay a regular 5% dividend, as no doubt it can, it is itself perfectly sound, and owners of its stock are quite needlessly ruining themselves by panic selling.

> Never let us be anxious about the Price of the Stock: If 100 *l.* Stock will sell but for 200 at the Books, but will pay me the Interest of 400 *l.* at the usual Periods of Dividends, it will soon come up to be worth 400 at the Books too, in spite of Stock-jobbing, in spite of Scarcity of Money, or Want of Credit.[25]

The directors, it argues, may be divided into 'active' and 'passive', and the latter, who betrayed their trust to investors out of indolence, are the more to blame. But it is for the committee appointed to investigate them to decide as to their guilt or innocence. As to the rumour that there are 'great men' active in the affair behind the scenes, the *Director* is sceptical.[26]

But then on 5 November 1720 the *London Journal*, a radical Opposition organ, printed the first of a series of 'Cato's Letters', by Thomas Gordon and Sir John Trenchard, which argued the 'great men' accusation with much acerbity. They made it fairly plain that their leading suspect was Defoe's sometime patron the Earl of Sunderland, now First Lord of the Treasury, and they would hint (what was true) that Sunderland had induced Walpole, for a long time his enemy, to screen him from prosecution.

The *Director* reacted indignantly to 'Cato'. It complained that its authors wanted to ruin not only the South Sea directors but the Company itself – whereas its own 'Bent' had always been to restore peace and 'calm the Minds of Men allarm'd by hot Spirits, and as much as may be to open their Eyes to the Advantages of the *South-Sea* Scheme if rightly manag'd'.[27] It printed a pair of letters to the Editor (perhaps fictitious) defending it from the charge of wanting to shield the directors:

> If the Writers of Letters publish'd in the *London Journal*, pretend to shelter themselves under the popular Clamour, to raise the Mob upon your Paper Call'd the DIRECTOR, on pretence of your being an Advocate for the *South-Sea* Directors: Tell them, you shall take it for an evidence of their Guilt, and that you defy the Scandal.[28]

The ensuing issue (16 January) presents a balance-sheet for the South Sea Company, showing it to be in good health, after which the *Director* disappears from the scene.

*   *   *   *   *   *

One could more or less say that here, on this quiet note, Defoe's political career ends. Over the next decade he would be amazingly productive; in addition to his novels (*Moll Flanders, A Journal of the Plague Year, Colonel Jacque, Roxana* and *A New Voyage Round the World*) we owe to it some of his best non-fictional writing, for instance the *Tour Thro' the Whole Island of Great Britain* (1724–7), the *Complete English Tradesman* (1726) and the *Political*[29] *History of the Devil* (1726). But as a writer he has, no doubt with some relief, turned his back on politics.[30] In a word, the 'return of the prodigal' was a lasting affair.

APPENDIX A

THREE RECENTLY-DISCOVERED LETTERS FROM DEFOE TO GODOLPHIN (1708)[1]

[*To* Sidney Godolphin, Earl of Godolphin]
26 June 1708

My Lord,

It is really work enough, and requires some Application and Time also, to heal and Allay the Ferment that This late Affair has raised here,[2] Or indeed my Ld but to lay it asleep for a while, for Once in Three yeares it must revive, and perhaps Encrease, for mischief Seldome Declines.

Tis hard my Ld That Medicine should Thus turn to Poison, and what was Contrived to secure a Nation Should Expose it: The Trienniall Bill has This irreparable Mischief in it, That it keeps alive Our Divisions, and Sets us Triennially together by the Eares all Over the Nation.[3]

The remainder of Strife which my Ld had its beginning in the Center, is Now Diffused into The Circle; the Intrest makeing, Heaving, and Struggling, tho' it be now Spread in the Countrys remote from hence, is yet as Eagerly Pusht, and has in proportion as mischievous Causes, and as ill Effects as here; Nay as if They were a sport (tho' I look on them I Confess with another view) and that the Gentlemen Could Divert Themselves with the Distractions of their Country. The D of Argile[4] and the E of Marr[5] have been as it were Playing a Game at Elections in Kinross and Clackmannon, two shires united by the Treaty. Both the Gentlemen They set up were of One Side, and both right, and both the Gentlemen Setting Them up are So also, But whether it were private respect to the Persons, or relation or Humour, or Triall of Skill, I kno' not, but they made the Election a meer Farce. Lieutenant Generall Ross[6] and Dalrymple of Glenmuir[7] are the Candidates; The Earl of Marr setts up the last *his Estate lying in The place* there. There are but 15 or 16 Voters in all, of These *Dalrymple* has 13, *Ross* however makes up Eight – and Then both fall to protesting. Ross protests against Dalrymple's Voters, that is Severall of them, Enough to bring him to a Majority. Mr Dalrymple Protests That of Rosses Eight Freeholders, Seavin of Them are Fagots,[8] Made Barons[9] but for the Day, a Sad Scandalous Method now taken up here, and which must I hope receiv some Checq in Parliament.

From This Strife in the Country they Come to Town, and Fall to a Pen and Ink Scuffle, Scandalous Enough. Dalrymple puts it into the Town News paper,[10] That he is Chosen; Ross Puts it in next day that he protests against the Election, and resolves to Dispute it, having protested against his Voters; Dalrymple Put it in again, That Ross had but Eight votes, and he protested against Seaven of them, and Thus they go on Exposeing themselves, *a la Mob*, and Serve for nothing but to make Their Enemyes Laugh at both.

In the North my Ld the Elections Go very well, and if the Ld Strathnaver[11] be right, There is none wrong; he is son to the E of Sutherland,[12] who it seems is revoted to the Squadr.,[13] and is one of those they call the *Squadruche* or little Squadroni, but he married the Daughter of Morrison of Prestongrange,[14] by whom and the E of Glasgow[15] he is Chiefly guided; besides That he has a regiment of Foot in the Forces here, without which he is hardly able to subsist, and ought by that to be Taught his Duty.

The Country Elections My Ld are not yet all Over, and Therefore I can not Draw your Ldpp The Table I mentioned and which I purpose to do, as soon as all the Names are known.

In my Last[16] my Lord I Lay'd before your Ldpp an Humble request on my own Account about the Audit of the Customs,[17] founded on your Ldpps former Goodness to me, and the Assurance I had from your Ldpps Letter, that if any Patent Place offered in the Customes here, your Ldpp would reserve one for me.

When I look Farther into This Case here, and See how Easily I may Enjoy this place Under your Ldpps Favour, and be Entirely Concealed from the wholl world, How it will Enable me to be allwayes Serving her Majtie both in Public, and private – Nay how I might even officiat Myself, and give very Little Umbrage here, but by a Deputy might have it entirely Concealed in England,[18] and so be Free to be Disposed as her Majties Pleasure should think fitt – when I see this, and look back on the many Occasions in which your Ldpp has done me Good, I Flatter My Self, that your Ldpp will Think of me in this affair.

I have now no Intercessors with your Ldpp, I have nothing but your Ldpps Meer Goodness, and the Favours of That Promise to Depend upon, And my Ld this puts me upon filling my Letters with This unwellcom Importunity – Nor my Lord do I plead any Merit, I have been willing to Merit, but I am none of those that put a great Vallue on their own Performances. My Chief Merit, My Ld, is the suffering part, by which I am reduc'd to a Circumstance I was ever unaccquainted with, and have little but my Integrity to recommend me to your Ldpp.

Yet my Ld according to the Common rate of Merit, I have some Merit too, *for Men now Think they Merit when they do Their Duty*. In the Affair of the Union My Ld I was placed here with assurance of Support; I did here my Uttmost, I had my Share of the Hazard of the Union More Than any man; Every man more or less (but I) reaped some share of her Majties Bounty on that Occasion.[19] But *had not your Ldpp Took me up* I was left 8 months with out Subsistence; Nay out of what your Ldpps Bounty remitted me, vizt. £100 to bring me away,[20] £18: – : – was stopt upon me at N Castle, in the hands of The Person it was remitted to for Postage of Letters; which Letters had been Frank't as I Thought upon the publick Account. So That upon the wholl, I can safely assure your Ldpp I had not subsistence while I was here, Till your Ldpps Goodness relieved me, which I can never Omit letting your Ldpp know, it is Impossible I can forgett.

Now My Lord an occasion offers to restore a Man Crusht by Inumerable Disasters, and to Make a Life Easy, that will for Ever be a Volunteer in your Ldpps Intrest, whether Private or Publick, that Dares be faithfull, and Can not be unthankfull. If your Ldpp shall Think fitt to bestow This Favour on me, and I may have a hint from your Ldpp of the method your Ldpp will be pleased to Direct it in, I shall then Trouble your Ldpp with my Farther Thoughts about it.

I kno' your Ldpp will be sollicited by Mr Tilson,[21] but my Ld That Gentleman Enjoys Two very Good Things allready; other Powerful Sollicitations your Ldpp may have, whereas I have nothing to move your Ldpp with but the same Bounty, and Goodness, That moved

your Ldpp to Think on me in a prison,[22] and to Fetch me back from a deserted Case in This Country, and to Honour me Since that with a Confidence which I am Endeavouring Faithfully to Improve to your Ldpps Service. I lay Therefore my request at your Ldpps Feet and am
   May it please your Ldpp
                    your Ldpps Most Humble & Obed't Servt
                           De Foe.
Edinb. June 26. 1708.

[*To* Sidney Godolphin, Earl of Godolphin]
29 June 1708

My Lord,

I have little of moment to Trouble your Ldpp with this Post. I am Applying, as I hinted to your Ldpp in my Last, to healing as much as Possible The breaches of This last Combustion, which I assure your Ldpp are not Small: This City My Ld seems to me like the City of Naples after a Vesuvian Eruption, when The people are Clearing Their streets and Cleaning their houses, of the Cinders, the Ashes, and Bituminous stuff the Emblem of Hell has Thrown out upon Them. The people here Universally Censure The Conduct of The nobillity and foresee that The Visible persuit of Private Intrest among Them gives Them very little Hopes of any Public Good from Them.

I have been in Conference with some of The Gentlemen Since the Election, and Find they are not a little anxious least her Majtie resenting Their behaviour should use them as They Deserv.

But I must not forget to remind your Ldpp how the party boast here, That the E of Orkney[23] is gone Directly to Harwich in Order for Flanders; and that as he Influenc'd severall of the officers of the Army here, so he is to Cultivate The same Intrest in the Army, and to form his Party there. It is Enough for mee to Accquaint your Ldpp of this; your Ldpp knows well who it is proper should be made Sencible of this Design,[24] which I believe is really their next Thing in view.

Enclosed I send your Ldpp the printed paper I promised (in my Last but one) should Come last Post,[25] but Could not be ready; your Ldpp will see by it The steps I am Taking. It would be a most usefull Encouragement to kno' if your Ldpp approves This, and My Design of Dispersing it over the wholl Island, in a Method I noted to your Ldpp was formally Done in the Case of the reply to the Memoriall.[26]

It is but a short piece, but I am perswaded it may be usefull, and I shall Follow it with Another,[27] and perhaps a Third, to expose the Conjunction of These men with the Enemies of the Government. I have sent this up this post to be printed in England;[28] your Ldpp will perceive I have Disguised the Stile, and I am perswaded no body will so much as guess it is mine.

I proposed to your Ldpp Spending Some Time among The Towns, and Gentlemen, &c., in Order to propagate the work I am alwayes Upon, Viz. of reconciling People here to Their Own Intrest and to the Government; and fortifying them against Such Notions as are now spread about to poison their Principles. I am waiting your Ldpps Approbation of That Design, or what other Commands your Ldpp May have for me, being ready to Obey your Ldpp Orders.

I am, May I Please your Ldpp

your Ldpps Most Humble & obedt Servt

(signed) De Foe.

Edinb. June 29. 1708.

I am oblig'd to ask your Ldpps pardon for not sending this last post; the Press kept the sheet so long I lost the Post.

[*To* Sidney Godolphin, Earl of Godolphin]

3 July 1708

My Lord,

I enclosed your Ldpp in my Last a Printed sheet Chiefly to show your Ldpp a Specimen of the Steps I am Takeing to Illuminate the Darkness of an Imposed-upon people, and to kno' if your Ldpp Approves my Thots upon That Subject.

I am Spending my time here, as I formerly Noted, to heal the wide breaches this Party making Season has made among the people, which are indeed too large, and may not be without Very Unhappy Consequences in the Course of Time. I Can not but say This affair has serv'd to highten the aversion to the Union, which I was in hopes had begun to lessen apace; But as the Uneasy people here are fond of Laying Every Thing to the charge of the Union, so now they say, and perhaps with too much Truth, That The Squadroni receiv all Their Support from England, and that all this Division is from the Union.

It were Therefore to be Wished that while The Squadroni really sink in Intrest here as They have done by These Elections They might be resolutely Discountenanced in England, and above all if Possible Divided; That as There is a Visible Inclination in This Nation against them it may be Encouraged from England, for my Ld the present Division here is Onely kept up on Two Accounts: *Hope* in Their Own Party that they will support them and be able by Their Influence above to do mighty Things for Them – and but for This some who fawned upon Them would not Dare'd to have appeared, I mean such of the Queens Servants as are Gone over to Them[29] – and *Secondly Fear* in the other Party Least they should prevail and That then Their resentment should affect Them here. My Ld Forbess,[30] a Poor Depending Gentleman with whom I had a Conversation on This head, is an Eminent Instance. Your Ldpp will Take his Own words to me in a Confidence to which I hope your Ldpp will Conceal his name.

> "What can such a man as I do, They pretend they are sure of Kings, They show me Letters from Noblemen,[31] that I kno' the Queen Trusts – I kno' my own Circumstances, if I appear against Them and they prevail I am undone, If I oppose the present Ministry I am in Danger – I kno' no better way Than to Vote for Some of both Those that I think are most in the Generall Intrest –"

This my Lord was the Principle That really Chose The *Six*[32] and with out which They had never been Elected, and if Their projects in England Fail, Their Intrest here will Entirely Sink with a very little good Mannagement.

I have had some farther occasion to hint[33] Letters sent hither, and am onely Cautious Least your Ldpp find it necessary to use These hints, where perhaps those Gentlemen May obtain some Guess, that they Come by my hand, or may See my writeing; I Entreat one word from your Ldpp if I may be assured that my letters are secured in your Ldpp's own hands and no hints of my Intelligence Comes near those persons, Since I shall be Utterly Unable to make the steps I am Takeing *another way* in the least Effectuall, if either My P. s. . . .[34] or any of the Noble men formerly Mentioned Can Come to the Knowledge of it. Besides my Ld it would sacrifice my Character as to Integrity, which

I do not Think I Injure at all in Serving your Ldpp, but should seem to blott by Maintaining a Counter Correspondence &c., tho' at the same Time *as your Ldpp noted* it is in the Main for those Gentlemens Services.

I Entreat your Ldpp for This Caution; I doubt not but your Ldpp will be Carefull *Even of Me* while I am Thus Engaged in your Service, but I also humbly Suggest, that it will be for your Ldpps Service to Keep me perfectly Concealed; Especially My Ld while I am Insinuating my Self into the Cabinet of the Party that are Acting Against your Ldpps Intrest – and My Ld if I am but preserved from being Suspected on the Subject of These Letters to your Ldpp I dare assure your Ldpp I shall be in the very Cabinet of your Ldpps Enemyes, where I shall never fail to promote your Ldpps Intrest.

This is a most Serious request, and I do not presume to make it to your Ldpp without Some little Ground of Apprehension that Some hints have been obtain'd of my Corresponding with your Ldpp. If I may have the Honour of one line from your Ldpp On This Affair, I shall be larger in Explaining particulars to your Ldpp in my next.

I am

    May it please your Ldpp

                Your Ldpps Most obedient Humble
                       and Faithfull Servt
                       De Foe.

Edinb. July 3. 1708.

I enclose to your Ldpp another of the prints Least the former be not arrived.

APPENDIX B

Sir Andrew Politick's Letter, *Mist's Journal*, 25 October 1718

MIST, thou Party Oracle, answer the Doubts of the Nation, if thou art able, or tell us thy Oracle is silent in these Things, and that we are to expect no Illuminations of this kind from thee. We are running into a War, I suppose, that, I find *No Body can deny, deny*,[1] &c. Prithee tell us, *Mist*, for I ask it now without any Reflection upon the King and Government, or any Offence to Scots George[2] or the Whigs; I say, tell us what it is we are going to fight for? Who it is we are going to fight with? Whose Quarrel embarks us? And what have we to do with that Quarrel? What are the Pretences? How are these Pretences made good? What Condition are we in to carry it on, and that will be the Consequences of the War, whether we are conquer'd or may conquer.

1st. We are supposed to be running into a War; this I think I might make good by looking back on what is past, viz. first, we have attack'd the Spanish Fleet and defeated them.[3] 2dly. They have rejected our Proposals of Peace, and have taken our Merchant Ships, seized our Effects, &c. and what can follow but A WAR?

But prithee, Man, tell me, is here not a Hole for the Spaniards to creep out at, a Way for them to trick all the Confederates *but one* into a Peace, and then fight *with that one*? They tell us the Spaniards have till the 2d of November their Stile.[4] Now if the King of Spain should answer the Regent of France and the Emperor, that he accepts of the Proposals, then there is an End of the War on their Side; but as the King of Spain may alledge that this has no Relation to the new Quarrel between England and Spain, viz. to our attacking the Spaniards, which the King of Spain calls a Rupture on our Side; so when this may be done the Peace is made with the rest; but may not the War be left to go on only between Us and Spain, pray tell me what you have to say to this, whether I am right or wrong?

If am wrong tell me how it is to be, if you can?

If I am right tell me what a fine Kettle of Fish we are frying?

2dly. *What is it we fight for?* The general Answer is *Peace*: I am to believe his Majesty's Design is to settle and preserve the Peace of Europe: But then our Tories, who you know are inquisitive People, say we had Peace before, and they do not see what need we have to break our own Peace to preserve other People's: They say they do not see how the Quarrel between the Spaniards and the Emperor would have affected our Peace, but that *as the Dutch said* they would be willing to have used all good Offices to preserve a Peace in Italy, but that they see no Concern so great in it, as that they should enter into a War about it: That in particular they think the Protestant Cause is not concerned in the Quarrel, seeing it was only one Papist Power against another: That they do not see there is any exorbitant Power to crush in the Case; for if there is any difference, it is the Emperor that is strongest, and much more likely by his Strength to be a Terror to his Neighbours than the King of Spain; so that *they say* they do not see what Occasion, much less what Necessity we had to meddle in a Quarrel, of which at most it might be said the Peace of all the Protestant Part of the World might have been preserved without it; pray what can you say to all these Objections?

3dly. *Whose Quarrel is it?* The Answer I suppose must be, that it is the Emperor's Quarrel, otherwise I cannot guess whose it is: Now several honest ignorant People ask me this Question, viz. What Business have we to take up the Emperor's Quarrel? And why must we pay for a War in the Emperor's Quarrel, to secure Kingdoms and Countries to the Emperor? They remember, *they say*, that it cost them a great many Taxes in former Times to send Men to fight for the Emperor, and the Effect of the War was to get Naples and Milan, and the Spanish Low Countries for the Emperor; and *they say*, they think it is hard if the Emperor cannot keep them when he has got them: That if it is our Business to keep him in Possession of our Dominions, as well as to conquer them for him, then we are a kind of Landlords to him, and they think he should pay us some Rent that we might the better afford it.

4thly. As for the Pretences which are made use of for this War by the Whigs, for I need not meddle with what the Government says, the most I have met with are, that the K of Great Britain is bound as Guarrantee of the Neutrality of Italy, to preserve the Possession of the Emperor there: Pray tell me if it be true, for I hear that the Spaniards say that the Guarrantee was at an End when the General Peace was made; and if not, pray why are not the Dutch engaged, and obliged to do it as well as we, and what need is there to ask them to come into a new Confederacy on that Account?

5thly. What Condition are we in to carry on this new War? and are the Advantages to us equal to the Loss of our Trade with Spain; and the encreasing our Debt at home? especially if the latter be as Mr. H[utcheson],[5] a Member of Parliament has represented it, viz. That instead of lessening the Publick Debts, we are run God knows how many Millions in Debt since the last Peace? And, prithee, tell me, if thou can'st, how the Advantages of a War or the Necessities of War can be equal to the Distresses of a Nation, whose Debt, as his Majesty himself has most justly expressed, is already insupportable?

6thly. Describe, if you can, or at least suggest in some rational Manner what will be the Consequences of this War, and under this Head I desire to be told, Mist, whether you think 'tis rational for us to believe that France who are the principal People to carry it on by Land, will be hearty in pushing Spain to Extremities in this War? Will France, who has spilt so much Blood and Treasure to set King Philip on the Throne of Spain, join heartily now and spend more Blood and Treasure to pull him down again? And will they do this for the Emperor, the ancient, and I may almost say hereditary Rival of the French Glory? And pray Mr. Oracle, tell us, how and whence comes this great Confidence in the French which we have taken up so lately,[6] that we the Whigs can depend with so much satisfaction upon France now, who [sic] so little while ago they treated us as the most perfidious Nation in the World; and if the French at last should not push the War on heartily by Land; pray what think you shall we make of it by Sea?

7thly. Besides, Mr. Mist, unless the French shall prohibite Trade too with Spain as well as make a War with them, will you inform me what the Consequence of the War will be, and whether they will not gain from us the Trade to Spain, and so make a politick Juggle of the War, viz. to carry off all their Manufactures, engross the Trade to Spain, import all the Spanish Wool, and sell it to us at second Hand, and so while they see us carry on the War in earnest, they may carry it on in jest, and gain the Trade from us by a pretended War with Spain, which it is evident they could not gain by the Peace: Therefore tell me, Mr. Mist, if the first Token of the French Sincerity in this War would not be a general Prohibition of Commerce with Spain, and whether you think they will come into that or we?

8thly. Father [*sic*], pray tell us, if you can, what Loss our Merchants will now sustain by seizing their Ships and Effects in Spain?[7] I do not say it will amount to so many Millions as some pretend it will; but if you can get a true Account of it, and calculate it at any positive Sum; then tell me if you think it is probable that ever Spain will be brought to make Restitution upon a Peace; and whether ever it was known that upon former Breaches with Spain, when the Spaniards have seized our Merchants Effects, as they have done now, they ever did make Restitution upon the Conclusion of a Peace? and then till [*sic*] us what amends will any Peace that bema may de [*sic*, may be made?] without such Restitutions to the poor ruined Families which suffer by it?

9thly. Tell us whether the King of Spain has not sufficiently paid himself for the Loss of 11 Men of War taken in the fight off Sicily, and what England in particular has gained by that Victory, besides what we may suffer still by the seizing our Ships in the Streights, and in the West-Indies before our Merchants may have a full Information that there is a War.

10thly. Though it may be true that in the Prosecution of this War, we may be able to commit great Spoil upon the Spanish Plate Fleets, and first and last may take great Quantities of rich Merchandizes from them, as well as immense Sums in Silver and Gold; yet will it be true, that in such Cases, 1st. The private Families which are ruined now may be never the better for the Gain, the Prizes taken from the Enemy being ever applied to make good the Loss of the Prizes taken by the Enemy from us: And 2dly. That in those Spoils made on the Spanish Plate Fleets, the Spaniards themselves abstractedly considered, are generally the least Sufferers; and we may rather be said in that Case, to rob our Friends, nay our selves, rather than spoil our Enemies, since the Effects of the Galleons are principally or chiefly the Estates of the Dutch, the English, the French, the Genoese, the Venetians, the Leghornese, and the Portuguese; and as to the

Spaniards, I have heard it affirm'd, that not one fifth Part is at any Time properly to be reckoned theirs.

Speak home to these Points if you can, Mist, and your Merit shall always be acknowledged by

Your old Friend,
Sir Andrew Politick.

APPENDIX C

An Appeal to Honour and Justice, tho' it be of his Worst Enemies. By Daniel De Foe. Being a True Account of his Conduct in Publick Affairs.

Jerem. xviii. 18. Come and let us smite him with the Tongue, and let us not give heed to any of his Words.

London: Printed for J. Baker, at the Black Boy in Pater-Noster-Row. 1715.[1]

An APPEAL to *Honour* and *Justice*, &c.

I Hope the Time is come at last, when the Voice of moderate Principles may be heard; hitherto the Noise has been so great, and the Prejudices and Passions of Men so strong, that it had been but in vain to offer at any Argument, or for any Man to talk of giving a Reason for his Actions: And this alone has been the Cause why, when other Men,[2] who, I think, have less to say in their own Defence, are appealing to the Publick, and struggling to defend themselves, I alone have been silent under the infinite Clamours and Reproaches, causeless Curses, unusual Threatnings, and the most unjust and injurious Treatment in the World.

I hear much of Peoples calling out to punish the Guilty; but very few are concern'd to clear the Innocent. I hope some will be inclin'd to Judge impartially, and have yet reserv'd so much of the Christian, as to believe, and at least to hope, that a rational Creature cannot abandon himself so as to act without some Reason, and are willing not only to have me defend my self, but to be able to answer for me where they hear me causlesly insulted by others, and therefore are willing to have such just Arguments put into their Mouths as the Cause will bear.

As for those who are prepossess'd, and according to the modern Justice of Parties are resolv'd to be so, *Let them go*, I am not arguing with them, *but against them*; they act so contrary to Justice, to Reason, to Religion, so contrary to the Rules of Christians and of good Manners, that they are not to be argued with, but to be expos'd, or entirely neglected. I have a Receipt against all the Uneasiness which it may be supposed to give me, and that is, to contemn Slander, and think it not worth the least Concern; neither should I think it worth while to give any Answer to it if it were not on some other Accounts, of which I shall speak as I go on.

If any Man ask me, why I am in such hast to publish this Matter at this time? Among many other good Reasons which I could give, these are some:

1. I think I have long enough been made *Fabula Vulgi*,[3] and born the Weight of general Slander; and I should be wanting to Truth, to my Family, and to my Self, if I did not give a fair and true State of my Conduct for impartial Men to judge of, when I am no more in being to answer for my self.

2. By the Hints of Mortality, and by the Infirmities of a Life of Sorrow and Fatigue, I have reason to think that I am not a great way off from, if not very near to the great Ocean of Eternity, and the time may not be long e're I embark on the last Voyage: Wherefore, I think, I should *even Accounts* with this World before I go, that no Actions (Slanders) may lie against my Heirs, Executors, Administrators, and Assigns, to disturb them in the peaceable Possession of their Father's (Character) Inheritance.

3. I fear, *God grant I have not a second Sight in it*, that this lucid Interval of Temper and Moderation which shines, *tho' dimly too* upon us at this time, will be but of short Continuance, and that some Men, who know not how to use the Advantage God has put into their Hands with Moderation, will push, in spight of the best Prince in the World, at such extravagant Things, and act with such an intemperate Forwardness, as will revive the Heats and Animosities which wise and good Men were in the hopes should be allay'd by the happy Accession of the King to the Throne.

It is and ever was my Opinion, that Moderation is the only Vertue by which the Peace and Tranquillity of this Nation can be preserv'd, even the King himself, *I believe his Majesty will allow me that Freedom*, can only be happy in the Enjoyment of the Crown by a moderate Administration; if his Majesty should be oblig'd, contrary to his known Disposition, to joyn with intemperate Councils, if it does not lessen his Security, I am perswaded it will lessen his Satisfaction. It cannot be pleasant or agreeable, and, *I think*, it cannot be safe to any just Prince to Rule over a divided People, split into incens'd and exasperated Parties: Tho' a skilful Mariner may have Courage to master a Tempest, and goes fearless thro' a Storm, yet he can never be said to delight in the Danger; a fresh fair Gale, and a quiet Sea, is the Pleasure of his Voyage, and we have a Saying worth Notice to them that are otherwise minded, *Qui amat periculum periibat in illo*.[4]

To attain at the happy Calm, which, as I say, is the Safety of *Britain*, is the Question which should now move us all; and he would Merit to be call'd the Nation's Physician that could prescribe the Specifick for it. I think I may be allow'd to say, a *Conquest of Parties* will never do it; *a Balance of Parties MAY*. Some are for *the former*; they talk high of Punishments, letting Blood, revenging the Treatment they have met with, and the like: If they, *not knowing what Spirit they are of*, think this the Course to be taken, let them try their Hands, I shall give them for lost, and look for their Downfal *from that time*; for the Ruin of all such Tempers slumbereth not.

It is many Years that I have profess'd my self an Enemy to all Precipitations in publick Administrations; and often I have attempted to shew, that hot Councils have ever been destructive to those who have made use of them: Indeed they have not always been a Disadvantage to the Nation, as in King *James* II's Reign, where, as I have often said in Print, his Precipitation was the Safety of us all; and if he had proceeded temperately and politickly, we had been undone, *Fælix quem faciunt*.[5]

But these things have been spoken when your Ferment has been too high for any thing to be heard; whether you will hear it now or not, *I know not*, and therefore it was that I said, *I fear* the present Cessation of Party-Arms will not hold long.

These are some of the Reasons why I think this the proper Juncture for me to give some Account of my self, and of my past Conduct to the World; and that I may do this as effectually as I can, being perhaps never more to speak from the Press, I shall, as concisely as I can, give an Abridgment of my own History during the few unhappy Years I have employ'd my self, or been employ'd in Publick in the World.

Misfortunes in Business having unhing'd me from Matters of Trade, it was about the Year 1694. when I was invited by some Merchants, with whom I had corresponded abroad, and some also at home, to settle at *Cadiz* in *Spain*, and that with Offers of very good Commissions; but Providence, which had other Work for me to do, placed a secret Aversion in my Mind to quitting *England* upon any account, and made me refuse the best Offers of that kind, to be concern'd with some eminent Persons at home, in proposing *Ways* and *Means* to the Government for raising Money to supply the Occasions of the War then newly begun. Some time after this, I was, without the least Application of mine, and being then seventy Miles from *London*, sent for to be Accomptant to the Commissioners of the Glass Duty, in which Service I continued to the Determination of their Commission.[6]

During this time, there came out a vile abhor'd Pamphlet, in very ill Verse, written by one Mr. *Tutchin*,[7] and call'd, THE FOREIGNERS: In which the Author, *who he was I then knew not*, fell personally upon the King himself, and then upon the *Dutch* Nation; and after having reproach'd his Majesty with Crimes, that his worst Enemy could not think of without Horror, he sums up all in the odious Name of FOREIGNER.

This fill'd me with a kind of Rage against the Book, and gave birth to a Trifle which I never could hope should have met with so general an Acceptation as it did, I mean, *The True-Born-Englishman*.[8] How this Poem was the Occasion of my being known to his Majesty; how I was afterwards receiv'd by him; how Employ'd; and how, above my Capacity of deserving, Rewarded, is no Part of the present Case, and is only mention'd here as I take all Occasions to do for the expressing the Honour I ever preserv'd for the Immortal and Glorious Memory of that Greatest and Best of Princes, and who it was my Honour and Advantage to call Master as well as Sovereign, whose Goodness to me I never forgot, neither can forget; and whose Memory I never patiently heard abused, nor ever can do so; and who had he liv'd, would never have suffered me to be treated as I have been in the World.

But Heaven for our Sins remov'd him in Judgment. How far the Treatment he met with, from the Nation he came to save, and whose Deliverance he finished, was admitted by Heaven to be a Means of his Death, I desire to forget for their sakes who are guilty; and if this calls any of it to mind, it is mention'd to move them to treat him better who is now with like Principles of Goodness and Clemency appointed by God, and the Constitution, to be their Sovereign; least he that protects righteous Princes, avenges the Injuries they receive from an ungrateful People, by giving them up to the Confusions their Madness leads them to.

And in their just acclamations at the happy accession of His present Majesty to the Throne, I cannot but advise them to look back, and call to mind who it was that first Guided them to the Family of *Hanover*, and to pass by all the Popish Branches of *Orleans* and *Savoy*, recognizing the just authority of Parliament, in the undoubted Right of Limiting the Succession, and Establishing that Glorious Maxim of our Settlement, (*viz.*) That *it is inconsistent with the Constitution of this Protestant Kingdom to the Govern'd by a Popish Prince.*[9] I say let them call to mind who it was that guided their Thoughts first to the Protestant Race of our own Kings in the House of *Hanover*, and that it is to King *William*, next to Heaven it self, to whom we owe the Enjoying a Protestant King at this time. I need not go back to the particulars of his Majesty's Conduct in that Affair, his Journey in Person to the Country of *Hanover*, and the Court of *Zell*; his particular management of the Affair afterwards at home, perfecting the Design, by naming the Illustrious Family to the Nation, and bringing about a Parliamentary Settlement to effect it,[10] entailing thereby the Crown in so effectual a manner as we see has been sufficient to prevent the worst Designs of our *Jacobite* People in behalf of the Pretender; a Settlement, together with the subsequent Acts which followed it, and the Union with *Scotland* which made it unalterable, that gave a compleat Satisfaction to those who knew and understood it, and removed those terrible apprehensions of the Pretender (which some entertain'd) from the minds of others who were yet as zealous against him as it was possible for any to be: Upon this Settlement, as *I shall shew presently*, I grounded my Opinion, *which I often express'd*, (*viz.*) that I did not see it possible the

Jacobites could ever set up their Idol here; and I think my Opinion abundantly justify'd in the Consequences, of which by and by.

This Digression, as a debt to the Glorious Memory of King *William*, I could not in Justice omit, and as the Reign of his present Majesty is esteem'd Happy, and look'd upon as a Blessing from Heaven by us, it will most necessarily lead us to bless the Memory of King *William* to whom we owe so much of it; How easily could his Majesty have led us to other Branches, whose Relation to the Crown might have had large pretences? What Prince but would have submitted to have Educated a Successor of their Race in the Protestant Religion for the sake of such a Crown – ? But the King, who had our Happiness in View, and saw as far into it as any humane sight could Penetrate, who knew we were not to be Govern'd by unexperienc'd Youths; that the Protestant Religion was not to be Establish'd by Political Converts; and that Princes under *French* Influence, or Instructed in *French* Politicks, were not proper Instruments to preserve the Liberties of *Britain*, fixt his Eyes upon the Family who now possesses the Crown, as not only having an undoubted Relation to it by Blood, but as being first and principally Zealous and Powerful assertors of the Protestant Religion and Interest against Popery; And *Secondly*, stored with a visible Succession of worthy and promising Branches, who appear'd equal to the Weight of Government, quallified to fill a Throne, and guide a Nation which, without Reflection, are not famed to be the most easy to Rule in the World.

Whether the Consequence has been a Credit to King *William*'s Judgment I need not say, I am not Writing Panegyricks here, but doing justice to the Memory of the King my Master, who I have had the Honour very often to hear express himself with great satisfaction, in having brought the Settlement of the Succession to so good an Issue; and to repeat his Majesty's own Words, *That he knew no Prince in* Europe *so fit to be King of* England*, as the Elector of* Hanover. I am persuaded, without any Flattery, that if it should not every way answer the Expectations his Majesty had of it, the fault will be our own: God Grant the King may have more Comfort of His Crown than we suffer'd King *William* to have.

The King being Dead, and the Queen Proclaim'd, the Hot Men of that Side, as Hot Men of all Sides do, Thinking the Game in their own Hands, and all other People under their Feet, began to run out into those mad Extreams, and precipitate themselves into such Measures, as according to the Fate of all intemperate Councils, ended in their own Confusions, and threw them at last out of the Saddle.

The Queen, who, tho' willing to favour the High Church Party, did not thereby design the Ruin of those of she did not Employ, was soon alarm'd at their wild Conduct, and turn'd them out,[11] adhering to the moderate Councils of those who better understood, or more faithfully pursued her Majesty's and their Countries Interest.

In this Turn fell Sir *Edw. Seymour's* Party,[12] for so the High Men were then call'd; and to this Turn, we owe the Conversion of several other Great Men, who became *Whigs* upon that Occasion, which it is known they were not before; which Conversion afterwards begat that unkind Distinction of Old Whig, and Modern Whig,[13] which some of the former were with very little Justice pleased to run up afterwards to an Extreme very pernicious to both.

But I am gone too far in this Part. I return to my own Story. In the Interval of these Things, and during the Heat of the first Fury of High-flying, I fell a Sacrifice for writing against the Rage and Madness of that High Party, and in the Service of the Dissenters: What Justice I met with, and above all what Mercy, is too well known to need a Repetition.[14]

This Introduction is made that it may bring me to what has been the Foundation of all my further Concern in publick Affairs, and will produce a sufficient Reason for my adhering to those whose Obligations upon me were too strong to be resisted, even when many things were done by them which I could not approve; and for this Reason it is that I think it is necessary to distinguish how far I did, or did not adhere to, or joyn in or with the Persons or Conduct of the late Government: And those who are willing to judge with Impartiality and Charity, will see reason to use me the more tenderly in their Thoughts, when they weigh the Particulars.

I will make no Reflections upon the Treatment I met with from the People I suffer'd for, or how I was abandon'd even in my Sufferings, at the same time that they acknowledg'd the Service it had been to their Cause; but I must mention it to let you know, that while I lay friendless and distress'd in the Prison of *Newgate*, my Family ruin'd, and my self, without Hope of Deliverance, a Message was brought me from a Person of Honour,[15] who, till that time, I had never had the least

Acquaintance with, or Knowledge of, other than by Fame, or by Sight, as we know Men of Quality by seeing them on publick Occasions. I gave no present Answer to the Person who brought it, having not duly weighed the Import of the Message; the Message was by Word of Mouth thus: *Pray ask that Gentleman, what I can do for him?* But in return to this kind and generous Message, I immediately took my Pen and Ink, and writ the Story of the blind Man in the Gospel, who follow'd our Saviour, and to whom our Blessed Lord put the Question, *What wilt thou that I should do unto thee?* Who, as if he had made it strange that such a Question should be ask'd, or as if he had said, *Lord, doest thou see that I am blind, and yet ask me what thou shalt do for me?* My Answer is plain in my Misery, *Lord, that I may receive my Sight.*[16]

I needed not to make the Application; and from this time, altho' I lay four Months in Prison after this, and heard no more of it, yet from this time, as I learn'd afterwards, this noble Person made it his Business to have my Case represented to Her Majesty, and Methods taken for my Deliverance.

I mention this Part, because I am no more to forget the Obligation upon me to the Queen, than to my first Benefactor.

When Her Majesty came to have the Truth of the Case laid before Her, I soon felt the Effects of her Royal Goodness and Compassion. And first, Her Majesty declar'd, That She left all that Matter to a certain Person,[17] and did not think he would have used me in such a Manner. Perhaps these Words may seem imaginary to some, and the speaking them to be of no Value, and so they would have been if they had not been follow'd with farther and more convincing Proofs of what they imported, which were these, That Her Majesty was pleased particularly to enquire into my Circumstances and Family, and by my Lord Treasurer *Godolphin*, to send a considerable Supply to my Wife and Family, and to send me to the Prison Money to pay my Fine, and the Expenses of my Discharge. Whether this be a just Foundation, let my Enemies judge.

Here is the Foundation on which I built my first Sense of Duty to Her Majesty's Person, and the indelible Bond of Gratitude to my first Benefactor.

Gratitude and Fidelity are inseparable from an honest Man. But to be thus oblig'd by a Stranger, by a Man of Quality and Honour, and after that by the Sovereign, under whose Administration I was suffering, let any one put himself in my stead and examine upon what Principles I could ever act against either such a Queen, or such a Benefactor; and what must my own Heart reproach me with, what blushes must have cover'd my Face when I had look'd in, and call'd myself ungrateful to him that sav'd me thus from distress? *Or* Her that fetch'd me out of the Dungeon, and gave my Family Relief? Let any Man, who knows what Principles are, what Engagements of Honour and Gratitude are, make this Case his own, and say what I could have done less or more than I have done.

I must go on a little with the Detail of the Obligation, and then I shall descend to relate what I have done, and what I have not done in the Case.

Being deliver'd from the Distress I was in, Her Majesty, who was not satisfy'd to do me Good by a single Act of Bounty, had the Goodness to think of taking me into her Service, and I had the Honour to be employ'd in several honourable, tho' secret Services, by the Interposition of my first Benefactor, who then appear'd as a Member in the publick Administration.

I had the Happiness to discharge my self in all these Trusts, so much to the Satisfaction of those who employ'd me, tho' often times with Difficulty and Danger, that my Lord Treasurer *Godolphin*, whose Memory I have always honour'd, was pleas'd to continue his Favour to me, and to do me all good Offices with Her Majesty, even after an unhappy Breach had separated him from my first Benefactor: The Particulars of which may not be improper to relate; and as it is not an Injustice to any, so I hope it will not be offensive.

When upon that fatal Breach, the Secretary of State was dismiss'd from the Service,[18] I look'd upon my self as lost, it being a general Rule in such Cases, when a great Officer falls, that all who came in by his Interest fall with him. And resolving never to abandon the Fortunes of the Man to whom I ow'd so much of my own, I quitted the usual Applications which I had made to my Lord Treasurer.

But my generous Benefactor, when he understood it, frankly told me, that I should by no means do so; for, said he, in the most engaging terms, My Lord Treasurer will employ you in nothing but what is for the publick Service, and agreeable to your own Sentiments of Things: And besides, it is the Queen you are serving, who has been very good to you. Pray apply your self as you used to do; I shall not take it ill from you in the least.

Upon this I went to wait on my Lord Treasurer, who receiv'd me with great Freedom, and told me smiling, *He had not seen me a long while.* I told his Lordship very frankly the Occasion, That the unhappy Breach that had fallen out, had made me doubtful whether I should be acceptable to his Lordship. That I knew it was usual, when great Persons fall, that all who were in their Interest fell with them. That his Lordship knew the Obligations I was under, and that I could not but fear my Interest in his Lordship was lessen'd on that Account. *Not at all Mr.* De Foe, reply'd his Lordship; *I always think a Man honest, till I find to the contrary.*

Upon this I attended his Lordship as usual, and being resolved to remove all possible Ground of Suspicion that I kept any secret Correspondence, I never visited, or wrote to, or any way corresponded with my principal Benefactor for above three Years; which he so well knew the Reason of, and so well approv'd that punctual Behaviour in me, that he never took it ill from me at all.

In Consequence of this Reception, my Lord *Godolphin* had the Goodness not only to introduce me for the second time to her Majesty,[19] and to the Honour of kissing her Hand, but obtain'd for me the Continuance of an Appointment which her Majesty had been pleas'd to make me in Consideration of a former special Service I had done,[20] and in which I had run as much risque of my Life as a Grenadier upon the Counterscarp; and which Appointment however was first obtain'd for me at the Intercession of my said first Benefactor, and is all owing to that Intercession, and Her Majesty's Bounty. Upon this second Introduction Her Majesty was pleas'd to tell me with a Goodness peculiar to Her self, That she had such Satisfaction in my former Services, that she had appointed me for another Affair, which was something Nice, and that my Lord Treasurer should tell me the rest; and so I withdrew.

The next Day his Lordship having commanded me to attend, told me, That he must send me to *Scotland*; and gave me but three Days to prepare my self. Accordingly I went to *Scotland*,[21] where neither my Business, not the manner of my discharging it is material to this Tract, nor will it be ever any part of my Character that I reveal what should be concealed; and yet my Errand was such as was far from being unfit for a Sovereign to direct, or an honest Man to perform; and the Service I did on that Occasion, as it is not unknown to the greatest Man[22] now in the Nation under the King and the Prince, so I dare say, his Grace was never displeased with the Part I had in it, and I hope will not forget it.

These things I mention upon this Account, and no other, (*viz.*) to state the Obligation I have been in all along to Her Majesty personally, and to my first Benefactor principally, by which, *I say I THINK*, I was at least obliged not to act against them even in those things which I might not approve. Whether I have acted with them farther than I ought, shall be spoken to by it self.

Having said thus much of the Obligations lay'd on me, and the Persons by whom, I have this only to add, That I think no Man will say a Subject could be under greater Bonds to his Prince, or a private Person to a Minister of State; and I shall ever preserve this Principle, that an honest Man cannot be ungrateful to his Benefactor.

But let no Man run away now with the Notion, that I am now intending to plead the Obligation that was upon me from Her Majesty, or from any other Person, to justify my doing any thing that is not otherwise to be justify'd in it self.

Nothing would be more injurious than such a Construction; and therefore I capitulate for so much Justice as to explain my self by this Declaration (*viz.*) That I only speak of these Obligations as binding me to a negative Conduct not to fly in the Face of, or concern my self in Disputes with those to whom I was under such Obligations, altho' I might not in my Judgment joyn in many things that were done. No Obligation could excuse me in calling Evil Good, or Good Evil; but I am of the Opinion, that I might justly think my self oblig'd to defend what I thought was to be defended, and to be silent in any thing which I might think was not.

If this a Crime, I must plead guilty, and give in the History of my Obligation above mention'd as an Extenuation, at least, if not a Justification of my Conduct; suppose a Man's Father was guilty of several things unlawful and unjustifiable, a Man may heartily detest the unjustifiable thing, and yet it ought not to be expected that he should expose his Father. I think the Case on my side exactly the same. Nor can the Duty to a Parent be more strongly obliging than the

Obligation laid on me: But I must allow the Case on the other side not the same.

And this brings me to the Affirmative, and to enquire what the Matters of Fact are, what I have done, or have not done, on Account of these Obligations which I have been under.

It is a general Suggestion, and is affirm'd with such Assurance, that they tell me it is in vain to contradict it; That I have been employ'd by the Earl of O—d,[23] late Lord Treasurer, in the late Disputes about Publick Affairs, to write for him, or to put it into their own Particulars, have written by Direction, taken the Materials from him, been dictated to, or instructed by him, or by other Persons from him, by his Order, and the like; and that I have receiv'd a Pension, or Sallery, or Payment from his Lordship for such Services as these.

If I could put it into Words that would more fully express the Meaning of these People, I profess I would do it.

One would think it was impossible, but that since these things have been so confidently affirm'd, some Evidence might be produc'd, some Facts might appear, some one Body or other might be found that could speak of certain Knowledge: To say things have been carry'd too closely to be discover'd, *is saying nothing*; for then they must own, *that it is not discover'd*: And how then can they affirm it, as they do, with such an Assurance, as nothing ought to be affirm'd by honest Men, unless they were able to prove it?

To speak then to the Fact: Were the Reproach upon *me only* in this Particular, I should not mention it; I should not think it a Reproach to be directed by a Man to whom the Queen had at that time entrusted the Administration of the Government. But as it is a Reproach upon his Lordship, Justice requires that I do Right in this Case. The Thing is true or false, I would recommend it to those who would be call'd honest Men, to consider but one Thing, (*viz.*) What if it should not be true? Can they justify the Injury done to that Person, or to any Person concern'd? If it cannot be prov'd, if no Vestiges appear to ground it upon, how can they charge Men upon Rumours and Reports, and joyn to run Men's Characters down by the Stream of Clamour.

Sed quo rapit impetus undæ.[24]

In Answer to the Charge, I bear Witness to Posterity, that every Part of it is false and forg'd; and I do solemnly protest, in the *Fear* and

Presence of him that shall Judge us all, both the Slanderers, and the Slandered, that I have not receiv'd any Instructions, Directions, Orders, *or let them call it what they will of that kind*, for the Writing any Part of what I have written, or any Materials for the putting together, for the Forming any Book or Pamphlet whatsoever from the said Earl of O—d, late Lord Treasurer, or from any Person, by his Order, or Direction, since the Time that the late Earl of G—in was Lord Treasurer: Neither did I ever shew, or cause to be shew'd to his Lordship, for his Approbation, Correction, Alteration, or for any other Cause, any Book, Paper, or Pamphlet, which I have Written and Publish'd before the same was Printed, work'd off at the Press, and Publish'd.

If any Man living can detect me of the least Prevarication in this, or in any Part of it, I desire him to do it by all means; and I challenge all the World to do it – *And if they cannot*, then I appeal, *as in my Title*, to the Honour and Justice of my worst Enemies, to know upon what Foundation of Truth or Conscience they can affirm these things, and for what it is that I bear these Reproaches.

In all my Writing, I ever capitulated[25] for my Liberty to Speak according to my own Judgment of Things; I ever had that Liberty allow'd me, nor was I ever imposed upon to write this way or that against my Judgment by any Person whatsoever.

I come now historically to the Point of Time when my Lord *Godolphin* was dismiss'd from his Employment,[26] and the late unhappy Division broke out at Court; I waited on my Lord the Day he was displac'd, and humbly ask'd his Lordship's Direction, what Course I should take? His Lordship's Answer was, *That he had the same good Will to assist me, but not the same Power; That I was the Queen's Servant, and that all he had done for me, was by Her Majesty's special and particular Direction; and that whoever should succeed him, it was not material to me, he supposed I should be employ'd in nothing relating to the present Differences: My Business was to wait till I saw things settled, and then apply my self to the Ministers of State, to receive Her Majesty's Commands from them.*

It occur'd to me immediately, as a Principle for my Conduct, that it was not material to me what Ministers Her Majesty was pleas'd to employ, my Duty was to go along with every Ministry, so far as they did not break in upon the Constitution, and the Laws and the Liberties of my Country; my Part being only the Duty of a Subject, (*viz.*) to submit to all lawful Commands, and to enter into no Service which was not justifiable by the Laws: To all which I have exactly oblig'd my self.

By this I was providentially cast back upon my Original Benefactor,[27] who, according to his wonted Goodness, was pleased to lay my Case before Her Majesty, and thereby I preserv'd my Interest in Her Majesty's Favour; but without any Engagement of Service.

As for Consideration, Pension, Gratification, or Reward, I declare to all the World I have had none; except only that old Appointment which Her Majesty was pleased to make me in the Days of the Ministry of my Lord *Godolphin*: Of which I have spoken already, and which was for Services done in a foreign Country some Years before. Neither have I been employ'd, or directed, or order'd, by my Lord T——r aforesaid, to do, or not to do, anything in the Affairs of the unhappy Differences which have so long perplex'd us, and for which I have suffer'd so many, and such unjust Reproaches.

I come next to enter into the Matters of Fact, and what it is I have done, or not done; which may justify the Treatment I have met with. And first, for the Negative Part, what I have not done.

The first Thing in the unhappy Breaches which have fallen out, is the heaping up Scandal upon the Persons and Conduct of Men of Honour on one Side, as well as on the other; those unworthy Methods of falling upon one another by personal Calumny and Reproach. This I have often in print complain'd of as an unchristian, ungenerous, and unjustifiable Practice. Not a Word can be found in all I have written reflecting on the Persons, or Conduct of any of the former Ministry, I serv'd Her Majesty under their Administration, they acted honourably and justly in every Transaction in which I had the Honour to be concern'd with them; and I never publish'd, or said any thing dishonourable of any of them in my Life: Nor can the worst Enemy I have produce any such thing against me. I always regretted the Change, and look'd upon it as a great Disaster to the Nation in general, I am sure it was so to me in particular; and the Divisions and Feuds among Parties, which follow'd that Change, were doubtless a Disaster to us all.

The next Thing which follow'd the Change was THE PEACE: No Man can say that ever I once said in my Life, that I approv'd of the Peace. I wrote a publick Paper at that time,[28] and there it Remains upon Record against me, I printed it openly, and that so plainly, as others durst not do; That I did not like the Peace, neither that which was made, nor that which was before a making; That I thought the Protestant Interest was not taken care of in either; That the Peace I was for, was such as should neither have given the *Spanish* Monarchy to the House of *Bourbon*, or the House of *Austria*; but that this Bone of Contention should have been broken to Pieces, that it should not have been dangerous to *Europe* on any Account, and that the Protestant Powers, (*viz.*) *Britain*, and the *States*, should have so strengthen'd and fortify'd their Interest by their sharing the Commerce and Strength of *Spain*, as should have made them no more afraid either of *France*, or the *Emperor*. So that the Protestant Interest should have been superior to all the Powers of *Europe*, and been in no more Danger of exhorbitant Power, whether *French* or *Austrian*. This was the Peace I always argued for, pursuant to the Design of King *William* in the Treaty of Partition, and pursuant to that Article of the Grand Alliance, which was directed by the same glorious Hand at the Beginning of this last War (*viz.*) That all we should conquer in the *Spanish West-Indies* should be our own.

This was with a true Design that *England* and *Holland* should have turn'd their Naval Power, which were eminently superiour to those of *France*, to the Conquest of the *Spanish West-Indies*, by which the Channel of Trade, and Return of Bullion, which now enriches the Enemies of both, had been ours; and as the Wealth, so the Strength of the World had been in Protestant Hands. *Spain*, whoever had it, must then have been dependant upon us; the House of *Bourbon* would have found it so poor without us, as to be scarce worth fighting for; and the People so averse to them for want of their Commerce, as not to make it ever likely *France* could keep it.

This was the Foundation I ever acted upon with relation to the Peace. It is true, that when it was made, and could not be otherwise, I thought our Business was to make the best of it, and rather to enquire what Improvements were to be made of it, than to be continually exclaiming at those who made it; and where the Objection lies against this Part I cannot yet see.

While I spoke of things in this manner, I bore infinite Reproaches from clamouring Pens of being in the *French* Interest, being hir'd and brib'd to defend a bad Peace, and the like; and most of this was upon a Supposition of my Writing, or being the Author of Abundance of

Pamphlets which came out every Day, and which I had no hand in. And indeed, as I shall observe again by and by, this was one of the greatest Pieces of Injustice that could be done me, and which I labour still under without any redress; that whenever any Piece comes out which is not liked, I am immediately charg'd with being the Author, and very often the first knowledge I have had of a Books being pub-lish'd, has been from seeing my self abused for being the Author of it, in some other Pamphlet publish'd in Answer to it.

Finding my self treated in this manner, I declin'd writing at all; and for a great Part of a Year never set Pen to Paper, except in the Publick Paper call'd the *Review*. After this I was long absent in the *North* of *Eng-land*, and observing the Insolence of the *Jacobite* Party, and how they insinuated fine things into the Heads of the Common People of the Right and Claim of the *Pretender*, and of the great Things he would do for us if he was to come in; of his being to turn a Protestant, of his being resolved to maintain our Liberties, support our Funds, give Lib-erty to Dissenters, and the like; and finding that the People began to be deluded, and that the *Jacobites* gain'd ground among them by these Insinuations, I thought it the best Service I could do the Protestant Interest, and the best way to open the Peoples Eyes to the Advantages of the Protestant Succession, if I took some Course effectually to alarm the People with what they really ought to expect if the *Pretender* should come to be King. And this made me set Pen to Paper again.

And this brings me to the affirmative Part, or to what really I HAVE DONE; and in this I am sorry to say, I have one of the foulest, most unjust, and unchristian Clamours to complain of, that any Man has suffer'd, I believe, since the Days of the Tyranny of King *James* the Second. The Fact is thus.

In order to detect the Influence of *Jacobite* Emissaries, as above, the first thing I wrote was a small Tract, call'd, *A Seasonable Caution*.[29]

A Book sincerely written to open the Eyes of the poor ignorant Country People, and to warn them against the subtle Insinuations of the Emissaries of the *Pretender*; and that it might be effectual to that Purpose, I prevail'd with several of my Friends to give them away among the poor People all over *England*, especially in the *North*; and several thousands were actually given away, the Price being reduced so low, that the bare Expense of Paper and Press was only preserv'd, that every one might be convinc'd, that nothing of Gain was design'd, but a sincere Endeavour to do a publick Good, and assist to keep the People entirely in the Interest of the Protestant Succession.

Next to this, and with the same sincere Design, I wrote Two Pamphlets, one entituled, *What if the* Pretender *should come?* The other, *Reasons against the Succession of the House of* Hanover. Nothing can be more plain, than that the Titles of these books were Amusements, in order to put the Books into the Hands of those People who the *Jacobites* had deluded, and to bring the Books to be read by them.[30]

Previous to what I shall farther say of these Books, I must observe, that all these Books met with so general a Reception and Approbation among those who were most sincere for the Protestant Succession, that they sent them all over the Kingdom, and recommended them to the Peoples reading as excellent and useful Pieces, insomuch, that about Seven Editions of them were Printed, and they were Reprinted in other Places; and I do protest, had his present Majesty, then Elector of *Hanover*, given me a thousand Pounds to have written for the Interest of his Succession, and to expose and render the Interest of the *Pretender* odious and ridiculous, I could have done nothing more effectual to those Purposes than these Books were.

And that I may make my worst Enemies, to whom this is a fair Appeal, Judges of this, I must take leave by and by to repeat some of the Expressions in those Books which were direct, and need no Explication, and which, I think, no Man that was in the Interest of the *Pretender*, nay which no Man but one who was entirely in the Interest of the *Hanover* Succession, could write.

Nothing can be severer in the Fate of a Man than to act so between two Parties, that both Sides should be provok'd against him. It is certain, the *Jacobites* curs'd those Tracts and the Author; and when they came to read them, *being deluded by the Titles according to the Design*, they threw them by with the greatest Indignation imaginable: Had the *Pretender* ever come to the Throne, I could have expected nothing but Death, and all the Ignominy and Reproach that the most inveterate Enemy of his Person and Claim could be suppos'd to suffer.

On the other hand, I leave it to any considering Man to Judge, what a Surprize it must be to me to meet with all the publick Clamour that Informers could invent, as being Guilty of writing against the *Hanover* Succession, and as having written several Pamphlets *in Favour of the* Pretender.

No Man in this Nation ever had a more riveted Aversion to the *Pretender*, and to all the Family he pretended to come of, *than I*: A Man that had been in Arms under the Duke of *Monmouth*,[31] against the Cruelty and Arbitrary Government of his pretended Father; That for twenty Years had, to my utmost, opposed him, (King *James*) and his Party after his Abdication; That had serv'd King *WILLIAM* to his Satisfaction, and the Friends of the Revolution after his Death, at all Hazards and upon all Occasions; That had suffer'd and been ruin'd under the Administration of *Highflyers* and *Jacobites*, of whom some are, *at this Day, COUNTERFEIT Whigs*;[32] It could not be! the Nature of the Thing could by no means allow it, it must be monstrous; and that the Wonder may cease, I shall take leave to quote some of the Expressions out of these Books, of which the worst Enemy I have in the World is left to Judge, whether they are in Favour of the *Pretender*, or no; but of this in its Place.

For these Books I was prosecuted, taken into Custody, and oblig'd to give Eight hundred Pound Bail.

I do not in the least object here against, or design to reflect upon the Proceedings of the Judges which were subsequent to this; I acknowledg'd *then*, and *now* acknowledge *again*, that, upon the Information given, there was a sufficient Ground for all they did, and my unhappy entring upon my own Vindication in Print, while the Case was before their Lordships in a Judicial Way, was an Error which I neither understood, and which I did not foresee; and therefore, altho' I had great Reason to reflect upon the Informers, yet I was wrong in making that Defence in the Manner and Time I then made it, and which, when I found, I made no scruple afterward to Petition the Judges, and acknowledge, that they had just Ground to resent it: Upon which Petition and Acknowledgment, their Lordships were pleas'd, with particular Marks of Goodness, to release me, and not take the Advantage of an Error of Ignorance, as if it had been consider'd and premeditated.[33]

But against the *INFORMERS*, I think, I have great Reason to complain; and against the Injustice of those Writers, who, in many Pamphlets, charged me with writing for the *Pretender*, and the Government, with pardoning an Author who wrote for the *Pretender*, and indeed the Justice of those Men can be in nothing more clearly stated, than in this Case of mine; where the Charge, in their Printed Papers and Publick Discourse was brought, not that they themselves believ'd me Guilty of the Crime, but because it was necessary to blacken the Man; That a general Reproach might serve for an Answer to whatever he should say that was not for their Turn: So that it was the Person, not the Crime they fell upon, and they may justly be said to persecute for the sake of Persecution, *as will thus appear.*

This Matter making some Noise, People began to enquire into it, and to ask what *De Foe* was prosecuted for, seeing the Books were manifestly written against the *Pretender*, and for the Interest of the House of *Hanover?* And my Friends expostulated freely with some of the Men who appear'd in it, who answer'd, *with more Truth than Honesty,* That they knew this Book had nothing in it, and that it was meant another way; but that *De Foe* had disoblig'd them in other things, and they were resolv'd to take the Advantage they had, both to punish and expose him. They were no inconsiderable People who said this; and had the Case come to a Tryal, I had provided good Evidence to prove the Words.

This is the Christianity and Justice by which I have been treated; and this Injustice is the thing that I complain of.

Now as this was a Plot of a few Men to see if they could brand me in the World for a *Jacobite*, and perswade rash and ignorant People that I was turn'd about for the *Pretender, I think they might as easily have prov'd me to be a Mahometan;* therefore, I say, this obliges me to state that Matter as it really stands, that impartial Men may judge whether those Books were written for, or against the *Pretender;* and this cannot be better done, than by the Account of what follow'd after the first Information, which in few Words is thus:

Upon the several Days appointed, I appear'd at the *Queen's Bench Bar* to discharge my Bail; and at last had an Indictment for High Crimes and Misdemeanours exhibited against me by Her Majesty's Attorney-General, which, as I was inform'd, contain'd two hundred Sheets of Paper.

What was the Substance of the Indictment I shall not mention here, neither could I enter upon it, having never seen the Particulars: But I was told, that I should be brought to Tryal the very next Term.

I was not ignorant that in such Cases it is easy to make any Book a Libel, and that the Jury must have found the Matter of Fact in the Indictment, (*viz.*) That I had written such Books, and then what might have follow'd I knew not: Wherefore I thought it was my only way to cast my self on the Clemency of her Majesty, whose Goodness I had had so much Experience of many ways; representing in my Petition, that I was far from the least Intention to favour the Interest of the *Pretender*, but that the Books were all written with a sincere Design to promote the Interest of the House of *Hanover*; and humbly laid before her Majesty, as I do now before the rest of the World, the Books themselves to plead in my behalf; representing farther, that I was maliciously inform'd against by those who were willing to put a Construction upon the Expressions different from my true Meaning, and therefore, flying to her Majesty's Goodness and Clemency, I entreated her Gracious PARDON.

It was not only the native Disposition of her Majesty to Acts of Clemency and Goodness, that obtain'd me this Pardon; but, as I was inform'd, her Majesty was pleas'd to express it in the Council, *She saw nothing but private Pique in the first Prosecution*; and therefore, I think, I cannot give a better and clearer Vindication of my self, than what is contain'd in the Preamble to the Pardon which her Majesty was pleas'd to grant me, and I must be allow'd to say, to those who are still willing to object, that, I think, what satisfy'd her Majesty might be sufficient to satisfy them; and I can assure them, that this Pardon was not granted without her Majesty's being specially and particularly acquainted with the things alledg'd in the Petition, the Books also being look'd in to find the Expressions quoted in the Petition. The Preamble to the Patent for a Pardon, as far as relates to the Matters of Fact, runs thus:

> *Whereas, in the Term of the* Holy Trinity *last past, our Attorney General did exhibit an Information, in our Court of* Queens Bench *at* Westminster, *against* DANIEL DE FOE, *late of* London, *Gent. for Writing, Printing, and Publishing, and causing to be Written, Printed, and Published,* THREE LIBELS, *the one entituled,* Reasons against the Succession of the House of *Hanover*, with an Enquiry, how far the Abdication of King *James*, supposing it to be legal, ought to affect the Person of the *Pretender. One other entituled,* And what if the *Pretender* should Come? *Or some* Considerations of the Advantages and real Consequences of the *Pretender's* possessing the Crown of *Great*

Britain. And one other entituled, An Answer to a Question that nobody thinks of (*viz.*) What if the Queen should Die?

And whereas the said Daniel De Foe *hath, by his humble Petition, represented to us, that he, with a sincere Design to propagate the Interest of the* Hanover Succession, *and to animate the People against the Designs of the* Pretender, *whom he always looked on as an Enemy to our Sacred Person and Government,* did publish *the said Pamphlets; In all which Books, altho' the Titles seem'd to look as if written in Favour of the* Pretender, *and several Expressions, as in all ironical Writing it must be, may be wrested against the true Design of the Whole, and turn'd to a Meaning quite different from the Intention of the Author, yet the Petitioner humbly assures us, in the solemnest Manner, that his true and only Design in all the said Books was, by an ironical Discourse of recommending the* Pretender, *in the strongest and most forcible Manner to expose his Designs, and the ruinous Consequences of his Succeeding therein; which, as the Petitioner humbly represents, will appear to our Satisfaction by the Books themselves, where the following Expressions are very plain,* (viz.) *That the PRETENDER is recommended* as a Person proper to amass the *English* Liberties into his own Soveraignty, supply them with the Privileges of wearing WOODEN SHOES; easing them of the trouble of chusing Parliaments; and the Nobility and Gentry of the Hazard and Expence of Winter Journeys, by governing them in that more righteous Method of his ABSOLUTE WILL, and enforcing the Laws by a Glorious STANDING ARMY; paying all the Nations Debts at once by stopping the Funds, and Shutting up the *Exchequer;* easing and quieting their Differences in Religion, by bringing them to the UNION of POPERY, or leaving them at Liberty to have no Religion at all: *That these were some of the very Expressions in the said Books which the Petitioner sincerely design'd to expose, and oppose as far as in him lies the* Interest of the Pretender, *and with no other Intention: NEVERTHELESS, the Petitioner, to his great Surprize, has been misrepresented, and his said Books misconstrued, as if written in Favour of the* Pretender, *and the Petitioner is now under Prosecution for the same; which Prosecution, if farther carried on, will be the utter Ruin of the Petitioner and his Family: Wherefore the Petitioner humbly assuring us of the Innocence of his Design, as aforesaid, flies to our Clemency, and most humbly prays our most Gracious and Free Pardon. WE taking the Premises, and the Circumstances aforesaid into our Royal Considera-tion, are graciously pleas'd,* &c.

Let any indifferent Man Judge whether I was not treated with par-ticular Malice in this Matter, who was, notwithstanding this, reproach'd in the daily Publick Prints with having written treasonable Books, in behalf of the *Pretender*, nay, and in some of those Books, as before, the Queen her self, was reproach'd, *with having granted her Pardon to an Author who writ for the* Pretender.

I think I might with much more Justice say, I was *the first Man* that ever was oblig'd to seek a Pardon for writing for the *Hanover* Succes-sion; and *the first Man* that these People ever sought to Ruin for writing against the *Pretender*. For if ever a Book was sincerely design'd to far-ther and propogate the Affection and Zeal of the Nation against the *Pretender*, nay, and was made use of, and that with success too, for that purpose, THESE BOOKS *were so*; and I ask no more Favour of the World to determine the Opinion of honest Men for or against me than what is drawn constructively from these Books. Let one Word, either written or spoken by me, either publish'd, or not publish'd, be produced, that was in the least disrespectful to the Protestant Succes-sion, or to any Branch of the Family of *Hanover*, or that can be judg'd to be favourable to the Interest or Person of the *Pretender*, and I will be willing to wave her Majesty's Pardon, and render my self to Publick Justice, to be punish'd for it as I should well deserve.

I freely and openly Challenge the worst of my Enemies to charge me with any Discourse, Conversation, or Behaviour in my whole Life, which had the least Word in it injurious to the Protestant Succession, unbecoming or disrespectful to any of the Persons of the Royal Fam-ily of *Hanover*, or the least favourable Word of the Person, the Designs, or Friends of the *Pretender*.

If they can do it, let them stand forth and speak, no doubt but they may be heard; and I, for my part, will relinquish all Pleas, Pardons, and Defences, and cast my self into the Hands of Justice.

Nay, to go farther, I defy them to prove, that I ever kept Company, or had any Society, Friendship, or Conversation with any *Jacobite*; so averse have I been to the Interest, and to the People, that I have studi-ously avoided their Company upon all Occasions.

As nothing in the World has been more my Aversion than the Society of *Jacobites*, so nothing can be a greater Misfortune to me than to be accus'd, and publickly reproach'd with what is, of all things in the World, most abhorr'd by me, and which has made it the more afflicting is that this Charge arises from those very things, which I did, with the sincerest Design, to manifest the contrary.

But such is my present Fate, and I am to submit to it, which I do with Meekness and Calmness, as to a Judgment from Heaven, and am practising that Duty which I have studied long ago, of *Forgiving my Enemies*, and *praying for them that despitefully use me.*[34]

Having given this brief History of the Pardon, *&c.* I hope the Impartial part of the World will Grant me, That being thus Graciously Deliver'd a second Time from the Cruelty of my Implacable Enemies, and the Ruin of a Cruel and unjust Persecution, and that by the meer Clemency and Goodness of the Queen, my Obligation to her Majesty's Goodness, was far from being made less than it was before.

I have now run through the History of my Obligation to Her Majesty, and to the Person of my Benefactor aforesaid. I shall state every thing that follow'd this with all the Clearness I can, and leave my self lyable to as little Cavil as I may; for I see my self assaulted by a sort of People who will do me no justice. I hear a Great Noise made of Punishing those that are GUILTY, but as I said before not one Word of Clearing those that are INNOCENT; and I must say in this Part, they Treat me not only as I were no Christian, but as if they themselves were not Christians. They will neither prove the Charge, nor hear the Defence, which is the unjustest thing in the World.

I foresee what will be alledged to the Clause of my Obligation, *&c.* to Great Persons: And I resolve to give my Adversaries all the Advantage they can desire; by acknowledging beforehand, That *no Obligation to the QUEEN, or to any Benefactor, can justify any Man's acting against the Interest of his Country, against his Principles, his Conscience, and his former Profession.*

I think this will Anticipate all that can be said upon that Head, and it will then remain to state the Fact as I am, or am not Chargeable with it; which I shall do as clearly as possible in few words.

It is none of my Work to enter into the Conduct of the Queen or of the Ministry in this Case, the Question is not what *they have done*, but what *I have done*? And tho' I am very far from thinking of them as some other People think, yet for the sake of the present Argument, I am to give them all up, and Suppose, *tho' not Granting,* that all which is suggested of them by the worst Temper, the most censorious Writer, the most scandalous Pamphlet or Lampoon should be True, and I'll go through some of the Particulars, as I meet with them in Publick.

1*st*, That they made a Scandalous Peace, unjustly Broke the Allyance, Betray'd the Confederates, and Sold us all to the *French.*

God forbid it should be all Truth, in the manner that we see it in Print; But that, I say, is none of my Business – *But what hand had I in all this?* I never wrote one word for the Peace *before it was made,* or to Justify it after *it was made,* let them produce it if they can; Nay, in a *Review* upon that Subject, while it was making I Printed it in plainer Words than other Men durst Speak it at that Time, That *I did not like the Peace,* nor did I like any Peace that was a making, since that of the PARTITION, and that the Protestant Interest was not taken Care of either in that or the Treaty of *Gertrudinburgh* before it.[35]

It is true, that I did say, That since the Peace was made, and we could not help it, that it was our Business and our Duty to make the best of it, to make the utmost Advantage of it by Commerce, Navigation, and all kind of Improvement that we could,[36] and this I SAY STILL; and I must think it is more our Duty to do so, than the Exclamations against the thing it self which it is not in our power to Retrieve. This is all that the worst Enemy I have can Charge me with: *After the Peace was made,* and the *Dutch* and the Emperor stood out, I gave my Opinion of what I foresaw would necessarily be the Consequence of that Difference, (*viz.*) That it would inevitably involve these Nations in a War with one or other of them; *any one* who was Master of Common Sense in the publick Affairs, might see that the standing out of the *Dutch* could have no other Event: For if the Confederates had Conquer'd the *French,* they would certainly have fallen upon us by way of Resentment, and there was no doubt, but the same Councils that led us to make a Peace, would Oblige us to maintain it, by preventing too great Impressions upon the *French.*

On the other hand, I alledged, that should the *French* prevail against the *Dutch,* unless he stopt at such Limitations of Conquest as the Treaty oblig'd him to do, we must have been under the same necessity to renew the War against *France;* and for this Reason, seeing we had made a Peace, we were oblig'd to bring the rest of the Confederates into it, and to bring the *French* to give them all such Terms as they ought to be satisfied with.

This way of Arguing was either so little Understood, or so much Malign'd, that I suffer'd innumerable Reproaches in Print, for having Written for a War with the *Dutch*, which was neither in the Expression, or ever in my Imagination:[37] But I pass by these Injuries as small and trifling compar'd to others I suffer under.

However one thing I must say of the Peace, *Let it be Good or Ill in its self*, I cannot but think we have all reason to Rejoyce in behalf of his Present Majesty, That at his accession to the Crown, He found the Nation in Peace; and had the Hands of the King of *France* tied up by a Peace, so as not to be able, without the most infamous breach of Articles, to offer the least Disturbance to his taking a Quiet and Leisurely possession, or so much as to Countenance those that would.

Not but that I believe, if the War had been at the height, we should have been able to have preserved the Crown for his present Majesty, its only Rightful Lord: But I will not say it should have been so Easy, so Bloodless, so Undisputed as now, and all the Difference must be acknowledged to the Peace, and this is all the Good I ever yet said of the Peace.

I come next to the general Clamour of *the Ministry being for the Pretender*; I must speak my Sentiments solemnly and plainly, as I always did in that matter, (*viz.*) That if it was so, I did not see it, nor did I ever see Reason to believe it; This I am sure of, that if it was so, I never took one step in that kind of Service, nor did I ever hear one Word spoken by any one of the Ministry that I had the Honour to know or Converse with, that favour'd the Pretender: But have had the Honour to hear them all Protest that there was no Design to Oppose the Succession of *Hanover* in the least.

It may be Objected to me, That they might be in the Interest of the Pretender for all that: *It is true they might*; But that is nothing to me, I am not Vindicating their Conduct, but my own; as I never was Employ'd in any thing that way, so I do still protest, I do not believe it was ever in their Design, and I have many Reasons to confirm my Thoughts in that Case, which are not material to the present Case: But be that as it will, it is enough to me that I acted nothing in any such Interest, neither did I ever Sin against the Protestant Succession of

Hanover in Thought, Word, or Deed; and if the Ministry did, I did not see it, or so much as suspect them of it.

It was a Disaster to the Ministry, to be driven to the Necessity of taking that Set of Men[38] by the hand, who, no body can deny, were in that Interest: But as the former Ministry answer'd, when they were charg'd with a Design to overthrow the Church, because they favour'd, joyn'd with, and were united to the *Dissenters*; I say they answer'd, *That they made use of the* Dissenters, *but granted them nothing* (WHICH BY THE WAY WAS TOO TRUE:) So these Gentlemen Answer, *That it is true, they made use of* Jacobites, *but did nothing for them.*

But *this by the by.* Necessity is pleaded by both Parties for doing things which neither Side can justify. I wish both Sides would for ever avoid the Necessity of doing Evil; for certainly it is the worst Plea in the World, and generally made use of for the worst Things.

I have often lamented the Disaster which I saw, employing *Jacobites*, was to the late Ministry, and certainly it gave the greatest Handle to the Enemies of the Ministry to fix that universal Reproach upon them of being in the Interest of the *Pretender.* But there was no Medium. The *Whigs* refused to shew them a safe Retreat, or to give them the least Opportunity to take any other Measures but at the Risque of their own Destruction; and they ventur'd upon that Course, in hopes of being able to stand alone at last without help of either the one or the other, in which no doubt they were mistaken.

However, in this Part, as I was always assur'd, and have good Reason still to believe, that her Majesty was steady in the Interest of the House of *Hanover*, and that nothing was ever offer'd to me, or requir'd of me to the Prejudice of that Interest, On what Ground can I be reproach'd with the secret reserv'd Designs of any, if they had such Designs as I still verily believe they had not?

I see there are some Men who would fain perswade the World, that every Man that was in the Interest of the late Ministry, or employ'd by the late Government, or that serv'd the late Queen, was for the *Pretender.*

God forbid this should be true; and I think there needs very little to be said in Answer to it. I can answer for my self, that it is notoriously false; and I think the easy and uninterrupted Accession of his Majesty to the Crown contradicts it: I see no End which such a Suggestion aims at, but to leave an Odium upon all that had any Duty or Regard to her late Majesty.

A Subject is not always Master of his Sovereign's Measures, nor always to examine what Persons or Parties the Prince he serves Employs; so be it that they break not in upon the Constitution; that they govern according to Law, and that he is employ'd in no illegal Act, or have nothing desir'd of him inconsistent with the Liberties and Laws of his Country: If this be not right, then a Servant of the King's is in a worse Case than a Servant to any private Person.

In all these things I have not err'd, neither have I acted or done any thing in the whole Course of my Life, either in the Service of her Majesty, or of her Ministry, that any one can say has the least Deviation from the strictest Regard to the Protestant Succession, and to the Laws and Liberties of my Country.

I never saw an Arbitrary Action offer'd at, a Law dispens'd with, Justice deny'd, or Oppression set up, either by Queen or Ministry, in any Branch of the Administration, wherein I had the least Concern.

If I have sin'd against the *Whigs*, it has been all NEGATIVELY, (*viz.*) that I have not joyn'd in the loud Exclamations against the Queen, and against the Ministry, and against the Measures; and if this be my Crime, my Plea is twofold.

1. I did not really see Cause for carrying their Complaints to that violent Degree.

2. Where I did see what, as before, I lamented and was sorry for, and could not joyn with, or approve, as joyning with *Jacobites*, the *Peace*, &c. My Obligation is my Plea for my silence.

I have all the good Thoughts of the Person, and good Wishes for the Prosperity of my Benefactor, that Charity, and that Gratitude, can inspire me with: I ever believ'd him to have the true Interest of the Protestant Religion, and of his Country in his view; if it should be otherwise, I should be very sorry. And I must repeat it again, that he always left me so entirely to my own Judgment in every thing I did, that he never prescrib'd to me what I should write, or should not write in my Life; neither did he ever concern himself to dictate to, or restrain me in any kind; nor did he see any one Tract that I ever wrote before it was Printed: So that all the Notion of my writing by his Direction, is as much a Slander upon him, as it is possible any thing of that kind can be; and if I have written any thing which is offensive, unjust, or untrue, I must do that Justice as to declare, He has had no hand in it; the Crime is my own.

As the Reproach of his directing me to write, is a Slander UPON THE PERSON I am speaking of; so that of my receiving Pensions and Payments from him for writing, is a Slander UPON ME; and I speak it with the greatest Sincerity, Seriousness, and Solemnity that is possible for a Christian Man to speak, That except the Appointment I mention'd before, which her Majesty was pleas'd to make me formerly, and which I receiv'd during the time of my Lord *Godolphin*'s Ministry, I have not receiv'd of the late Lord Treasurer, or of any one else by his Order, Knowledge, or Direction, one Farthing, or the Value of a Farthing, during his whole Administration; nor has all the Interest I have been suppos'd to have in his Lordship, been able to procure me the Arrears due to me in the time of the other Ministry. SO HELP ME GOD.

I am under no Necessity of making this Declaration. The Services I did, and for which her Majesty was pleas'd to make me a small Allowance, are known to the greatest Men in the present Administration; and some of them were then of the Opinion, and I hope are so still, that I was not unworthy of her Majesty's Favour. The Effect of those Services, however small, are enjoy'd by those Great Persons, and by the whole Nation to this Day; and I had the Honour once to be told, *That they should never be forgotten.* It is a Misfortune, that no Man can avoid, to forfeit for his Deference to the Person and Services of his Queen, to whom he was inexpressibly oblig'd: And if I am fallen under the Displeasure of the PRESENT Government, for any thing I ever did in Obedience to her Majesty in THE PAST, I may say it is my Disaster; but I can never say it is my Fault.

This brings me again to that other Oppression which as I said I suffer under, and which, I think, is of a Kind, that no Man ever suffer'd under so much as my self: And this is to have every Libel, every Pamphlet, be it ever so foolish, so malicious, so unmannerly, or so dangerous, be laid at my Door, and be call'd publickly by my Name. It has been in vain for me to struggle with this Injury; It has been in vain for me to protest, to declare solemnly, nay if I would have sworn that I had no hand in such a Book, or Paper, never saw it, never read it, and the like, it was the same thing.

My Name has been hackney'd about the Street by the Hawkers, and about the Coffee-Houses by the Politicians, at such a rate, as no Patience could bear. One Man will swear to the Style; another to this or that Expression; another to the Way of Printing; and all so positive, that it is to no purpose to oppose it.

I publish'd once, to stop this way of using me, that I would Print nothing but what I set my Name to, and I held it for a Year or Two; but it was all one, I had the same Treatment. I now have resolv'd, for some time, to write nothing at all; and yet I find it the same thing. Two Books lately publish'd being called mine,[39] for no other reason that I know of, than that, at the Request of the Printer, I revised two Sheets of them at the Press,[40] and that they seem'd to be written in Favour of a certain Person; which Person also, as I have been assur'd, had no Hand in them, or any knowledge of them, till they were publish'd in Print.

This is a Flail which I have no Fence against, but to complain of the Injustice of it, and that is but *the shortest Way* to be treated with more Injustice.

There is a mighty Charge against me for being Author and Publisher of a Paper call'd, *The MERCATOR*. I'll state the Fact first, and then speak to the Subject.

It is true, that being desir'd to give my Opinion in the Affair of the Commerce with *France*, I did, as I often had done in Print many Years before, declare, That it was my Opinion we ought to have an Open Trade with *France*, because I did believe we might have the Advantage by such a Trade; and of this Opinion I am still. What Part I had in the *Mercator*, is well known; and would Men Answer with Argument, and not with personal Abuses, I would, at any time, defend every Part of the *Mercator* which was of my doing. But to say the *Mercator* was mine, is false; I neither was the Author[41] of it, had the Property of it, the Printing of it, or the Profit by it. I had never any Payment or Reward for writing any Part of it; Nor had I the Power to put what I would into it: Yet the whole Clamour fell upon me, because they knew not who else to load with it. And when they came to Answer, the Method was, instead of Argument, to threaten, and reflect upon me; reproach me with private Circumstances and Misfortunes,[42] and give Language which no Christian ought to give, and which no Gentleman ought to take.

I thought any *Englishman* had the Liberty to speak his Opinion in such things; for this had nothing to do with the Publick. The Press was open to me as well as to others; and how, or when I lost my *English* Liberty of speaking my Mind, I know not; neither how my speaking my Opinion without Fee or Reward could authorize them to call me Villain, Rascal, Traytor, and such opprobrious Names.

It was ever my Opinion, and is so still, that were our Wooll kept from *France*, and our Manufactures spread in *France* upon reasonable Duties, all the Improvement which the *French* have made in Woolen Manufactures would decay, and in the End be little Worth, and consequently the Hurt they could do us by them, would be of little Moment.

It was my Opinion, and is so still, that the Ninth Article of the Treaty of *Commerce* was calculated for the Advantage of our Trade, let who will make it, *that is nothing to me.* My Reasons are, because it TYED up the *French* to open the Door to our Manufactures at a certain Duty of Importation THERE, and left the Parliament of *Britain* at Liberty to shut theirs out by as high Duties as they pleas'd HERE, there being no Limitation upon us as to Duties on *French* Goods; *but that other Nations should pay the same.*

While the *French* were thus bound, and the *British* free, I always thought we must be in a Condition to Trade to Advantage, or it must be our own Fault: This was my Opinion, and IS SO STILL, and I would venture to maintain it against any Man upon a publick Stage, before a Jury of fifty Merchants, and venture my Life upon the Cause, if I were assured of fair Play in the Dispute. But that it was my Opinion, That we might carry on a Trade with *France* to our great Advantage, and that we ought for that reason to Trade with them, appears in the Third, Fourth, Fifth, and Sixth Volume of the *Reviews*, above Nine Year before the *Mercator* was thought of; it was not thought Criminal to say so then, how it comes to be Villainous to say so now God knows, I can give no account of it; I am still of the same Opinion, and shall never be brought to say otherwise, unless I see the state of Trade so altered, as to alter my Opinion; and if ever I do, I will be able to give good Reasons for it.

The Answer to these things, whether mine or no, was all pointed at me, and the Arguments were generally in the Terms of Villain, Rascal, Miscreant, Lyer, Bankrupt, Fellow, Hireling, Turn-Coat, *&c.* what the

Arguments were better'd by these Methods, that I leave to others to Judge of. Also most of those things in the *Mercator*, for which I had such Usage, were such as I was not the Author of.

I do grant, had all the Books which have been called by my Name been written by me, I must of Necessity have exasperated every Side, and perhaps have deserved it; but I have the greatest Injustice imaginable in this Treatment, as I have in the perverting the Design of what really I have written. To sum up therefore my Complaint in few Words:

I was from my first entring into the Knowledge of publick Matters, and have ever been to this Day, a sincere Lover of the Constitution of my Country; zealous for Liberty, and the Protestant Interest; but a constant Follower of moderate Principles, a vigorous Opposer of hot Measures in all Parties: I never once changed my Opinion, my Principles, or my Party; and let what will be said of changing Sides, this I maintain, That I never once deviated from the Revolution Principles, nor from the Doctrine of Liberty and Property, on which it was founded.

I own I could never be convinc'd of the great *Danger* of the PRETENDER, in the Time of the late Ministry: Nor can I be now convinc'd of the great *Danger* of the CHURCH under this Ministry. I believe the Cries of one was politically made use of then to serve other Designs; and I plainly see the like Use made of the other now. I spoke my Mind freely then, and I have done the like now, in a small Tract to that purpose not yet made publick; and which, if I live to publish, I will publickly own, as I purpose to do, every thing I write, that my Friends may know when I am abused, and they impos'd on.

It has been the Disaster of all Parties in this Nation to be very HOT in their Turn, and as often as they have been SO, I have differed with them all, and ever must and shall do so. I'll repeat some of the Occasions on the *Whigs* Side, because from that Quarter the Accusation of my turning about comes.

The first Time I had the Misfortune to differ with my Friends, was about the Year 1683. when the *Turks* were besieging *Vienna*, and the *Whigs* in *England*, generally speaking, were for the *Turks* taking it; which I having read the History of the Cruelty and perfidious Dealings of the *Turks* in their Wars, and how they had rooted out the Name of the Christian Religion in above Threescore and Ten

Kingdoms, could by no means agree with: And tho' then but a young Man, and a younger Author, I opposed it, and wrote against it;[43] which was taken very unkindly indeed.

The next Time I differed with my Friends was when King *James* was wheedling the *Dissenters* to take off the Penal Laws and Test, which I could by no means come into. And as *in the first* I used to say, I had rather the Popish House of *Austria* should ruin the Protestants in *Hungaria*, than the Infidel House of *Ottoman* should ruin both Protestant and Papist, by over-running *Germany*; So in the other, I told the *Dissenters* I had rather the Church of *England* should pull our Cloaths off by Fines and Forfeitures, than the Papists should fall both upon the *Church*, and the *Dissenters*, and pull our Skins off by Fire and Fagot.[44]

The next Difference I had with good Men, was about the scandalous Practice of *Occasional Conformity*, in which I had the Misfortune to make many honest Men angry, rather because I had the better of the Argument, than because they disliked what I said.[45]

And now I have lived to see the *Dissenters* themselves very quiet, if not very well pleased with an Act of Parliament to prevent it.[46] Their Friends indeed laid it on; they would be Friends indeed if they would talk of taking it off again.

Again, I had a Breach with honest Men for their Male-treating King *William*; of which I say nothing: Because, I think, they are now opening their Eyes, and making what amends they can to his Memory.

The fifth Difference I had with them, was about the *Treaty of Partition*, in which many honest Men were mistaken, and in which I told them plainly then, That they would at last End the War upon *worse Terms*; and so it is my Opinion they would have done, tho' the Treaty of *Gertrudenburgh* had taken Place.

The sixth Time I differed with them, was when the *Old Whigs* fell upon the *Modern Whigs*; and when the Duke of *Marlborough* and my Lord *Godolphin* were used by the *Observator* in a Manner worse, *I must confess for the Time it lasted*, than ever they were used since;[47] nay tho' it were by *Abel*[48] and the *Examiner*. But the Success failed. In this dispute my Lord *Godolphin* did me the Honour to tell me, *I had served him* and *his Grace also*, both *faithfully* and *successfully*. But his Lordship is Dead, and I have now no Testimony of it but what is to be found in the *Observator*, where I am plentifully abused for being an Enemy to my Country, by acting in the Interest of my Lord *Godolphin*, and the Duke of *Marlborough*: *What Weather-Cock can Turn with such Tempers as these!*

I am now in *the seventh* Breach with them and my Crime now is, That I will not believe and say the same things of the *Queen*, and the late *Treasurer*, which I could not believe before of my Lord *Godolphin*, and the Duke of *Marlborough*, and which in Truth I cannot believe, and therefore could not say it of either of them; and which, if I had believed, yet I ought not to have been the Man that should have said it, for the Reasons aforesaid.

In such Turns of Tempers and Times a Man must be tenfold *a Vicar of* Bray,[49] or it is impossible but he must one Time or other be out with every Body. This is my present Condition, and for this I am reviled with having abandon'd my Principles, turn'd *Jacobite*, and what not: God Judge between me and these Men. Would they come to any Particulars with me, what real Guilt I may have I would freely acknowledge; and if they would produce any Evidence, of the Bribes, the Pensions, and the Rewards I have taken, I would declare honestly, whether they were true or no. If they would give a List of the Books which they charge me with, and the Reasons why they lay them at my Door, I would acknowledge any Mistake, own what I have done, and let them know what I have not done. But these Men neither shew Mercy, or leave place for Repentance, in which they act not only unlike their Maker, but contrary to his express Commands.

It is true, good Men have been used thus in former times; and all the Comfort I have is, that these Men have not the last Judgment in their Hands, if they had, dreadful would be the Case of those who oppose them. But that Day will shew many Men and Things also in a different State from what they may now appear in; some that now appear clear and fair, will then be seen to be black and foul; and some that are now thought black and foul, will then be approved and accepted; and thither I cheerfully appeal, concluding this Part in the Words of the Prophet, *I heard the Defaming of many; Fear on every side; Report,* say they, *and we will Report it; All my Familiars watch'd for my halting, saying, Peradventure he will be enticed, and we shall prevail against him, and we shall take our Revenge on him,* Jerem. 20.10.

Mr. *Pool's Annotations* has the following Remarks on these Lines, which, I think, are so much to that Part of my Case which is to follow, that I could not omit them. His Words are these.

'The Prophet, *says he*, here rendreth a Reason why he thought of giving over his Work as a Prophet; his Ears were continually filled with the Obloquies and Reproaches of such as reproached him; and besides, he was afraid on all Hands, there were so many Traps laid for him, so many Devises devised against him. They did not only take Advantage against him, but sought Advantages, and invited others to raise Stories of him. Not only Strangers, but those that he might have expected the greatest Kindness from; those that pretended most courteously, they watch, *says he*, for opportunities to do me Mischief, and lay in wait for my Halting, desiring nothing more than that I might be enticed to speak, or do something which they might find Matter of a colourable Accusation, that so they might satisfie their Malice upon me. This hath always been the Genius of wicked Men; *Job* and *David*, both made Complaints much like this.' These are Mr. *Pool's* Words.[50]

And this leads me to several Particulars, in which my Case may, without any Arrogance, be likened to that of the Sacred Prophet; except only the vast Disparity of the Persons.

No sooner was the Queen Dead, and the King as Right required, proclaim'd, but the Rage of Men encreased upon me to that Degree, that the Threats and Insults I receiv'd were such as I am not able to express: If I offered to say a word in favour of the present Settlement, it was called fawning and turning round again; on the other hand, tho' I have meddled neither one way or other, nor written one Book since the Queen's Death, yet a great many things are call'd by my Name, and I bear every Day the Reproaches which all the Answerers of those Books cast as well upon the Subject as the Authors. I have not seen or spoken to my Lord of *Oxford* but once since the King's Landing,[51] nor receiv'd the least Message, Order, or Writing from his Lordship, or any other way Corresponded with him, yet he bears the Reproach of my Writing in his Defence,[52] and I the Rage of Men for doing it. I cannot say it is no Affliction to me to be thus used, tho' my being entirely clear of the Facts, is a true support to me.

I am unconcerned at the Rage and Clamour of *Party-men*; but I can not be unconcern'd to hear Men, who I think are good Men and good Christians, prepossess'd and mistaken about me: However I cannot doubt but some time or other it will please God to open such Mens Eyes. A constant, steady adhering to *Personal Vertue*, and to *Publick Peace*, which, I thank God, I can appeal to him, has always been my Practice; will AT LAST restore me to the Opinion of Sober and Impartial Men, and that is all I desire: What it will do with those who are resolutely Partial and Unjust I cannot say, neither is that much my Concern. But I cannot forbear giving one Example of the hard Treatment I receive, which has happened, even while I am Writing this Tract: I have six Children, I have Educated them as well as my Circumstances will permit, and so as I hope shall recommend them to better Usage than their Father meets with in the World. I am not indebted One Shilling in the World for any part of their Education, or for any thing else belonging to bringing them up; yet the Author of the *Flying-Post* Published lately, That I never pay'd for the Education of any of my Children.[53] If any Man in *Britain* has a Shilling to demand of me for any part of their Education, or any thing belong to them, let them come for it.

But these Men care not what Injurious Things they Write, nor what they Say, whether Truth or Not, if it may but raise a Reproach on me, tho' it were to be my Ruine. I may well Appeal to the Honour and Justice of my worst Enemies in such Cases as this.

Conscia Mens Recti fama Mendacia Ridet.[54]

CONCLUSION by the Publisher.

While this was at the Press, and the Copy thus far finish'd, the Author was seiz'd with a violent Fit of an Apoplexy, whereby he was disabled finishing what he design'd in his farther Defence, and continuing now for above Six Weeks in a Weak and Languishing Condition, neither able to go on, or likely to recover, at least in any short time, his Friends thought it not fit to delay the Publication of this any longer; if he recovers, he may be able to finish what he began; if not, it is the Opinion of most that know him, that the Treatment which he here complains of, and some others that he would have spoken of, have been the apparent Cause of his Disaster.

NOTES

Introduction

1. His suggestions for employing seamen and reforming the law on bankruptcy eventually caught the attention of the Government. See *Letters*, pp. 73–7, and Introduction to *PEW*, vol. 8, ed. W. R. Owens, pp. 14–18.
2. John Robert Moore, *A Checklist of the Writings of Daniel Defoe* (2nd edn, Hamden, Connecticut, 1971).
3. See P. N. Furbank and W. R. Owens, *The Canonisation of Daniel Defoe* (New Haven and London, 1988), *Defoe De-Attributions: A Critique of J. R. Moore's 'Checklist'* (London and Rio Grande, 1994) and *A Critical Bibliography of Daniel Defoe* (London, 1998).
4. William Lee, *Daniel Defoe: His Life, and Recently Discovered Writings*, 3 vols (London, 1869). For an account of Lee, see P. N. Furbank and W. R. Owens, 'William Lee of Sheffield: Defoe Bibliographer and Sanitary Inspector', *The Book Collector*, 37 (1988), pp. 185–206.
5. P. N. Furbank and W. R. Owens, 'The Myth of Defoe as "Applebee's Man"', *Review of English Studies*, n.s. 48 (1997), pp. 198–204. We should make it clear, as we do in this article, that it is Lee's *blanket* attribution of leading articles in *Applebee's Journal* that we are objecting to, as altogether unconvincing. One occasionally meets with an article in the journal that seems, at first sight, as if it might very well be by Defoe.
6. See above, p. 58.
7. See Defoe to Charles Delafaye, 26 April, 10 May, 23 May, 4 June and 13 June 1716; *Letters*, pp. 450–60. These letters are discussed above, pp. 166–71.

Chapter 1
Poetry, Pamphleteering and the Pillory

1. Charles II in 1672 brought *quo warranto* proceedings against the City and succeeded in compelling it, and the livery companies, to give up their charters.
2. 'At which Work, I myself, then but a Boy, Work'd like a Horse, till I Wrote out the whole *Pentateuch*, and then was so tyr'd, I was willing to run the Risque of the rest'; *Review*, 22 December 1705.
3. *An Essay on the History of Parties* (London, 1711), p. 13.

4. On 24 January 1686 a number of people were arrested for attending an unlawful conventicle in Little Moorefields. They were indicted and released on bail, and Defoe stood for recognizance for two of them, Mary Deering and Jane Foe (or Du Foe), the latter presumably being one of his relatives. See Paula R. Backscheider, *Daniel Defoe: His Life* (Baltimore and London, 1989), p. 43. The use of the particle 'Du' puts one in mind of Defoe's own adopted 'De'.

5. See Backscheider, *Daniel Defoe: His Life*, p. 37.

6. *Review*, 31 March 1713.

7. See *An Appeal to Honour and Justice*, above, p. 216. See also Peter Earle, *Monmouth's Rebels* (London, 1977), pp. 180, 223, n. 39.

8. *Review*, 16 September 1710.

9. *Review*, 23 September 1710.

10. He is eulogized, among many other places, in Defoe's novel *Memoirs of a Cavalier* (London, 1720).

11. Defoe admits that he cannot remember Love's exact wording and is paraphrasing. A fuller and no doubt more accurate version is given in *Parliamentary Debates* for the year 1673, pp. 44–5.

12. See *PEW*, vol. 3, ed. W. R. Owens, pp. 27–36.

13. He mentions it again in *An Appeal to Honour and Justice*; see above, p. 230.

14. Included in *SFS*, vol. 1, ed. W. R. Owens, pp. 35–56.

15. Mary Elizabeth Campbell, in her *Defoe's First Poem* (Bloomington, Indiana, 1938), did a remarkable job in elucidating the poem, though a few passages defeated even her.

16. See *SFS*, vol. 1, p. 27, n. 30.

17. Rapparees were savage Irish marauders; others as well as Defoe applied this epithet to the 117 petitioners. 'Modesty' is a reference to a pamphlet, *A Modest Inquiry into the Causes of the Present Disasters in England* (London, 1690), which blamed the defeat of the English navy in 1690 on Jacobites and nonjurors. When Defoe reprinted *A New Discovery* in *A Second Volume of the Writings of the Author of the True-Born Englishman* (London, 1705), he emended 'Mathematicks' to 'City Mathematicks', meaning 'town politics'.

18. See pp. 52–4 above.

19. See *SFS*, vol. 1, p. 76, ll. 419–21.

20. Ibid., p. 52, ll. 505–16.

21. Ibid., p. 53, ll. 537–8.

22. Ibid., p. 160, ll. 115–18.

23. Ibid., p. 172, ll. 573–5.

24. Ibid., pp. 341–80.

25. Ibid., p. 42, l. 146; p. 56, ll. 633–6.

26. See *Some Reflections On a Pamphlet Lately Publish'd* (1697), *An Argument Shewing, That a Standing Army … Is not Inconsistent with a Free Government* (1698) and *A*

Brief Reply to the History of Standing Armies (1698), in *PEW*, vol. 1, ed. P. N. Furbank, pp. 37–98.

27. See *PEW*, vol. 3, p. 55.
28. Ibid., pp. 45, 48.
29. See *PEW*, vol. 5, ed. P. N. Furbank, pp. 23–40.
30. Quoted in Lee, *Daniel Defoe: His Life and Recently Discovered Writings*, vol. 1, p. 42.
31. *The Present State of Jacobitism Considered* (London, 1701), Preface (unpaginated).
32. See above, p. 15.
33. *The True-Born Englishman*, in *SFS*, vol. 1, p. 86, l. 32.
34. Ibid., pp. 88–9, ll. 106–44.
35. Ibid., pp. 89–90, ll. 150–87.
36. Ibid., pp. 91–2, ll. 212–58.
37. Ibid., p. 92, ll. 277–84.
38. Furbank and Owens, *The Canonisation of Daniel Defoe*, p. 136.
39. *The True-Born Englishman*, in *SFS*, vol. 1, pp. 100–1, ll. 572–77.
40. Ibid., p. 107, ll. 814–19. ('Conference' in l. 815 is a mistake, and should read 'Conscience'.)
41. Ibid., p. 110, ll. 915–18.
42. Ibid., p. 113, l. 1057.
43. Ibid., p. 118, ll. 1191–216.
44. See, for example, *The Fable of the Cuckoo: or the Sentence on the Ill Bird that defiled his own Nest. Shewing in a Dissenter's Dream, some Satyrical Reflections on a late Infamous Libel, call'd The True-Born Englishman* (London, 1701).
45. *A Satyr upon Thirty Seven Articles* (London, 1701), p. 1.
46. *The True-Born Hugonot* (London, 1703), p. 2.
47. *Some Reflections on a Pamphlet lately Publish'd* (1697), in *PEW*, vol. 1, p. 44.
48. See Backscheider, *Daniel Defoe: His Life*, p. 79
49. *Legion's Memorial*, in *PEW*, vol. 2, ed. J. A. Downie, pp. 39–46.
50. See *An Account of Some Late Designs to Create a Misunderstanding Betwixt the King and his People* (London, 1702), pp. 16–18.
51. Defoe's first major piece of non-fictional writing was the lengthy treatise on social reform, *An Essay upon Projects* (1697); see *PEW*, vol. 8, pp. 27–142.
52. It was reprinted half a century later during John Wilkes's struggle over the rights of citizens *vis-à-vis* Government and Parliament.
53. Mackworth, *A Vindication of the Rights of the Commons of England* (London, 1701), p. 5.
54. *The Original Power … of the People of England*, in *PEW*, vol. 1, p. 112.
55. Ibid., p. 121.
56. Sacheverell, *The Political Union: A Discourse Shewing the Dependance of Government on Religion in General: And of the English Monarchy on the Church of England in Particular* (Oxford, 1702), p. 50.
57. See *PEW*, vol. 3, pp. 77–93.

58. *The Shortest Way with the Dissenters*, in *PEW*, vol. 3, pp. 95–109.
59. See *The Dissenters Answer to the High-Church Challenge* (1704), in *PEW*, vol. 3, p. 177.
60. Defoe to Daniel Finch, Earl of Nottingham, 9 January 1703; *Letters*, pp. 1–3.
61. Defoe to William Penn, 12 July 1703; *Letters*, p. 8.
62. See Backscheider, *Daniel Defoe: His Life*, p. 110.
63. *Letters*, p. 8.
64. See *More Reformation* (1703), in *SFS*, vol. 1, p. 238, ll. 890–94.
65. Letter from Godolphin to Nottingham, 17 July 1703, quoted in John Robert Moore, *Daniel Defoe: Citizen of the Modern World* (Chicago, 1958), p. 135.
66. See, for instance, the reference to 'Empty N[ottingham]' in *A Hymn to Victory* (1704), in *SFS*, vol. 1, p. 306, l. 383; the portrait of 'Finski' in *The Dyet of Poland* (1705), in ibid., p. 353, ll. 295–320; the description of 'Dismal', in *Review*, 9 June 1713.
67. *A Hymn to the Pillory*, in *SFS*, vol. 1, pp. 239–53.
68. D. W. Hayton, 'Robert Harley' in Eveline Cruickshanks, Stuart Handley and D. W. Hayton, *The History of Parliament: The House of Commons 1690–1715*, 5 vols (Cambridge, 2002), vol. 4, p. 244.
69. Quoted by Hayton in ibid., p. 245.
70. See the excellent account of this in the first two chapters of J. A. Downie's *Robert Harley and the Press* (Cambridge, 1979).

Chapter 2
Defoe and the Dead King

1. *An Appeal to Honour and Justice*, p. 202 above.
2. *Letters*, pp. 17, 68.
3. See *Review*, 22 October 1709; 31 October 1710; vol. VIII, Preface.
4. *The History of the Union*, in *TDH*, vol. 7, ed. D. W. Hayton, pp. 112, 117.
5. 'The Storm. An Essay', in *An Elegy on the Author of The True-Born Englishman. With an Essay on the Late Storm* (1704), in *SFS*, vol. 1, p. 285, ll. 72–4.
6. Defoe to Charles Montagu, Baron Halifax, 5 April 1705; *Letters*, pp. 81–83.
7. *A Reply to a Pamphlet entituled, The L—d H—'s Vindication of his Speech* (London, 1706), pp. 8–9.
8. *Review*, 20 March 1707.
9. See J. A. Downie, 'Daniel Defoe: King William's Pamphleteer?', *Eighteenth-Century Life*, 12 (1988), pp. 105–17.
10. *The Succession of Spain Consider'd* (1711), in *PEW*, vol. 5, p. 127.
11. In fact, as we saw from his letter to Harley of May/June 1704 (p. 26), he claimed that it was King William's 'bounty' that enabled him to set up a tile-making business at Tilbury, the implication being that it flourished until the débâcle of *The Shortest Way*. The truth, however, seems to be that the business was already in a bad way in the preceding year, and suppliers were boycotting

Defoe because of his non-payment of debts. On 20 May 1702 he was arrested for debt and appeared before a judge at the Fleet. See Backscheider, *Daniel Defoe: His Life*, p. 119.

12. *The Succession of Spain Consider'd* (1711), in *PEW*, vol. 5, p. 127.

13. Ibid., p. 126.

14. See Furbank and Owens, *A Critical Bibliography of Daniel Defoe*, p. 19.

15. 'I have, within these 20 Years past, Travelled … to every Nook and Corner of that part of the Island, call'd *England*, either upon Publick Affairs, when I had the Honour to serve his late Majesty King *William* … Or upon my private Affairs'; *Review*, 22 February 1711.

16. British Library, Add. MS 29595 (f. 239, for 22 July 1703); quoted by Backscheider, *Daniel Defoe: His Life*, p. 108. She comments: 'This important note seems to corroborate Defoe's acquaintance with his king' (p. 558, n.).

17. For which, of course, it is perfectly possible that he had been paid by the Ministry, though no record of this has been discovered.

18. See above, p. 145.

19. Bodleian Library, MS Rawl D 132.

20. Healey describes the moment of realization in a letter to J. R. Moore of 21 March 1951; uncatalogued Moore papers, University Archives, Indiana University, Bloomington.

21. See Saxe Bannister, *The Life of William Paterson* (Edinburgh, 1858), ch. 21.

22. William Minto, *Daniel Defoe* (London, 1879), p. 169.

Chapter 3
The Author of the *Review*

1. Laurence Hanson, *Government and the Press 1695–1763* (Oxford, 1936), p. 1.

2. *An Essay on the Regulation of the Press* (1704), in *PEW*, vol. 8, pp. 143–59.

3. See *To the Honourable the C—s of England Assembled in P—t* [1704], in ibid., pp. 161–6. This pamphlet and the spy's report were first brought to light by J. A. Downie; see his 'An Unknown Defoe Broadsheet on the Regulation of the Press?', *The Library*, 33 (1978), pp. 51–8. As Downie rightly says, the Petition is not really another *Shortest Way*, since its irony is not intended to deceive.

4. For a full account of the circumstances of publication of the *Review*, see John McVeagh's Introduction to his edition of *Defoe's Review* (London, 2003), vol. 1, pp. x–xli.

5. Defoe's complex, subtle and adventurous-minded stance towards French 'greatness' seems very impressive to us, and we cannot quite go along with Alan Downie's argument that it represented merely the execution of a 'task' that had been set Defoe, 'to build up an "official" picture of the might of France' (*Robert Harley and the Press*, p. 65). How can we even be sure that his supposed taskmaster Harley absolutely understood Defoe's train of thought?

Godolphin most certainly did not. Downie quotes him as writing to Harley, in high indignation, that such scandalous 'magnifying of France' was a thing 'so odious in England' that no pains or expense should be spared to find and punish the author (ibid., p. 66).

6. *Review*, 2 September 1707.

7. See *Memorandum to Robert Harley* [1704], in *PEW*, vol. 1, pp. 151–63.

8. See *Review*, 1 July 1704.

9. *Memorandum*, in *PEW*, vol. 1, pp. 158–9.

10. *The Dissenters Answer to the High-Church Challenge* (1704), in *PEW*, vol. 3, pp. 159–86.

11. *A New Test of the Church of England's Honesty* (1704), in ibid., pp. 187–205.

12. In a letter to William Paterson in April 1703 he wrote bitterly that 'Even the Dissenters like Casha to Caesar Lift up the first Dagger at me: I Confess it makes me Reflect on the wholl body of the Dissenters with Something of Contempt More Than Usuall, and gives me the More Regrett That I Suffer for Such a People'; *Letters*, p. 4.

13. *Letters*, p. 68.

14. Defoe to Harley, August–September 1704; *Letters*, pp. 53–4.

15. Defoe to Harley, July–August 1704; *Letters*, p. 27.

16. Defoe to Harley, September 1704; *Letters*, p. 57.

17. Defoe to Harley, 28 September 1704; *Letters*, p. 59.

18. See [Anon.], *A True State of the Difference between Sir George Rook, Knt., and William Colepeper, Esq.* (London, 1704); *Review*, 20 May 1704; Frank H. Ellis (ed.), *Poems on Affairs of State, Vol. 7: 1704–1714* (New Haven and London, 1975), p. 97, n.

19. See *The Spanish Descent* (1702), in *SFS*, vol. 1, pp. 193–205.

20. See Defoe to Harley, June[?] 1704; *Letters*, pp. 20–5.

21. See *Review*, 4 November 1704.

22. Defoe to Harley, 28 September 1704; *Letters*, p. 59.

23. *The Address* (1704), in *PEW*, vol. 2, pp. 67–76.

24. See *Review*, 3 June 1704.

25. Defoe to Harley, 28 September 1704; *Letters*, p. 59.

26. See *Giving Alms no Charity* (1704), in *PEW*, vol. 8, pp. 167–91.

27. See *The Dissenter Misrepresented and Represented* (probably published in 1704), in *PEW*, vol. 3, pp. 207–23.

28. *The Consolidator* (1705), in *SFS*, vol. 3, ed. Geoffrey Sill, pp. 27–158.

29. Ibid., p. 64.

30. Ibid., p. 65.

31. Ibid., p. 42.

32. Ibid., p. 47.

33. Ibid., p. 43.

34. Ibid., pp. 43–5.

35. Ibid., pp. 104–6.

36. Ibid., p. 67.
37. *The History of the Union*, in *TDH*, vol. 7, p. 135.
38. The story duly appeared in the *London Post* for 14 May 1705 under the heading 'Resolutions upon the present Posture of Affairs by TRUTH and HONESTY'.
39. See Tutchin's account of his family background in the *Observator* for 22–5 August 1705.
40. Thomas Babington Macaulay, *The History of England* (London, n.d.), vol. 1, p. 581.
41. See *The True-Born Englishman*, in *SFS*, vol. 1, pp. 102–3; ll. 623–53.
42. See *Review*, 31 May 1705.
43. *Observator*, 16–19 May 1705.
44. See Defoe's letter to Owen, 26 and 27 October 1705; *Letters*, pp. 105–8.
45. *Observator*, 16–19 May 1705.
46. See Defoe's letter to Halifax, 5 April 1705; *Letters*, pp. 81–3. Healey identifies the bill as the 'Act for giving like remedy upon promissory notes as is now used upon bills of exchange' (ibid., p. 82, n.).
47. The Junto comprised Thomas Wharton (1648–1715), first Marquis of Wharton; John Somers (1651–1716), Lord Somers; Edward Russell (1653–1727), first Earl of Orford; Charles Montagu (1661–1715), Earl of Halifax; and Charles Spencer (1674–1722), third Earl of Sunderland.
48. *Letters*, p. 82.
49. Defoe to Halifax, early summer 1705; *Letters*, p. 86.
50. *Letters*, p. 89.
51. *Letters*, p. 100.
52. *A Challenge of Peace* (London, 1703), p. 23.
53. Defoe to Harley, *c.* 6 November 1705; *Letters*, p. 113.
54. Ibid., p. 112.
55. Defoe to Harley, 10 September 1705; *Letters*, pp. 103–4.
56. These events are described in a letter to Harley of 14 August 1705; *Letters*, pp. 97–9.
57. Defoe to Hugh Stafford, 14 August 1705; *Letters*, pp. 101–2.
58. Stafford's letter to Hedges is quoted in *Letters*, pp. 101–2, n.
59. *Review*, 17 October 1705.
60. Defoe to Edward Owen, 26 and 27 October 1705; *Letters*, pp. 105–6.
61. The Earl of Peterborough had entered Barcelona on 3 October.
62. Blue was the party colour of the Tories.
63. Jeremy Withers was a Whig attorney in Coventry.
64. I.e. Jacobites.
65. *Letters*, p. 107.
66. *Jure Divino*, in *SFS*, vol. 2, ed. P. N. Furbank, p. 35.
67. Ibid., p. 71, ll. 1–4.
68. Ibid., ll. 15–18.

69. Ibid., p. 75, l. 149.
70. Quoted by Defoe in the Preface to *Jure Divino*, *SFS*, vol. 2, pp. 54–5. The passage was in fact left out of the preamble to the second Occasional Conformity Bill.
71. See Defoe's *A Short View of the Present State of the Protestant Religion in Britain* (Edinburgh, 1707), pp. 34–5.
72. *Jure Divino*, in *SFS*, vol. 2, p. 57.
73. *Reformation of Manners*, in *SFS*, vol. 1, p. 173, ll. 607–10.
74. Toland later printed it in *The Second Part of the State Anatomy* (London, 1717), pp. 51–60. For further details, see James Dybikowski, 'John Toland's Letter Concerning Toleration to the Dissenting Ministers', *Enlightenment and Dissent*, 18 (1999), pp. 57–83.
75. *A Short View*, pp. 34–5.
76. Toland, *The Second Part of the State Anatomy*, p. 48.
77. Ibid., p. 67.
78. Ibid., p. 47.
79. Edmund Calamy, *An Historical Account of My Own Life*, ed. John R. Rutt, 2 vols (London, 1829), vol. 2, pp. 38, 461–2.
80. Toland, *The State-Anatomy of Great Britain* (1717), p. 31.
81. R. J. Leslie, *Life and Writings of Charles Leslie* (London, 1885), p. 164.
82. *Review*, 8 May 1705.
83. *Rehearsal*, 9–16 June 1705.
84. See *Rehearsal* for 3 August 1706.
85. *Review*, 13 July 1706.
86. *Rehearsal*, 27 July 1706.
87. *Review*, 13 July 1706; *Rehearsal*, 31 July 1706.
88. *Review*, 10 September 1706. There is, in fact, no ambiguity in what Defoe meant, as is seen by his remark in a note to *Jure Divino*, Book IV, where he says that Sidney's book 'remains unanswerable to this day'; see *SFS*, vol. 2, p. 169, n.
89. *Rehearsal*, 13 November 1706.

Chapter 4
Propagandist for the Union

1. *Review*, 14 July 1709.
2. *An Essay at Removing National Prejudices against a Union with Scotland … Part I* (1706), in *PEW*, vol. 4, ed. D. W. Hayton, pp. 35–61.
3. *An Essay … Part II* (1706), in ibid., pp. 63–87.
4. See Backscheider, *Daniel Defoe: His Life*, p. 207, and Backscheider, 'Defoe and the Clerks of Penicuik', *Modern Philology*, 84 (1987), pp. 372–81.
5. Backscheider, *Daniel Defoe: His Life*, pp. 207–8.

6. See Maximillian E. Novak, *Daniel Defoe: Master of Fictions* (Oxford, 2001), p. 309.

7. Quoted in Backscheider, *Daniel Defoe: His Life*, p. 208.

8. Defoe to Harley, 6 May 1706; *Letters*, p. 121.

9. A report of his examination by the Commissioners appeared in the *London Gazette* for 8 August 1706; quoted in *Letters*, p. 124, n. It would seem that Defoe in fact failed to obtain a certificate of quittance from his creditors, as the law prescribed, which would lead to trouble for him later. See his account of the matter in *Mercator*, 12–14 January 1714.

10. *Cantabit vacuus coram latrone viator* ('the traveller without possessions will sing in the robber's face'), Juvenal, *Satires*, X.22.

11. Defoe to Harley, 13 September 1706; *Letters*, pp. 126–7. The account Defoe gave of this expedition in his later *History of the Union* (1709) was discreetly misleading: 'My curiosity prest me to take a Journey thither [to Scotland], and being by all my Friends, to whom I communicated my Design, encouraged, to think I might be useful there to prompt a Work that I was fully convinced was for the general Good of the whole Island; and particularly necessary for the strengthening the Protestant Interest, I was moved purely on these Accounts to undertake a long Winter, a Chargeable, and as it proved, a Hazardous Journey'; see *TDH*, vol. 7, p. 259.

12. *Letters*, p. 126.

13. Quoted in *Letters*, p. 130, n.

14. Defoe to Harley, 30 September 1706; *Letters*, p. 131.

15. Harley to Defoe, October 1706; *Letters*, p. 132.

16. Defoe to Harley, 24 October 1706; *Letters*, pp. 133–5.

17. The text of the 'Articles of Union' is included in Defoe's *History of the Union*; see *TDH*, vol. 7, p. 242.

18. *TDH*, vol. 8, ed. D. W. Hayton, p. 32.

19. Ibid., pp. 33–4.

20. Defoe to Harley, 14 November 1706; *Letters*, p. 148.

21. For the texts of all three poems, see *PEW*, vol. 4, pp. 199–204, 205–8, 378–80.

22. He was imprisoned in Edinburgh Castle after the abortive Jacobite invasion of March 1708 and later sent in custody to England, on the (unjustified) suspicion of treason.

23. *Review*, 10 July 1708.

24. *TDH*, vol. 8, p. 43.

25. In November 1706 the Earl of Mar reported that 'Defoe … is still here. I'm not acquainted with him, but he really takes a great deall of pains in this affair'; quoted in Ellis (ed.), *Poems on Affairs of State: Vol. 7, 1704–1714*, p. 211.

26. This was the lump sum payment to be given from the English public revenue to compensate the Scots for the massive financial losses they incurred following the failure of the Darien expedition in 1699–1700, and in recognition

of the fact that Scots would be paying taxes after the Union towards the satisfaction of the English national debt.

27. See Defoe to Harley, 22 November 1706; *Letters*, pp. 155–8.
28. See *TDH*, vol. 8, pp. 92–6.
29. Defoe to Harley, 2 November 1706; *Letters*, p. 139.
30. Godolphin to Harley, 16 January 1707; quoted in Backscheider, *Daniel Defoe: His Life*, p. 231.
31. *Letters*, pp. 133, 140.
32. *An Essay, at Removing National Prejudices ... Part III*, in *PEW*, vol. 4, p. 93.
33. Ibid., p. 95.
34. Ibid., pp. 96, 105.
35. Ibid., p. 111.
36. See [James Hodges], *The Rights and Interests of the Two British Monarchies, Treatise III* (London, 1706), pp. 11–12.
37. *A Fourth Essay, at Removing National Prejudices*, in *PEW*, vol. 4, p. 119.
38. Ibid., p. 125.
39. The story is related in William Drummond's *The History of Scotland from the Year 1423 until the Year 1542* (London, 1655), p. 134.
40. *A Fourth Essay, at Removing National Prejudices*, in *PEW*, vol. 4, pp. 142–3.
41. *Letters*, p. 155.
42. Defoe to Harley, 26 November 1706; *Letters*, pp. 158–60.
43. One thinks of the lamentations of the letter-writer in his *A Continuation of Letters Written by a Turkish Spy at Paris* (1718) (see *SFS*, vol. 5, ed. David Blewett), and Defoe's description of himself, in a famous letter to Charles Delafaye of 1718, as being, like the Turkish spy, forced to live and work among 'a Generation who I profess My Very Soul abhorrs'; *Letters*, p. 454.
44. Defoe to Harley, 4 January 1707; *Letters*, p. 189.
45. *Letters*, p. 181.
46. See W. R. Owens and P. N. Furbank, 'New Light on John Pierce, Defoe's Agent in Scotland', *Edinburgh Bibliographical Society Transactions*, 6 (1998), pp. 134–43.
47. *Letters*, pp. 183, 188.
48. *Letters*, p. 193.

Chapter 5
'Maintaining a Counter Correspondence'

1. *Review*, 29 March 1707.
2. *Review*, 28 January 1707; 'Miscellanea'.
3. *Review*, 29 March 1707.
4. See Backscheider, *Daniel Defoe: His Life*, p. 235.
5. Defoe to Harley, 27 January 1707; *Letters*, pp. 196–7.
6. *Letters*, p. 188.

7. Defoe to Harley, 13 November 1706; *Letters*, p. 147.
8. *Letters*, p. 202.
9. Ibid.
10. Godolphin to Marlborough, 18 October 1706; in William Coxe, *Memoirs of the Duke of Marlborough*, 3 vols (London, 1907), vol. 2, pp. 22–3.
11. Godolphin to Marlborough, 24 June 1707; in ibid., p. 106.
12. Harley's letter is missing, but Defoe refers to it in his reply of 27 January; *Letters*, p. 196.
13. See *Letters*, pp. 202, 207, 213, 215.
14. *Letters*, p. 214.
15. Defoe to Godolphin, 22 February 1707; *Letters*, pp. 203–5.
16. Coxe, *Memoirs of the Duke of Marlborough*, vol. 2, p. 35.
17. *Letters*, pp. 220–1.
18. *Letters*, pp. 219, 223, 226–7.
19. Defoe had referred several times in earlier letters to meetings with Queensberry and his promises to 'Recommend' Defoe to Godolphin and the Queen; see *Letters*, pp. 213, 216, 224.
20. *Letters*, pp. 227–9.
21. *Letters*, p. 227.
22. Quoted in Winston S. Churchill, *Marlborough: His Life and Times*, 2 vols (London, 1947), vol. 2, p. 290.
23. It no doubt would have had to be in Scotland, since the Test Act did not operate there.
24. Defoe to Harley, 19 June 1711; *Letters*, pp. 331–2.
25. Defoe to Harley, 5 and 7 August 1707; *Letters*, pp. 232–6.
26. Defoe to Harley, 8 July 1707; *Letters*, pp. 229–30.
27. Godolphin wrote to Harley on 14 August 1707: 'I don't like D F's letter, but I have often observed that he gives you the worst side of the picture'; cited in *Letters*, p. 236, n.
28. *Review*, 2 September 1707.
29. *Review*, 21 October 1707.
30. *Dyers News Examined as to His Sweddish Memorial against the Review* ([Edinburgh, 1707]), p. 1. See also *De Foe's Answer, to Dyer's Scandalous News Letter* ([Edinburgh, 1707]).
31. See Narcissus Luttrell, *A Brief Historical Relation of State Affairs*, 6 vols (Oxford, 1857), vol. 6, p. 224, entry for Saturday 18 October 1707.
32. He was an insatiable reader of history, and indeed wrote in *The Two Great Questions Further Considered* (1700), 'I have Read all the Histories of *Europe*, that are Extant in our Language, and some in other Languages'; see *PEW*, vol. 5, p. 46.
33. See D. W. Hayton, Introduction to *The History of the Union*, in *TDH*, vol. 7, pp. 20–1.
34. *TDH*, vol. 7, p. 110.

35. Ibid., pp. 153–4.
36. *Letters*, pp. 242–3.
37. *Letters*, p. 245.
38. *Letters*, p. 246.
39. Defoe to Harley, 28 November 1707; *Letters*, p. 247.
40. See letter from Harley to Marlborough, 16 September 1707, in Churchill, *Marlborough*, vol. 2, p. 293.
41. See G. V. Bennett, *The Tory Crisis in Church and State 1688–1730: The Career of Francis Atterbury, Bishop of Rochester* (Oxford, 1975), p. 95.
42. See Coxe, *Memoirs of the Duke of Marlborough*, vol. 2, p. 192.
43. *Letters*, p. 250.
44. See *An Appeal to Honour and Justice*, above, pp. 208–9.
45. They are reprinted above, pp. 187–93.
46. Above, pp. 188–9.
47. See above, pp. 192–3.
48. *Review*, 8 June 1708.
49. *Review*, 8 May 1708.
50. *Review*, 15 May 1708.
51. *Review*, 4 May 1708.
52. We may suppose that the intermediary was not the MP Shute Barrington, as Healey suggests (*Letters*, p. 256, n. 2), but John Shut, a councillor of Lincoln's Inn, sent on a mission to Scotland by Lord Wharton (see *Letters*, p. 184, n. 5).
53. *Letters*, pp. 257–8.
54. *Review*, 22 June 1708. Coxe, in his *Memoirs of the Duke of Marlborough*, speaks of Defoe's 'extreme surprise and embarrassment' at these novel phenomena (vol. 2, p. 231), and likewise J. A. Downie, in his 'Defoe and the General Election of 1708', *Eighteenth-Century Studies*, 8 (1974–5), pp. 315–28, speaks of Defoe's 'utter ignorance' of the rift between his two patrons. They may well be right, but one reflects that, even if Defoe had known what Sunderland had been up to, it would have been altogether tactless to admit it.
55. *Letters*, pp. 256–9.
56. *Letters*, pp. 259–61.
57. *Review*, 14 September 1712. See P. W. J. Riley, *The English Ministers and Scotland 1707–1727* (London, 1964), p. 107.
58. See *The Old Whig and Modern Whig Revived* (1717), in *SFS*, vol. 4, ed. P. N. Furbank, p. 189.
59. William Forbes (d. 1716), thirteenth Lord Forbes. In his 'Preface to the Parliament' in his poem *Caledonia* Defoe writes of his 'extraordinary Obligations' to the Forbes family, but it is not known what they consisted in. See *PEW*, vol. 4, p. 215.
60. Above, p. 192.
61. The pamphlet Defoe is referring to is probably *A Memorial to the Nobility of Scotland* (Edinburgh, 1708).

62. Above, p. 193.
63. *Review*, 22 June 1708.
64. *Review*, 24 June 1708.
65. *Review*, 24 July 1708.
66. *Review*, 30 October 1708.
67. *Review*, 2 November 1708.
68. *Review*, 18 November 1708.
69. La Rochelle, a centre for the Huguenots, was forced to surrender to Louis XIII and Richelieu in 1627, after a long siege.
70. *Review*, 12 April 1708.
71. In the *Review* for 9 April he quotes his own famous opening lines to *Jure Divino*: '*Nature has left this Tincture in the Blood, / That all Men would be Tyrants if they could; / If they forbear their Neighbours to devour, / 'Tis not for Want of Will, but Want of Power*'.
72. *Review*, 19 April 1709.
73. *Review*, 16 April 1709.
74. *Review*, 19 April 1709.
75. See H. T. Dickinson, 'The Poor Palatines and the Parties', *English Historical Review*, 82 (1967), pp. 464–85.
76. *Review*, 24 February 1709.
77. *Review*, 25 June 1709.
78. *Review*, 2 July 1709.
79. *Review*, 5 July 1709.
80. *Canary-Birds Naturaliz'd in Utopia* (London, [1709]), p. 17.
81. *Review*, 8 September 1709, 'Miscellanea'.
82. See *Tour*, in *TDH*, vol. 1, ed. John McVeagh, p. 232.
83. See Moore, *Daniel Defoe: Citizen of the Modern World*, p. 190.
84. See Backscheider, *Daniel Defoe: His Life*, pp. 300–1.
85. Ibid., p. 264.
86. William Bissett, quoted by Geoffrey Holmes in *The Trial of Dr. Sacheverell* (London, 1973), p. 64.
87. See ibid., p. 68.

Chapter 6
1710: The Fateful Step

1. Quoted in Holmes, *The Trial of Dr. Sacheverell*, p. 57.
2. Ibid., p. 170.
3. 'Captain Tom' was the proverbial ringleader of riots.
4. *Review*, 18 March 1710.
5. *Review*, 21 March 1710.
6. *A Letter from Captain Tom to the Mobb* (London, 1710), p. 3.

7. As a result of a debate in the Lords in December 1705 it was made a penal offence to suggest that the Church was in danger.
8. Quoted in Holmes, *The Trial of Dr. Sacheverell*, pp. 186–7.
9. Defoe's argument, stated, for example, in the *Review* for 20 May 1710, is obviously correct. From a hereditary point of view the Pretender, being male, had a superior right to the throne.
10. *Review*, 11 March 1710.
11. Holmes, *The Trial of Dr. Sacheverell*, pp. 197–200.
12. *Review*, 9 May 1710.
13. *Review*, 17 June 1710.
14. *Review*, 20 June 1710.
15. *Review*, 22 June 1710.
16. See George Macaulay Trevelyan, *England Under Queen Anne*, 3 vols (London, 1934), vol. 3, p. 66.
17. *Letters*, pp. 270–1.
18. *Letters*, p. 272.
19. *Review*, 12 August 1710.
20. *Review*, 15 August 1710.
21. *Review*, 19 August 1710.
22. See *PEW*, vol. 6, ed. John McVeagh, pp. 49–61.
23. Defoe to Harley, 5 September 1710; *Letters*, pp. 276–7.
24. See *PEW*, vol. 6, pp. 63–76.
25. Moreover the Queen was adamantly against him.
26. The Treaty of Union did not give Scottish peers an automatic right to membership of the House of Lords, but it provided that, at a general election, they should appoint sixteen of their number to represent them in it.
27. Defoe to Harley, 18 November 1710; *Letters*, pp. 293–6.
28. Defoe to Harley, 26 December 1710; *Letters*, pp. 306–7.
29. *Letters*, p. 307.
30. See P. N. Furbank and W. R. Owens, 'The Dating of Defoe's *Atalantis Major*', *Notes and Queries*, n.s. 44 (1997), pp. 189–90.
31. Defoe to Harley, 13 February 1711; *Letters*, pp. 310–13.
32. Trevelyan, *England Under Queen Anne*, vol. 3, p. 96.
33. See *PEW*, vol. 2, pp. 139–76.
34. Ibid., pp. 153–55.
35. Ibid., pp. 159, 172.
36. That is, members of the notoriously High Church lower House of Convocation.
37. Quoted in David Nokes, *Jonathan Swift: A Hypocrite Reversed* (Oxford, 1985), p. 56.
38. *Examiner*, 9 November 1710.
39. *Examiner*, 28 December 1710.
40. *Examiner*, 16 November 1710.

41. Defoe, who certainly read the *Examiner*, riposted in the *Review* for 14 December, asking for an answer to a 'civil question: if *Mr. Examiner* had so much learning, how did he come to have so little manners?'.

42. *Examiner*, 19 April 1711.

43. In *The Conduct of the Allies* (1711), in *The Prose Works of Jonathan Swift*, ed. Temple Scott, 12 vols (London, 1900–25), vol. 5, p. 103.

44. *Review*, 1 May 1711.

45. Curiously, as Trevelyan points out in his *Blenheim* (London, 1930), p. 303, it was also, from the beginning of the war, the attitude of the arch-Tory Nottingham.

46. *Review*, 19 April 1709.

47. See *PEW*, vol. 2, p. 185.

48. Ibid., p. 201.

49. *Review*, 17 July 1711.

50. There was a clause in the treaty of the Grand Alliance which could be regarded as permitting this.

51. See further P. N. Furbank and W. R. Owens, 'Defoe's "South-Sea" and "North-Sea" Schemes: A Footnote to *A New Voyage Round the World*', *Eighteenth-Century Fiction*, 13 (2001), pp. 501–8.

52. See *PEW*, vol. 2 p. 222.

53. Ibid., pp. 223, 224.

54. Ibid., pp. 227, 230. For 'sinking the Ship', see the passage from the *Review* for 12 August 1710, quoted above, pp. 110–11.

55. See *Political State* for November 1711, p. 652; [A. Maynwaring], *A Letter to a High Churchman, in Answer to a Pamphlet, intitled, Reasons Why this Nation ...* (London, 1711), p. 4.

56. Gallas was banished from the Court for doing so. Maynwaring, however, surmised that it might have been a put-up job on the part of the Ministry, the author of *Reasons Why this Nation* painting so grim a picture of Britain's war-weariness as to make any kind of peace seem acceptable, thus causing the relatively advantageous provisions of the 'preliminaries' to come as a pleasant surprise.

57. Defoe to Harley, 14 February 1712; *Letters*, p. 370.

58. *Letters*, pp. 363, 380, 386.

59. See David Green, *Queen Anne 1665–1714* (London, 1970), p. 260.

60. He was still brooding over the Whigs' treachery a year and a half later. 'The People and Party I always loved and espous'd have forsaken the Spirit of Peace, and the knowledge of their real Interest, and have sold their Christian Liberty, O DISMAL! to thy empty and foolish Projects'; *Review*, 6 June 1713.

61. Defoe to Harley, 10 January 1712; *Letters*, p. 366.

62. Bolingbroke later did his best to suggest that Harley was behind these 'restraining orders', but he seems in fact to have devised them himself,

without telling his colleagues; see Trevelyan, *England under Queen Anne*, vol. 3, p. 217.

63. Defoe to Harley, 27 May 1712; *Letters*, p. 375.
64. *Letters*, p. 395.
65. *Review*, 25 December 1711.
66. *Review*, 21 February 1712.
67. *Review*, 10 July 1712.
68. Defoe to Harley, 1 April 1713; *Letters*, pp. 401–2. See also Defoe's later account of the affair in his journal *Mercator*, 14 January 1714.
69. *Flying Post*, 16 April 1713.
70. Nor, amazing as it must seem, were such as the author of *Judas Discuver'd, and Catch'd at Last: or, Daniel de Foe in Lobs Pound* (London, 1713) willing to read Defoe's titles as other than literal and as plain evidence of high treason.
71. See Backscheider, *Daniel Defoe: His Life*, p. 323.
72. Defoe to Harley, 19 April 1713; *Letters*, pp. 409–12.
73. See *Review* for 16 and 18 April 1713.
74. *And What if the Pretender Should Come?* (1715), in *PEW*, vol. 1, p. 195.
75. There is evidence in the Stuart Papers that Harley was continuously in touch with the Pretender's court, even during his spell in the Tower in 1715–17; see Wolfgang Michael, *England under George I*, 2 vols (London, 1939), vol. 2, p. 156. Henry St John was also in contact with it, through French intermediaries, for instance in regard to the Pretender's hoped-for conversion to Protestantism; see Sheila Biddle, *Bolingbroke and Harley* (London, 1975), p. 55, n. 2.
76. See above, p. 218.
77. See above, p. 212.
78. *Review*, 7 and 11 April 1713.
79. *An Essay on the Treaty of Commerce* (London, 1713), p. 39.
80. *Review*, 12 December 1704.
81. *An Essay on the Treaty of Commerce*, p. 40.
82. See above, p. 173.
83. See *Memoirs of Count Tariff* (1713), in *SFS*, vol, 3, pp. 159–97.
84. *The Late Tryal and Conviction of Count Tariff* (London, 1713), pp. 9–10.
85. *Memoirs of Count Tariff*, in *SFS*, vol. 3, p. 163. 'Coopman' is Dutch for 'merchant'.
86. Ibid., pp. 168–70.
87. Ibid., p. 173.
88. Ibid., p. 174.
89. Ibid., pp. 176–77.
90. *Review*, 19 May 1711 and 24 January 1712.
91. *Mercator*, 26–29 September 1713.
92. Defoe to Harley, 19 February 1714; *Letters*, pp. 429–30.
93. *Letters*, p. 433–38.
94. See [John Dunton], *Queen Robin* (London, [1714]), p. 31; cf. p. 58.

95. *Monitor*, 29 July 1714.
96. *The Reader*, 7–10 May 1714.
97. *Monitor*, 22 April 1714.
98. In April 1706, at the Emperor's behest, but in some degree at his own expense, Marlborough was installed as Prince of Mindelheim (a small principality in Bavaria).
99. *Monitor*, 31 July 1714.
100. *Monitor*, 17 June 1714.

Chapter 7
Defoe and the Whig Split

1. See *The Family Instructor*, 2nd edn (1715), Preface (unpaginated).
2. For further details, see P. N. Furbank and W. R. Owens, 'Defoe and the Sham *Flying-Post*', *Publishing History*, 43 (1998), pp. 5–15.
3. Arthur Moore, Commissioner of Trade, who had been associated with Defoe in the publication of the *Mercator*.
4. *Letters*, pp. 445–7.
5. See *The True-Born Englishman*, in *SFS*, vol. 1, p. 89, ll. 159–61; *Robinson Crusoe*, 'Shakespeare Head' edn, 3 vols (Oxford, 1927), vol. 2, p. 13.
6. *Letters*, pp. 443–4.
7. *The Secret History of the White-Staff*, in *PEW*, vol. 2, p. 269.
8. Ibid., pp. 270–3.
9. Ibid., p. 273.
10. Ibid., p. 277.
11. Symbolizing the Exchequer.
12. *The Secret History of the White-Staff*, in *PEW*, vol. 2, p. 294.
13. *The Secret History of the White Staff, Part II* (London, 1714), p. 64.
14. Ibid., p. 61.
15. *The History of the Mitre and Purse* (London, 1714), p. 14.
16. See Bennett, *The Tory Crisis in Church and State*, p. 192.
17. *The History of the Mitre and Purse*, p. 4.
18. Quoted in Novak, *Daniel Defoe: Master of Fictions*, pp. 461–2. Some months later Oxford also inserted a notice in the *London Gazette* (5–9 July 1715) formally denying all connection with the *Secret History*.
19. See Bennett, *The Tory Crisis in Church and State*, p. 190.
20. *The Secret History of the Secret History of the White Staff*, in *PEW*, vol. 2, p. 299.
21. Ibid., pp. 300–3
22. Ibid., pp. 303–5. The reader will not be surprised to hear that the anonymous author of *Queen Anne Vindicated from the Base Aspersions of Some Late Pamphlets* (London, 1715), pp. 12–15, reports Pittis as solemnly denying this story and putting it down to the invention of 'one Whose Christian Name is *Daniel*'.
23. See *The Minutes of the Negotiations of Monsr. Mesnager*, in *SFS*, vol. 4, p. 64.

24. Above, p. 199.
25. Above, p. 214.
26. Above, p. 210.
27. Above, p. 212.
28. Above, p. 227.
29. Above, p. 226.
30. See Laurence Hanson, *Government and the Press 1696–1760*, p. 96. See also J. A. Downie, 'Secret Service Payments to Daniel Defoe, 1710–1714', *Review of English Studies*, n.s. 30 (1979), pp. 437–41.
31. *A Friendly Epistle* (London, 1715), p. 17.
32. *Letters*, p. 448, n.
33. Samuel Keimer, *A Brand Pluck'd from the Burning* (London, 1718), pp. 96, 105.
34. The author of a (fictitious) letter from the Jacobite rebel General Forster to the Earl of Mar includes a postscript saying that he will make sure to have the letter 're-publish'd with Advantage, by Friend *Keimer*, and *D.F.* his *Amanuensis*, in the *London Post*' (*Political State* for December 1715).
35. It decrees that if twelve or more persons refuse to disperse, having been ordered to do so by a Justice of the Peace and the Act having been read out to them, violence can legitimately be used against them.
36. See *Robin's Last Shift*, 14 April 1716; *The Shift Shifted*, 19 May, 23 June and 7 July 1716.
37. This account is given by Defoe in a letter to Charles Delafaye, 26 April 1716; *Letters*, pp. 450–4.
38. See H. M. Imbert-Terry, *A Constitutional King: George the First* (London, 1927), pp. 230–1.
39. *The Quarrel of the School-Boys at Athens*, in *SFS*, vol. 3, p. 211.
40. *The State-Anatomy of Great Britain* (London, 1717), p. 3.
41. Ibid., p. 88.
42. Ibid., p. 60.
43. Ibid., p. 57.
44. *An Argument Proving* (London, 1717), pp. 5, 13.
45. Ibid., p. 18.
46. Ibid., p. 19.
47. Ibid., pp. 5–6.
48. *Political State*, June 1717, p. 632.
49. *The Second Part of the State Anatomy* (London, 1717), pp. 27–8.
50. *A Farther Argument* (London, 1717), pp. 4–5.
51. Ibid., pp. 5–6.
52. *The Old Whig and Modern Whig Revived*, in *SFS*, vol. 4, p. 198.
53. See Wolfgang Michael, *England under George I* (London, 1936), vol. 2, p. 21.
54. *Minutes of the Negotiations of Monsr. Mesnager*, in *SFS*, vol. 4, pp. 42
55. *Mercurius Politicus* for July 1717 reprinted a letter published by Defoe in the *St. James's Post* denying his authorship of the *Minutes*.

56. *Political State* for June 1717, p. 632.

57. *A Declaration of Truth to Benjamin Hoadly* (London, 1717), p. 19.

58. See *The Conduct of Christians* (1717) and *A Continuation of Letters Written by a Turkish Spy at Paris* (1718), in *SFS*, vol. 5.

59. See Geoffrey Sill's Introduction to *SFS*, vol. 3, p. 23.

60. *The Second Part of the State Anatomy*, p. 29.

61. *Mercurius Politicus*, July 1716, p. 134.

62. Ibid., p. 141.

63. See further, P. N. Furbank and W. R. Owens, 'Defoe, the De la Faye Letters and *Mercurius Politicus*', *British Journal for Eighteenth-Century Studies*, 23 (2000), pp. 13–19.

64. Lee, *Daniel Defoe: His Life, and Recently Discovered Writings*, vol. 1, chs 11, 12 and 14. See further Furbank and Owens, *The Canonisation of Daniel Defoe*, pp. 62–74.

65. Defoe to Charles Delafaye, 26 April 1718; *Letters*, p. 453.

66. See further, P. N. Furbank and W. R. Owens, 'Defoe and "Sir Andrew Politick"', *British Journal for Eighteenth-Century Studies*, 17 (1994), pp. 27–39.

67. In 1717, for instance, he was tried for printing trial proceedings without permission. See Jeremy Black, 'An Underrated Journalist: Nathaniel Mist and the Opposition Press during the Whig Ascendancy', *British Journal for Eighteenth-Century Studies*, 10 (1987), pp. 27–41.

68. See National Archives, SP 35/13, fo. 58.

69. National Archives, SP 35/13, fo. 59.

70. Quoted in George Aitken, 'Defoe and Mist's "Weekly Journal"', *Athenaeum*, 26 August 1893, p. 288.

71. *Read's Weekly Journal* for 18 October reports that Mist dares not admit that Defoe writes the *Weekly Journal* 'because he's strickly [*sic*] bound in the Penalty of 500 l. to the contrary'.

72. See Aitken, 'Defoe and Mist's "Weekly Journal"', pp. 287–8.

73. James Sutherland, *Defoe* (London, 1937), pp. 223–5.

74. *Read's Weekly Journal*, 26 July 1718.

75. See *London Review*, 4 and 11 June, 1864, pp. 590–1, 617–18. The letters, of 12 and 26 April, 10 and 23 May, and 4 and 13 June 1718, are in *Letters*, pp. 450–60.

76. See William Lee, 'Daniel Defoe, the News Writer', *Notes and Queries*, 3rd series, 7 (1865), pp. 244–6.

77. Although in quotations from Defoe's letters elsewhere we have followed the text in *Letters*, we have thought it convenient here, since so much turns on the exact wording of this important letter, to modernize spelling and punctuation.

78. See p. 173 above.

79. See Laurence Hanson, *Government and the Press 1695–1763*, p. 102.

80. William Lee, *Daniel Defoe: His Life, and Recently Discovered Writings*, vol. 1, p. 265.
81. Defoe to Delafaye, 23 May 1718; *Letters*, p. 456.
82. Backscheider, *Daniel Defoe: His Life*, pp. 387–9.

Chapter 8
The Return of the Prodigal

1. There is solid evidence for Defoe's directing the *White-Hall Evening Post*. In the number for 30 October, the journal published an item concerning a letter written by Sir David Dalrymple to the Earl of Stair. Dalrymple, who complained of the unauthorized use of his name, obtained an apology, and he identifies the editor as Defoe. (See Backscheider, *Daniel Defoe: His Life*, pp. 434–5.)
2. His admission comes in the 'Supplement' to the issue of the *Manufacturer*, a journal commissioned from Defoe by the London Company of Weavers, for 2 December 1719. The text is reprinted in Furbank and Owens, *A Critical Bibliography of Daniel Defoe*, p. 254.
3. *Mercurius Politicus*, December 1718, pp. 726–7.
4. *Robinson Crusoe*, vol. 1, pp. 60, 128, 164, 175, 178.
5. Ibid., pp. 114, 171.
6. This was a point stressed by Manuel Schonhorn, in his *Defoe's Politics: Parliament, Power, Kingship, and Robinson Crusoe* (Cambridge, 1991); see ch. 6, 'The politics of *Robinson Crusoe*', pp. 141–64.
7. *Jure Divino*, Book V, in *SFS*, vol. 2, p. 174, ll. 70–9.
8. Ibid., p. 71, ll. 1–4.
9. *Robinson Crusoe*, vol. 3, p. 80.
10. *Jure Divino*, Book II, in *SFS*, vol. 2, pp. 105–6, ll. 121–4.
11. *Robinson Crusoe*, vol. 1, p. 3.
12. *The Commentator*, 1 January 1720.
13. *The Commentator*, 8 January 1720.
14. *The Commentator*, 11 January 1720
15. This was a bill to restrict the royal prerogative in the creating of new peerages. It was introduced by Stanhope in March 1719 but was defeated, partly through a masterly speech by Walpole. The defeat was a major blow for the Government.
16. *The Commentator*, 11 January 1720.
17. I.e. Drury Lane and the new theatre in Lincoln's Inn Fields.
18. *The Commentator*, 15 February 1720.
19. In the famous comedy *The Rehearsal* (1672), by the Duke of Buckingham, Prince Pettyman (who was found abandoned by a fisherman and was brought up by him as his own child) muses: 'What Oracle this darkness can evince? / Some Times a Fishers Son, sometimes a Prince' (III.iv).

20. In number 6 of Steele's *The Reader* (May 1714) it was announced that he was preparing a history of Marlborough's campaigns in Flanders, but he failed to produce anything, and the papers were eventually passed on to Glover, and then to Mallet.

21. *The Commentator*, 17 March 1720.

22. See *The Chimera*, in *PEW*, vol. 6, p. 160.

23. See *The Director*, 21 October 1720, in *PEW*, vol. 6, p. 225.

24. *The Director*, 19 December 1720, in *PEW*, vol. 6, p. 273.

25. *The Director*, 28 November 1720, in *PEW*, vol. 6, p. 256.

26. *The Director*, 21 November 1720, in *PEW*, vol. 6, p. 249.

27. *The Director*, 16 January 1721, in *PEW*, vol. 6, p. 293.

28. *The Director*, 13 January 1721, in *PEW*, vol. 6, p. 289.

29. The word 'Political' here refers to devilish politics, not the Whig and Tory kind.

30. There might be said to be an exception in two pamphlets belonging to 1727, concerned with the danger of a new war with Spain (*The Evident Approach of a War*, and its sequel *The Evident Advantages to Great Britain and its Allies from the Approaching War*), but these do not reveal anything new as regards his political loyalties.

Appendix A

1. These letters exist in the form of transcripts preserved among the Yarborough papers on deposit in the Lincolnshire County Archives, Yarb 16/7/1 and 2. For a full account, see W. R. Owens and P. N. Furbank, 'Defoe as Secret Agent: Three Unpublished Letters', *The Scriblerian*, 25 (1993), pp. 145–53. In editing the letters for publication we have followed the principles adopted by George Harris Healey, editor of Defoe's *Letters*. The three letters here would come between letters 130 and 131 in Healey's edition. We are grateful to Lord Yarborough for giving us permission to publish the letters.

2. The general election of 1708, the first for an all-British Parliament. For an account of the conduct of the election in Scotland, see P. W. J. Riley, *The English Ministers and Scotland 1707–1727* (London, 1964), ch. viii.

3. Defoe also wrote about the unfortunate effects of the Triennial Act in the *Review* for 19 June 1708.

4. John Campbell (1678–1743), second Duke of Argyll; distinguished general. Though a leading architect of the Union Treaty, Argyll remained something of an independent.

5. John Erskine (1675–1732), eleventh Earl of Mar, whose seat was Alloa House in Clackmannan. Familarly known as 'Bobbing John' from his practice of changing political loyalties, he was now attached to the Court interest, and had just been appointed Keeper of the Signet.

6. Charles Ross (d. 1732), son of George, eleventh Lord Ross; MP for Ross-Shire 1709–22.

7. William Dalrymple (1678–1744), son of John, first Earl of Stair; MP for Clackmannanshire 1708–10.

8. 'Faggots' were dummy voters.

9. In Scotland the term 'baron' signified any freeholder.

10. The quarrel was reported in the *Edinburgh Courant*, 21–3 June 1708.

11. William Gordon (1683–1720), Lord Strathnaver, heir apparent of John, sixteenth Earl of Sutherland. He was elected, but subsequently disqualified as the eldest son of a peer. See Riley, *The English Ministers and Scotland*, p. 110.

12. John Gordon (*c.* 1660–1733), sixteenth Earl of Sutherland.

13. I.e. the '*Squadrone Volante*', or 'New Party', a coalition of lesser Presbyterian magnates who had, albeit with some reluctance, combined with the Scottish Court party (headed by the Duke of Queensberry) to bring about the Union.

14. William Morison (d. 1737) of Prestongrange, Haddingtonshire; Scottish MP 1707–8.

15. David Boyle (1666–1733), first Earl of Glasgow; a Court Tory.

16. This letter is untraced.

17. For Defoe's attempts to procure a post in Scotland, see above, pp. 79–80.

18. It was common for those given a post in the Scottish administration to avoid the necessity of going to Scotland by appointing a deputy; thus Defoe is evidently assuming that to appoint a deputy would be an effective disguise for his actual presence in Scotland.

19. For similar complaints, see letters to Harley, 10 June and 17 July 1707; *Letters*, pp. 226, 231.

20. See letter to Harley of 28 November 1707; *Letters*, pp. 247–8.

21. George Tilson (d. 1738), had become undersecretary to Henry Boyle in February 1708, and was appointed Auditor of the Scottish Excise by Godolphin. See J. C. Sainty, *Office-Holders in Modern Britain, II: Officials of the Secretaries of State 1660–1782* (London, 1973), pp. 109–10. See also Riley, *English Ministers and Scotland*, p. 64.

22. Godolphin had been instrumental in securing Defoe's release from Newgate in 1703; see above, p. 24.

23. George Hamilton (1666–1737), first Earl of Orkney, brother to the Duke of Hamilton; general. He would be frequently chosen as a representative peer. He publicly criticized Marlborough; see Defoe to Harley, 3 August 1708; *Letters*, p. 262.

24. Presumably Marlborough.

25. This is probably *A Memorial to the Nobility of Scotland* (Edinburgh, 1708). See Furbank and Owens, *A Critical Bibliography of Daniel Defoe*, p. 91.

26. Defoe is probably referring to his earlier *The High-Church Legion: Or, The Memorial Examin'd* (London, 1705), a reply to James Drake's notorious *Memorial of the Church of England* (London, 1705). See *Letters*, pp. 90–3.

27. Almost certainly *Scotland in Danger* (Edinburgh, [1708]), which reprints the *Reviews* for 1, 3 and 5 June, with minor adjustments for a Scottish audience.

28. No English printing of the *Memorial to the Nobility of Scotland* is known to exist.

29. According to Riley, *English Ministers and Scotland*, p. 108, important defectors from the Court party to the Squadrone included the Earls of Eglinton, Glencairn, Forfar and Buchan.

30. William Forbes (d. 1716), thirteenth Lord Forbes.

31. This is probably a reference to the famous letter, supposedly written by Sunderland to the Squadrone leader, the Earl of Roxburgh, suggesting that Queen Anne was now inclining towards the Junto. See above, p. 92.

32. These were peers not on the Court list, i.e. Montrose, Roxburgh, Rothes, Hamilton, Crawford and Orkney. See Riley, *English Ministers and Scotland*, p. 109.

33. Defoe seems to mean 'pass on extracts from'.

34. It is difficult to interpret this except as a misreading of the original manuscript. One possibility is that an 'L' has been misread as a 'P', an easy mistake with handwriting of this period, and the name intended is Lord Sunderland.

Appendix B

1. This is the refrain of a well-known song printed in *Rump Songs* (London, 1662): 'If none be offended with the scent, / Though I foul my mouth, I'le be content / To sing of the Rump of a Parliament, / Which nobody can deny', etc.

2. The Whig journalist George Ridpath, of the *Flying Post*.

3. A British fleet under Admiral Byng attacked and heavily defeated the Spanish off Cape Passaro on 11 August 1718, though the two countries were not then at war.

4. I.e. according to their calendar.

5. Archibald Hutcheson (*c.* 1659–1740), an Independent Whig and MP for Hastings, who published in 1718 *Some Calculations and Remarks Relating to the Present State of the Publick Debts and Funds*.

6. Upon the death of Louis XV in 1715 George I made a radical change in policy, concerting an alliance with France, which was signed in November 1716 and joined by the Dutch in January 1717.

7. I.e. by the seizing of their ships and effects by the Spanish.

Appendix C

1. *An Appeal to Honour and Justice* was advertised as published 'this day' in the *Post-Man* for 22–4 February 1715.

2. I.e. members of the Harley administration.

3. 'A byword among the people'.

4. 'Whoever loves danger, let him perish by it'; *Ecclesiasticus* (Vulgate), 3:26.

5. 'Happy is he who is made cautious by the disaster of others' (a Latin proverb).

6. In 1685 Dalby Thomas, one of three commissioners of the newly imposed Glass Duty recruited Defoe to serve as 'Accomptant to the Commissioners', a post worth £100 and later £180 a year, and which Defoe held until the Glass Duty was abolished in 1699. See John M. Parkinson, 'Daniel Defoe: Accomptant to the Commissioners of the Glass Duty', *Notes and Queries*, 143 (1998), pp. 455–6.

7. John Tutchin (1661?–1707), best known as author of the Whig periodical *The Observator* (1702–1707). See above, pp. 45–8.

8. See above, pp. 14–17.

9. This was one of the provisions of the Declaration of Right, which was given legislative form in the Bill of Rights (1689). Defoe claimed to have been present when Richard Hampden, the Presbyterian Whig MP, delivered the resolution quoted here to the House of Lords; see *Review* for 6 September 1705, and for 23 September 1710.

10. Under the Act of Settlement, passed in June 1701, the succession was settled on the House of Hanover.

11. During April 1704 Queen Anne compelled the Earl of Nottingham, the Earl of Jersey and Sir Edward Seymour, all High Tories, to resign.

12. Sir Edward Seymour (1633–1708), a prominent Tory, held office under Queen Anne as Comptroller of the Household. He was dismissed from the post in April 1704.

13. See above, p. 92.

14. The reference here is to the *Shortest Way with the Dissenters* episode. See above, pp. 21–2.

15. I.e. Robert Harley, who arranged, with the help of Godolphin, for Defoe's release from Newgate.

16. See Mark 10:51; Luke 18:41.

17. The Earl of Nottingham, as Secretary of State.

18. Harley was dismissed in February 1708.

19. This introduction took place in March 1708.

20. I.e. Defoe's work in the promotion of the Union with Scotland, in 1706–7.

21. Defoe arrived in Edinburgh in early April (see letter to Godolphin, 20 April 1708; *Letters*, pp. 254–6).

22. Defoe possibly means the Duke of Shrewsbury.

23. I.e. Oxford. (Harley had been created Earl of Oxford in May 1711.)

24. 'But whither does the tide sweep us?', Ovid, *Metamorphoses*, XI.531.

25. I.e. stipulated.

26. Godolphin was dismissed in August 1710.

27. I.e. Harley.

28. Defoe is referring to his discussion of the terms of the Peace in the *Review*; see above, pp. 128–9.

29. *A Seasonable Warning and Caution against the Insinuations of Papists and Jacobites* (London, 1712).

30. See above, p. 127.

31. See above, p. 7.

32. The Earl of Nottingham entered into an alliance with the Whigs in 1711.

33. See above, p. 128.

34. See Luke 6:28.

35. See above, p. 129.

36. See above, pp. 129–30.

37. See above, p. 126.

38. I.e. the October Club; see above, pp. 113–15.

39. I.e. the two parts of *The Secret History of the White-Staff*; see above, pp. 140–3.

40. The same statement appears in *The Secret History of the Secret History of the White Staff*; see above, pp. 143–5.

41. By 'Author' Defoe means here publisher, or promoter.

42. Henry Martyn, the author of the *British Merchant*, a periodical intended as a counterblast to the *Mercator*, took his hostility so far as to accuse Defoe of dishonesty in regard to his bankruptcy. See Defoe's lengthy retort to this in *Mercator*, 9–12 January 1713.

43. No copy of this work, assuming it was published, is known.

44. King James, on 4 April 1687, issued a Declaration of Indulgence, suspending the Test Acts and the oaths of allegiance and supremacy. Some Dissenters expressed gratitude for this, but others, including Defoe, saw it as a plot to promote popery. See above, p. 8.

45. See above, pp. 20–1.

46. The Act outlawing Occasional Conformity was passed in December 1711. See above, pp. 123–4.

47. Defoe is harking back to the election in 1708, when the Junto Whigs (according to him) were eager for the impeachment of Marlborough and Godolphin. Coxe, *Memoirs of the Duke of Marlborough*, vol. 2, p. 227, prints a letter of May/ June 1708 from Godolphin to Marlborough, complaining of the threats against himself by the Junto Whigs for his failure to overcome the refusal of the Queen to bring Lord Somers into her Privy Council, and hinting that he would like to resign.

48. The Tory journalist Abel Roper (1665–1726), author of the thrice-weekly *Post Boy* (1695–1714).

49. This was the proverbial name for a time-serving cleric, immortalized in an eighteenth-century popular song.

50. Quoted (with some minor omissions) from the comment on Jeremiah 20:10 in Matthew Poole, *Annotations upon the Holy Bible*, 2 vols (London, 1688), vol. 2, *s.v.*

51. George I arrived in England on 18 September 1714.
52. See above, p. 143.
53. See *Flying Post* for 4–7 December 1714.
54. 'The mind conscious of its own rectitude laughs at the lies of rumour', Ovid, *Fasti*, 4.311.

INDEX

Works assigned to Defoe (DD) appear directly under title; works by others under author's name.